*Voices of American Indian Assimilation
and Resistance*

Voices of American Indian Assimilation and Resistance

HELEN HUNT JACKSON, SARAH WINNEMUCCA, AND VICTORIA HOWARD

SIOBHAN SENIER

UNIVERSITY OF OKLAHOMA PRESS : NORMAN

Quotations from the Melville Jacobs Archives are used with the permission of the Whatcom Foundation. Parts of chapters 3 and 4 of the present work have appeared, in abbreviated and varied form, in *Legacy: A Journal of Women Writers* 14 (Spring 1997): 51–58, and in *Northwest Review* (September 1997): 46–56.

Published with the assistance of the National Endowment for the Humanities, a federal agency which supports the study of such fields as history, philosophy, literature, and language.

Library of Congress Cataloging-in-Publication Data

Senier, Siobhan, 1965–
    Voices of American Indian assimilation and resistance: Helen Hunt Jackson, Sarah Winnemucca, and Victoria Howard / Siobhan Senier.
      p.   cm.
    Includes bibliographical references and index.
    ISBN 0-8061-3293-0 (hc : alk. paper)
    1. Indians of North America—Cultural assimilation.   2. Indians of North America—Government relations—1869–1934.   3. Folk literature, Indian—History and criticism.   4. Indians in literature.   5. Jackson, Helen Hunt, 1830–1885.   6. Hopkins, Sarah Winnemucca, 1844?–1891. 7. Howard, Victoria, 1870–1930.   I. Title.

E98.C89 S46 2001
323.1'197073'09034—dc21

                           00–061595

1 2 3 4 5 6 7 8 9 10

CONTENTS

ILLUSTRATIONS

FIGURES

MAP

PREFACE

In this time of intense scholarly fascination with ethnicity and resistance, this book seeks to locate a specific kind of resistance—that of American Indians[1] to the so-called "Era of Assimilation," from 1879 to 1934. It locates that resistance in written and oral narratives by three women—the white novelist Helen Hunt Jackson, the Paiute autobiographer and performer Sarah Winnemucca, and the Clackamas Chinook storyteller Victoria Howard.

Women's history and literature are now happily garnering attention, but my focus on women, and on an apparently arbitrary triumvirate of them, still needs a word of explanation. I am not claiming that only women ever challenged assimilation; I am not even claiming that only women ever challenged it in the particular, complex ways I'll be describing here. A book in fact needs to be written that would read these and other women artists alongside male writers and orators, both Indian and non-Indian. But I'm interested in women because, for all of its ugliness, the Era of Assimilation also generated new opportunities for women to write and speak publicly—opportunities they seized with gusto. White women became public reformers, writers, and speakers, much as they had done decades earlier as abolitionists. Indian women, some of whom had been forced to learn how to speak, read, and write in English in boarding schools as part of the assimilative effort, also capitalized on this wave of reform by recording their stories themselves or relating them to others. And beyond gaining unique visibility in the Era of Assimilation, women of both races figured themselves as especially resistant. In other words, women and American Indians conceived of women and American Indians as uniquely qualified to confront assimilation. The pitfalls and possibilities of their so imagining will be part of my subject.

While many scholars nowadays cover wide ranges of writers and historical figures, I have zeroed in on three, partly because my readings, within history and across genres, call for a good deal of contextual work, and partly because (naturally) I think Jackson, Winnemucca, and Howard deserve much more attention than they have heretofore received. Are they "representative"? Yes, but not in the sense of being just like all other writers or storytellers of the period. Rather, at various times and in various contexts, they have all been culturally selected as representative, whether by popular consumption or scholarly scrutiny. And as speakers *for* and *as* American Indians, all three women claimed the status of representativeness for themselves. Finally, and most importantly, each woman in this study represents the Era of Assimilation, not just because she produced her work then, but because each, in her own way, helped produce or challenge the Era itself.

Helen Hunt Jackson is probably the most dramatically representative. Her best-selling romance, *Ramona* (1884), has been dubbed "the 'Indian' *Uncle Tom's Cabin*," a phrase that indicates how readers and Jackson herself envisioned the book's impact and cultural work. By the time of its publication, Jackson was already a well-established writer of sentimental novels. Born in 1830, she grew up in Amherst, Massachusetts, and was a friend of Emily Dickinson. Indeed, she was a more visible poet than her friend in her lifetime, ranking for inclusion in Ralph Waldo Emerson's *Parnassus*.

Jackson's life, as she liked to tell it, changed dramatically in 1879 when she heard Chief Standing Bear lecture in Boston on the forced removal of the Poncas from their homes. She began pouring out letters to editors and wrote a history of broken treaties, *A Century of Dishonor* (1881), which she distributed personally to members of Congress. *Ramona* was her last major work; Jackson died in 1885. The book was hailed by reformers and has even been claimed responsible for the passage, in 1887, of the Dawes (General Allotment) Act, an assimilative piece of legislation that called for tribal ownership of Indian lands to be converted into individual ownership.

It is not entirely clear that Jackson would have approved of the Dawes Act, nor certainly of its disastrous effects on American Indian lives. So in chapter 1, I read against the "pro-Dawes" interpretation of *Ramona* to glean how Jackson, not herself an American Indian, could nevertheless point radically to the legitimacy of indigenous traditions and sovereignty. Because she ultimately relies on a model of female agency that is intensely individualistic, I do find her less successful than Winnemucca and Howard at challenging racial hierarchies. Still, Jackson is a hugely important figure in the period, and in re-reading her I wish to model re-readings of other white authors who, for better or worse, represented American Indians.

Sarah Winnemucca, the subject of chapter 2, was already out of fashion by the time *Ramona* came on the scene, but her fame, in its day, was equally intense. Winnemucca (c. 1844–1891) was a member of the Paiute tribe, which had reservations in western Nevada but covered a larger territory, including parts of southern Oregon and California. The granddaughter of a chief who was friendly to whites, she was educated in white schools and served in her young adulthood as a translator for the U.S. Army and a mediator in Indian-white disputes. In 1879, Winnemucca created a sensation when she dressed in "Indian princess" garb of her own making and traveled to the East to lecture about the abuses of the reservation system. She also wrote what is believed to be the first Indian woman's autobiography, *Life Among the Piutes* (1883).[2]

Like Jackson, Winnemucca is often read as pro-assimilationist, even though she worked hard for American Indian self-determination, most notably when she established a Paiute school at the end of her life. I will therefore look at the complicated business of her self-representation: how she worked to represent the Paiutes and herself to white audiences who made conflicting demands on her, while still preserving a sense of traditional culture as vital and enduring. Perhaps the most vexed figure in this study, Winnemucca illustrates that while the Era of Assimilation generated opportunities for women to write and speak, those opportunities were by no means uncomplicated.

I devote two chapters to the little-known Victoria Howard, both to give her the filling-in she seems to require and to make the case for including oral storytellers in our literary histories. Howard lived her life (c. 1865–1930) on the Grand Ronde reservation on the northern coast of Oregon not far from the Columbia River. She was, in anthropological parlance, "an informant," working in 1929 and 1930 with the renowned linguist Melville Jacobs to record over one hundred traditional narratives, ethnographic accounts, and songs. Published in the 1950s as *Clackamas Chinook Texts*, these give us a unique opportunity to look at the work of one female indigenous storyteller.

As Jack Forbes maintains in an article on indigenous intellectual sovereignty, linguistic texts like Howard's "must be evaluated as sources coming from a particular Native author, one who may have his or her own story to tell."[3] I seek, then, not only to read Howard from a feminist standpoint (for her stories are full of women, powerful and otherwise, and full of the voices of her women relatives and acquaintances) but also to recover her as an indigenous author who can make contributions to American and Indian literary and intellectual histories. Working several decades after Jackson and Winnemucca, when the push for assimilation was beginning to wane, Howard is much more sophisticated than these earlier women in pointing to the endurance of indigenous traditions while juggling her readers/listeners out of hierarchical positions into more mutual and examined relationships.

None of these women critiques assimilation very directly. Indeed, one could also write a book on their complicity with assimilation, as the above synopses may suggest. But surprisingly few public figures during the Era of Assimilation generated direct challenges to the incorporation of American Indians into Euro-American lifestyles. In literary history specifically, we are left with a surfeit of braves plunging off cliffs and childlike, peaceful agrarian races, and comparatively few depictions of the intricate social, political, religious, and cultural institutions that long enabled indigenous peoples to survive. In part, this is because the people who were doing most of the writing at the turn of the last century—namely, whites and American Indians schooled by whites—were themselves invested in Euro-American institutions, albeit to varying degrees.

But I will argue that recovering resistance to Indian assimilation is difficult also because the artists who addressed assimilation critically were not primarily interested in representing tribal practices for the non-Indian readers who comprised much of their audience. They were more interested in restructuring the relations between those readers and themselves, and between Indians and non-Indians. Reading and writing, after all, can be assimilative in their own way: people read for, among other things, information about other peoples, about what they see as different and exotic ways of life, information which they can convert into some kind of colonizing knowledge. And people write, often, for compatible reasons: to master subjects and convey that mastery to others. This was surely at least part of the case during the Era of Assimilation, when, not coincidentally, the American public thirsted for fictions and ethnographies about the very peoples it was trying to incorporate. Jackson, Winnemucca, and Howard shake up these relationships among narrators and interlocutors. They seek not merely to represent American Indian ways of life as alternatives to assimilative ideals, but to get their readers and listeners to examine their own desires, motives, and positions.

Much literary criticism, I suspect, emerges from just such examinations, as critics struggle to understand why and how particular works have moved them. I did graduate work in central Illinois and teach now in northern New England, and while each place certainly has its own kinds of diversity, neither ranks among the United States' most talked-about hotbeds of cultural and racial variety. So I've worked, in my scholarship and my teaching, to understand and describe how literature seeks to help often distant and separated American communities talk with each other. That communication is not always transparent or simple, and it is not always just about transmitting cultural information from one group to another. In ferreting out American Indian resistance to assimilation, then, this book has become a meditation on the politics, the perils, and the possibilities of cross-cultural communication.

Nothing can make one feel so lucky, or reinvigorate one's love of academic life and fellow human beings, quite like writing acknowledgments. An awe-inspiring assembly of friends and colleagues read parts of this manuscript and challenged me, nourished me, humored me: Kurt Austin, Jill Bergman, Alice Bloom, Lisa Botshon, Claire Chantell, Beth Coleman, Jon D'Ericco, Jolly Donlon, Daniel P. Gunn, Rebecca Herzig, Jane Juffer, Melinda Plastas, Lee Sharkey, Vivian Wagner, Henry Zenk, and participants in the May 1999 Maine Women's Studies retreat. I also benefited from some extraordinary mentors, including Michael Bérubé and Stephanie Foote; Robert Dale Parker's incisive reading, guidance, and friendship have been unwavering.

In addition, I received some more material support in the form of money and the time that, in academe, money really can buy. The University of Illinois at Urbana-Champaign provided generous fellowships for course release as well as a Mary Kay Peer grant for travel to Grand Ronde and to the Melville Jacobs Archives. The

University of Maine at Farmington helped fund a trip to the Nevada Historical Society and the Pyramid Lake Reservation. Among indispensable professionals, Janine Bonk at the University of Maine at Farmington was the most resourceful and indefatigable of interlibrary loan librarians. The staffs at the Melville Jacobs Archives at the University of Washington, especially Gary Lundell, and at the Nevada Historical Society in Reno were also enormously helpful. Stacey Cuppernell provided invaluable research assistance, and Jesse Edwards helped as a talented and efficient graphic artist. I am also grateful to the interested and interesting people who took time to talk with me at and near the Grand Ronde reservation, including the late Vincent Mercier and Sister Kateri Petite.

The editors and readers at the University of Oklahoma Press deserve many thanks. In particular, Patricia Heinicke, Jr., made this a much more lucid, patient, and readable work. I credit all these people with this project's successes; any errors in fact or judgment are mine alone.

Without all of these people, I could not have completed this project. But I *would* not have completed it without my family: Jack, Phyllis, Laura, and Amy Senier, and Greg Tillman. To them this book is dedicated.

*Voices of American Indian Assimilation
and Resistance*

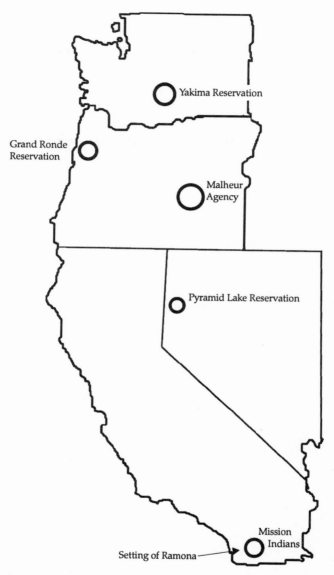

Setting of *Ramona*, by Helen Hunt Jackson; the Paiute territories, home of Sarah Winnemucca; and the Grand Ronde Reservation, home of Victoria Howard.

AMERICAN WOMEN'S NARRATIVES ABOUT INDIANS, 1879–1934

Although this book examines the work of three particular women, it is more broadly an attempt to locate and understand resistance to American Indian assimilation. My readings of Helen Hunt Jackson, Sarah Winnemucca, and Victoria Howard as paradigms of this resistance will make more sense with some historical and cultural background. In this introduction, then, I would like to survey the Era of Assimilation itself, showing that while that period saw its share of change and conflict, it was nevertheless quite uniform in its agreement that assimilation was the only thing that could be "done" with Indians. Disappointingly few people questioned assimilation, at least in writing; few suggested that American Indian ways of life might be legitimate or valuable in themselves, or that American Indians should be entitled to self-determination.

I will then map out some of the more complicated, sometimes evasive forms that resistance to assimilation takes. In a number of cases, American Indian and non-Indian people protested the policy outright. More often, those who represented indigenous culture, both artistically and politically, did so in canny ways that both pointed to and protected sacred and cultural traditions. Since I approach such texts as cross-cultural products and encounters, it is not my central aim to describe a formal, systematic "indigenous aesthetic."

I do, however, want to call attention to *moments* of an alternative aesthetic—moments that draw on communally shared lands and stories as resources, for instance, or that don't tell a story in ways that Euro-American culture might expect. These moments, in turn, resist assimilation and its nationalizing, individualizing drives.

THE ERA OF ASSIMILATION: A MONOLITHIC HISTORY

Scholars today are primed to find in literature and history such things as conflict, contest, polyphony. The Era of Assimilation, though, seems relatively monolithic. Historian Frederick Hoxie pinpoints its beginning at 1879, when several widely publicized tragedies garnered non-Indian sympathy for American Indians. Among these was the arrest of a group of Poncas as they tried to escape Indian Territory in Oklahoma, where they had been forcibly removed from their traditional homes in the southeastern part of Dakota Territory. They were led by Chief Standing Bear, the same man who so moved Helen Hunt Jackson to turn her writing over to American Indian subject matter.[1] In another incident, a group of Utes at White River in Utah killed the reservation agent, a Horace Greeley acolyte named Nathan Meeker. With assistance from the military, Meeker had tried to force the Utes to use certain farming practices that were at odds with their traditional land uses. Jackson was again among the many who took note: she wrote in the *Rocky Mountain News* that the Utes had merely "attempted, by force of arms, to restrain the entrance upon their own lands—lands bought, owned and paid for—of soldiers that the Government had sent there, to be ready to make war upon them, in case the agent thought it best to do so!"[2]

Jackson was a good barometer of public sentiment toward American Indians. That sentiment had shifted from the intense hostility surrounding the Battle of the Little Bighorn only three years earlier to a marked sympathy for indigenous peoples and outrage against the abuses of a corrupt reservation system. An Indian reform movement was soon underway, culminating in the Dawes (General Allotment) Act of 1887. This landmark legislation proposed to divide communally held tribal lands "in severalty," allotting a Jeffersonian 160 acres to each head of family. The Indian land would be held in trust for twenty-five years, at the end of which time American Indians would be made U.S. citizens and given individual titles to that land. Between lands sold or leased before the Indians got full title and "surplus" lands transferred to white settlers as soon as 160-acre parcels were allotted, American Indians lost some 90 million acres—two-thirds of the land base they had in 1887.[3]

Allotment had been bandied about in one form or another since before the Civil War and was indeed already under way among some tribes by 1887. Reformers claimed that the policy would protect Indian lands from white encroachment by giving the Indians individual titles that could be defended in court and by eliminating their dependence on unreliable agencies and government handouts.[4]

Allotment depended on two nationalizing assumptions: one, that only individuals, and in particular individuals who owned property, were entitled to government protection and rights; the other, that Indians had to cease to exist as collective entities, assimilating to Euro-American, agricultural, and capitalistic ways of life. Allotment was only the beginning of Indian reform: missionaries went to the reservations to teach Indians Christian doctrine; field matrons went to teach them domestic practices; and off-reservation boarding schools were established to "kill the Indian and save the man," in Carlisle Indian school founder Richard Pratt's infamous words.

In all of this, we can see the processes that Alan Trachtenberg has called "the incorporation of America," in which a rapidly consolidating national identity finds itself threatened by an array of new and disturbing forces: immigration, labor strikes, rapid industrialization, urbanization.[5] Among all those threats, the presence of American Indians as a political and cultural force remains little discussed, perhaps because Indians are assumed to have been vanishing, or at least to have been constructed by nineteenth-century culture as vanishing. But as the anxious efforts to incorporate them suggest, the sovereign nations within national borders were just as profoundly disruptive as any other threats coming from within or without. Indigenous populations were in fact keenly visible in the decades following the Civil War, as a rapidly westward-expanding population began to press more adamantly at the borders of reservations.

The push for American Indian citizenship and allotment coincided with the rise of anthropology as a profession. In 1879, the same year that Standing Bear made his speeches and the Utes killed Nathan Meeker, John Wesley Powell established the Bureau of American Ethnology (BAE) at the Smithsonian Institution. Powell, well known for his geographic surveys, was at the crux of a national drive to map and control the country's domestic interiors. Mapping and classifying Indians became an integral part of this project: taking for granted Lewis Henry Morgan's famous savagery-barbarism-civilization continuum, members of the BAE wanted to study Indians in their savage "stage" and to draw distinctions among tribes, especially by linguistic and cultural classification.[6]

These were more than simply academic discourses. Anthropologists joined forces with legislators, as when Powell advised Colorado Senator Henry Teller that the "removal of the Indians"—through allotment—should be the first step in "civilizing" them, as indigenous lands constituted "everything most sacred to Indian society."[7] Anthropologists also moved into more mainstream media; in 1883, for instance, Frank Cushing popularized his ethnographic findings in his "Adventures at Zuni" series, publishing them in *Century* magazine. Popular consumption of ethnography continued to grow, as did the drive to "document" so-called vanishing races; hordes of anthropologists, photographers, artists, and tourists rushed westward in this interest. By the early 1900s, led by Franz Boas, anthropologists like Melville Jacobs were urgently seeking out people like Victoria Howard as the "last" of certain tribes.[8] Few, perhaps, really believed that American Indians were declining numerically, but most still felt that the "pure" state of indigenous culture was ready to disappear. Hence, researchers sought to accumulate as much raw data about Indians as they could, as quickly as possible.

Meanwhile, American sentiment about assimilation was turning. The reformers' hope that allotment would protect indigenous land ownership had clearly been a pipe dream. As Brian Dippie explains, the 1920s saw many attempts to adjudicate land disputes between American Indians and white settlers who had been living on tribal lands for several years. Most always, the result was a division of tribal lands and a severance of tribal ties—as opposed, for instance, to letting Indians keep their lands and giving monetary settlements to whites to move away. In 1922, for example, New Mexico Senator H. O. Bursum tried to pass a bill giving an enormous portion of Pueblo lands to non-Indian claimants who had been occupying them, often illegally.[9] The notorious bill motivated activists anew to defeat it and push for changes in Indian policy.

Among those activists was John Collier, commissioner of Indian Affairs under Franklin D. Roosevelt and creator of the famous "Indian New Deal," the 1934 Indian Reorganization Act (IRA). This act aimed to give American Indian peoples more autonomy by recognizing their right to set up their own constitutions and operate under governments of their own design; it also tried to reverse the division of tribal lands into individual allotments. Tribes could supposedly operate under governments of their own choosing, with "appropriate" constitutions and bylaws, and could establish business corporations to "own, hold, manage, operate, and dispose of property of every description, real and personal."[10] The act provided that the secretary of the interior could return those "surplus" lands created by the Dawes Act to tribal ownership, and it established a revolving fund for economic development as well as annual appropriations for land purchase to increase the indigenous land base. Since then, American Indian scholars including D'Arcy McNickle and Robert Allen Warrior have praised the act, but it has also been attacked by Indians and non-Indians as failing to recognize Indian sovereignty fully.[11] Historically, though, this controversial piece of legislation did halt the allotment process, thus bringing the Era of Assimilation to an end.

There are two things to take away from this history. First, despite the dramatic changes in U.S. Indian policy between 1887 and 1934 and despite the surge in anthropology and ethnographic-style representation of indigenous peoples, white attitudes toward American Indians ultimately changed little. The United States remained centered on *managing* the threat that Indians posed to national borders from within: whether Indians were envisioned as potential yeoman farmers, as in the 1880s, or as a permanent underclass, as they came to be by the 1930s,[12] they were always to be contained within Euro-American norms.

Second, U.S. culture witnessed an intense struggle over individualism and community during this period. Early reformers believed that Indians were dangerously "communistic" and sought to refashion them as individuals by bestowing individual land ownership and citizenship on them. Conversely, Collier and his allies, in Dippie's words, believed that "inside every Indian, no matter how assimilated, there lurked a Pueblo waiting to be freed, a communal being eager to shuck off the trappings of individualistic society."[13] American Indian writers, meanwhile, oscillated between individualistic models in which they claimed personal agency and identity, and communal models that they either asserted as legitimate and enduring, or posited as alternatives to the American ideology of possessive individualism. All of this complicates any facile distinctions between Indians as communal and whites as individualistic and shows that, far from being mere descriptions of cultural realities, words like *individualistic* and *communistic* came to be markers with distinct *political* uses. Our brief history shows, moreover, that debates over individualism and community were central to debates about citizenship in the Era of Assimilation. We will see these debates played out again and again in Jackson's, Winnemucca's, and Howard's stories.

COUNTERING ASSIMILATION: EVASIVE REPRESENTATIONS OF INDIGENOUS CULTURE

Despite these tensions between individualistic and communal practices and discourses, the Era of Assimilation ultimately sought to eradicate indigenous community, land, and ways of life. Against this backdrop, the written record of American Indian resistance looks somewhat less than rich. Consider an apparently assertive performance of cultural difference like the 1902 *Atlantic Monthly* essay rather ironically entitled "Why I Am a Pagan." Written by the prominent Sioux activist Zitkala-Sa, the piece celebrates tribal identity, but it also celebrates a world where "both great and small are so surely enfolded in His magnitude that, without a miss, each has his allotted individual ground of opportunities."[14] Many early American Indian authors, like Zitkala-Sa, seem to have been quite willing to endorse Christianity, individual property, and other Euro-American institutions and to show that even if they were not ready to abandon tribal traditions, these traditions could still be easily amalgamated with white institutions.

Such writers pose an acute problem for American Indian intellectual history, for as Warrior has observed, they tended to silence their opposition and, "unfortunately, did not produce an organization of intellectuals that could create a written ideology for their traditionalist-nationalist stance. In this," he continues, "American Indian intellectual history is markedly different from that, for instance, of African-Americans, who have produced political organizations that have countered with forms of black nationalism the dominant ideologies of integration."[15] Put another way, the people most likely to articulate stiff resistance to allotment—like those Utes who attacked Nathan Meeker—may not have had access to literacy or to publication, or may simply not have been interested in writing their histories down. How, then, can we glean something about Indians' historical opposition to integration?

Uncovering resistance to American Indian allotment and assimilation, if such a thing is possible, depends partly on the forms one expects such resistance to take and on the complex, often canny ways that Indian and some non-Indian people chose to represent that resistance. Say one looks, for instance, for Indian-authored short stories, novels, and nonfiction depicting traditional social, political, cultural, and religious institutions. In such sources one would find, not necessarily resistance, but images of indigenous cultures that seem already oddly acculturated. For example, in Omaha writer Francis LaFlesche's account of allotment leasing, published in 1900, the problem the author describes is not that white settlers have found yet another way to divest Indians of their lands (by actually renting them away), but that the Indians are collecting rent money and spending it on alcohol and railroad fares to visit other tribes instead of working. LaFlesche "delivers a message" for an industrious Omaha man: "Labor is the only thing that will maintain the dignity of man and command respect from every one."[16] Alongside such pronouncements of seemingly Euro-American-style virtue, one will find in late-nineteenth century American Indian writings some rather familiar stereotypes, as in "The Sick Child" by Angel DeCora (Winnebago). In this very short narrative, a medicine man proves unable to heal a dying child—a vanishing-race scenario that, Bernd Peyer suggests, laments the inefficacy of traditional practices.[17]

Further complicating the picture, one finds in Indian writings a real taciturnity about traditional cultures. But that taciturnity should not be read as compliance with the forces attempting to eradicate traditional cultures. A good deal of tribal information, after all, is considered sacred or private, not for outsiders' gazes. Indian writers at the turn of the century were often laconic in explaining and describing traditional cultures, even as they seemed willing to offer detailed ethnographic accounts. They were, perhaps, just as worried about *whether* to represent their cultures as about *how* to represent them. Their works therefore oscillate dramatically between revealing those cultures and concealing them, between trying to render traditional ways of life intelligible or legitimate to non-Indian readers, and holding those readers at bay.

A brief reading will illustrate. LaFlesche's sister Suzette was like him a public figure; the two traveled together with Standing Bear on his East coast lecture tour as interpreters. Suzette was a journalist and did a good deal of her own writing, including the preface to her husband Thomas Tibbles's book, *The Ponca Chiefs*. She published one short story, "Nedawi," in the children's magazine *St. Nicholas* in 1881.[18] The narrative follows the young heroine of its title through her day: she plays a plum-seed dice game with friends; she carelessly loses track of her infant brother, then learns a stern lesson from her mother; and she enjoys the company of her family around their campfire at the end of the day.

The story arguably gave its young, predominantly white readers a nostalgic picture of an exotic and ostensibly disappearing culture; of the evening fireside scene, the narrator declares, "It seemed as if nature were trying to protect the poor waifs of humanity clustered in that spot."[19] Further, those readers can hardly have been surprised or alienated by this "little savage," who sanctimoniously chides a friend for ostracizing another, ragged-looking girl: "My father says we must be kind to poor little girls, and help them all we can; so *I'm* going to play with her if *you* don't."[20] Indeed, the story seeks to make its subjects intelligible not just by promoting values that Christians like to call their own, but also by reassuring its readers that the Indian children at their play acted "pretty much as white children do when reciting the multiplication table"[21] and that Nedawi was "no more perfect than any little white girl who gets into a temper now and then."[22] LaFlesche thus appears a gentle mediator between her culture and the dominant culture.

Mediation has in fact become one of American Indian studies' buzzwords, one I would like to pry at. One of the best discussions of the term has been James Ruppert's important book, *Mediation in Contemporary Native American Fiction* (1995), where he defines it thus: "an artistic and conceptual standpoint, constantly flexible, which uses the epistemological frameworks of Native American and Western cultural traditions to illuminate and enrich each other"; mediation, in this reading, "brings different cultural codes into confluence."[23] Ruppert focuses usefully on implied readers, on the varying and sometimes competing audiences a single American Indian text can address and the strategies these texts use to address those audiences (a project whose success cannot be guaranteed, he notes). He also proposes that "mediational texts" are geared "toward Native concerns such as nurturing survival, continuance, and continual reemergence of cultural identity."[24] As we will see when we turn to critical discussions of Sarah Winnemucca, other scholars writing on mediation have sometimes elided this complicated and often troubled two-way dynamic in an apparent eagerness to embrace "the harmonizing and unifying [of] dual perspectives."[25] Such readings promote an image of the American Indian writer who, seemingly without effort, chooses among cultural codes and blends them to bring white and Indian happily together.

Mediation, as Jace Weaver wryly remarks, "has always been more of a concern for Amer-Europeans than for Natives, who do not view their own cultural responses as 'old and isolating' and who often express scant interest in bridging their worldview with that of the dominant culture."[26] Reading for mediation, in other words, can have a disturbing way of keeping Euro-Americans at the center of the discussion; it can frame American Indian writing mainly in terms of what that writing can do for non-Indian readers.

As a non-Indian reader myself, I am perhaps almost inevitably concerned in this project to explore how indigenous writings talk to outsiders. However, I find that, far from making traditional cultures available or transparent to me, such writings often pointedly refuse to annotate and explicate, and further, that they dramatize the business of cross-cultural communication as politically vexed.

At the end of "Nedawi," for example, the girl's grandmother tells her a story of how turkeys came to have red eyes: A wily young boy, seeking food for his grandmother, traps a bunch of turkeys by convincing them to keep their eyes shut while he sings to them, otherwise—he threatens—their eyes will turn red. When one of the turkeys peeks and sees what the boy is up to, it escapes, but "ever after that the turkeys had red eyelids."[27] While LaFlesche includes the boy's song, first in Omaha, then with a bracketed "literal translation," this oral narrative is more elliptical than other passages in "Nedawi." The narrator, who has been at considerable pains to explain and smooth over various Indian practices, does not intervene here to explain what the story might have meant to the grandmother or to Nedawi. The story cuts off such an opportunity, actually, when "Nedawi gave a sigh of satisfaction when the story was finished, and would have asked for more, but just then her brothers came in from a dance. . . ."[28]

It is possible that the young readers of *St. Nicholas* could have assimilated the story as a lesson about youthful resourcefulness, or—from the turkeys' punishment—perhaps as a lesson about obedience. It is possible, too, to read the story as a reduction of oral tradition to simplistic etiological functions—or, if one wanted to push the matter, as a message about self-preservation. But such readings seem beside the point. The embedded oral story seems more invested in connections among family and community, as evidenced by Nedawi's satisfied sigh. It illustrates the continuing vibrancy of a tradition that conveys a particular cosmology and a sense of community, despite the framing story's apparent nostalgia for "old" ways of life. Fundamentally, "Nedawi" is invested neither in explicating that cosmology nor in sharing that sense of community with non-Indians.

The inclusion of this oral story in LaFlesche's narrative can thus throw non-Indian readers off center. Many writers have observed that one of the unstated goals or effects of ethnography has been to give colonizing cultures information about subjugated peoples so that they can continue their domination of those peoples.[29] Ethnographic texts, therefore, often put readers in a position of power; they purport to tell all about a culture while reassuring readers, usually, that the culture under scrutiny has disappeared or is under Western control. In this vein, "Nedawi" invites non-Indian readers, whether intentionally or not, to feel privileged in their newfound knowledge about Indian lives, knowledge that is seldom very disruptive to Euro-American value systems. But when the story gestures toward the oral tradition without fully annotating that tradition, when it lets the Indian version *precede* the English translation, the story also slyly repositions these readers. It deliberately obscures the apparently privileged glimpse it affords of Indian culture, while asserting the legitimacy and endurance of that culture.

Even DeCora's failed-medicine-man vignette contains a veiled critique of the new white ways it purportedly accepts as inevitable. Its narrator, the sister of the dying child, searches according to the medicine-woman's instructions for a spot of bare winter ground on which to lay an offering. During this search, she wonders, "where was a spot of earth to be found in all that white monotony?"[30] Against this canny expression of "white monotony," the story actually contains several assertions of the vitality of traditional practice. The medicine-woman's prediction that the sick child will not live turns out to be correct. And the medicine man who is called in later does not actually promise to save the child's life, only to make her dying more comfortable; in this he succeeds, and DeCora's rendering is sympathetic. Further, at key junctions, most notably when the narrator expresses concern that her offering didn't work, she repeats, "I was a silent child" and "I said nothing." This silence implies an understanding among the American Indian characters, one that the non-Indian reader is not necessarily invited to probe or master. It implies, moreover, that those understandings and ways of life are legitimate and continuous. In the Era of Assimilation, any such assertion, however muted, was radical.

We can, then, find ways of reading the literature of this period with an eye not just to how it mediates American Indian culture for white culture (or vice versa), nor just for how it seems to comply with the values of the consolidating nation-state. Victoria Howard, Sarah Winnemucca, and to a lesser degree Helen Hunt Jackson ask readers to reconsider their relationships to the material they are consuming. In so doing, they attempt to restructure the relationship between readers and writers, listeners and speakers, non-Indians and Indians.

REWRITING LITERARY HISTORY: COMMUNITISM AND ORALITY

My readings of these women are informed by several strands in current literary and cultural criticism. Most significantly, scholars have been reconsidering the canon in general and the history of the late nineteenth and early twentieth centuries in particular, as informed, contested, and reshaped by various minority traditions.[31] If, up to now, we have read that history as a master narrative about national consolidation around a model of individualized citizens and ownership, then Jackson, Winnemucca, and Howard help us rewrite that story. They draw on communally held lands and stories as resources for resistance and American Indian self-determination.

One of the most promising articulations of an alternative indigenous tradition, and one that speaks well to the Era of Assimilation, is Jace Weaver's theory of "communitism." Weaver wants to keep this term supple, to be worked out further in an ongoing dialogue with American Indian writers and critics. But he proffers this useful starting point:

> I would contend that the single thing that most defines Indian literatures relates to this sense of community and commitment to it. It is what I term "communitism." Communitism, or its adjectival form "communitist," is a neologism of my own devising. Its coining . . . is necessary because no other word from the Latin roots *communis* or *communitas*—communitarian, communal, communist, and so on—carries the exact sense necessary. It is formed from a combination of the words "community" and "activism" or "activist." Literature is communitist to the extent that it has a proactive commitment to Native community, including the wider community.[32]

Given that the push in the United States between 1879 and 1934 was to *erode* communally held Indian lands and practices, "communitism" proves an apt way to think about indigenous resistance to such despoliation. To return to Suzette LaFlesche, my reading of her story as merely reflecting white values back to white readers when her characters exhibit qualities like sharing or charity toward the poor seems unfair and reductive. LaFlesche may be deploying these similarities not only to mollify white readers and make Indians less "other" but also to promote particular values for Indian *and* non-Indian cultures, *at the same time* marking an indigenous communitist ethos that opposes the ethos of individualism and acquisition underlying the push for assimilation. Indeed, her story explicitly denotes some of these values as Indian: "Little Indian children are taught to share everything with one another, so it did not seem strange to Nedawi to have her gift [of fruit from a new friend] looked on as common property."[33] The notion of "common property," so threatening to the United States (especially in 1881, when LaFlesche published this story), is here underlined, claimed as specifically Indian, and proposed as an ethos intelligible to and crucial for Christian colonizers.

Communitism is an especially cogent concept because it avoids theorizing American Indian literature as somehow separatist in its resistance. Instead, Weaver refers to indigenous literature's "commitment to Native community, including the wider community," which I take to refer to non-Indian communities while still giving precedence to a desperately needed political and social commitment to Indian community. In this sense, I would like to follow him in his cautious deployment of current ideas we might group under the somewhat infelicitous heading "nonoppositionality." Postcolonial theorists, most notably Homi Bhabha, have argued that it is neither possible nor desirable to resist colonizing powers by separating from them and retreating into some supposedly pristine notion of an "authentic," "original" indigenous culture. This is a highly persuasive position; one has only to think of late-twentieth-century white supremacist groups to see the danger of such a separatist reclaiming of "authentic" culture—which is never a true reclamation, but a construction.[34]

James Clifford puts it this way: "Claims to purity are in any event always subverted by the need to stage authenticity *in opposition to* external, often dominating alternatives. Thus the 'Third World' plays itself against the 'First World,' and vice versa. . . . If authenticity is relational, there can be no essence except as a political, cultural invention, a local tactic."[35] The idea of cultural authenticity is not only chimerical, but also often highly damaging: the whole myth that Indians can "vanish" at all is predicated on an idea of culture as static, pristine, clearly delimited and bounded, when in fact *all* cultures, including indigenous cultures, have always been dynamic and multivalent. Postcolonial critics thus seek not to itemize the distinct features of individual cultures, but to describe those cultures' interrelations and mutualities.

At the same time, I wonder whether, like the concept of mediation, the current scholarly fascination with nonoppositionalism might not, in effect, merely preserve the comfortable place of Euro-Americans in the critical conversation. The challenge has to be to disrupt this comfort: to acknowledge the constructedness and dynamism of culture without disavowing the material losses and dispossession of indigenous peoples or erasing their genuine contributions. As Clifford puts it, we need to "preserve culture's differentiating functions while conceiving of collective identity as a hybrid, often discontinuous inventive process."[36] Readings that focus on "borders," "liminality," and other kinds of "cultural interstices," to pick up just a few now-popular phrases, keep American Indian literature, somehow, always about *their* relation to *us*. Like readings that trumpet successful "mediation," they ignore the subtle voice of resistance.

Relations, again, are a central focus of my study and of Jackson's, Winnemucca's, and Howard's work; it is impossible and undesirable, as writers like Bhabha and Clifford have shown, to talk about culture without discussing it relationally. Still, these women also flirt with forms of oppositionalism, if we can talk of such a thing, and sometimes with what has been called strategic essentialism—the deployment, for political purposes, of an idea of American Indian or female identity as ultimately and even innately different. I am not trying to rehabilitate such notions, which have been powerfully debunked by feminist and postcolonialist theorists.[37] Rather, I am pointing out that American Indian writers, especially under direct threat of assimilation, explored a wide range of resistant strategies that included forms of separatism and strategic essentialism, but were never limited to those.

For example, Winnemucca and Howard allude repeatedly to practices like oral storytelling or shamanism while pointedly evading much concrete description of those practices. Such cagey allusions offer the non-Indian reader anything but smooth mediation, and their purpose is clearly *not* to "bridge borders." These allusions certainly make it difficult to maintain any facile, felicitous notion of multicultural togetherness and cultural "sharing," although they do not preclude the possibility of such sharing. Instead, gestures such as coy references to shamanism put the burden of cross-cultural communication, if there is to be any such communication at all, squarely on the non-Indian reader. The narrative using such tactics does not simply move toward this reader but insists that the reader also move toward it—or let it be. Weaver's concept of communitism allows for this range of tactics because it includes the idea of cross-cultural community while still giving political primacy to the American Indian community under duress, and because it acknowledges the dynamism of culture while giving primacy to what Clifford calls culture's "differentiating functions."

Jackson, Winnemucca, and Howard help us see American Indian culture at the turn of the century as dynamic and intercultural, while also revealing indigenous traditions as bulwarks against and conceivable responses to nationalizing Euro-American traditions. There is some evidence that they are neither alone in this, nor alone in this as women. Here is Carol Batker's introduction to her exciting study of American Indian women journalists during the Era of Assimilation:

> In an apparent contradiction, Native American women argued both for Pan-Indianism and for many of the assimilationist policies of the Dawes Era in their early journalism. The journalism examined here reproduces, at times, dominant assimilationist discourse. However, it does not predicate assimilation on a rejection of Native identity and culture. Native women refused to accept Dawes Era ideologies that defined white dominant culture and traditional Native American cultures simply as binary opposites. Their early journalism demonstrates, I argue, a complex negotiation between Native and non-Native practices that suggests cultural dynamism rather than cultural loss as a paradigm for assimilation.[38]

Batker's work points suggestively to a specifically female tradition of resistance to assimilation. It makes sense that feminist theorists are finding some of their foremothers among early women writers and activists, just as postcolonial theorists are finding some of their forebears among early writers of color. Batke reminds us that feminist theory is sustaining a tradition that interrogates cultural and racial hierarchies. A female tradition of resistance, if such can be found, will not be based on some mystified biological essences or women's ways of knowing but rather on particular strategies that women developed collectively, out of their shared (albeit hugely varied) material dispossession.

This does not mean that men do not also have contributions to make to this history of resistance; indeed, as we continue writing these histories, we must take up the many groups that overlap with American Indian women and non-Indian women, and those include Indian and non-Indian men. In so doing we would find a range of provocative similarities *and* differences. The Salish scholar D'Arcy McNickle's beautiful 1936 novel *The Surrounded*, for example, uses a sophisticated and diffuse narrative voice to represent a community's complex continuance of its own tribalism (bringing their "pagan wailing" to church services, for instance). On the other hand, the trajectory for its strongest female character is a complete shunning of her conversion to Christianity and her return to traditional religion, residence, and speech. The autobiographies of Sioux physician Charles Eastman similarly depict his grandmother as an isolated, wholly traditional, older woman who refuses any commerce with white practices. Both men write of assimilation in complex, ambivalent, even productive ways. But both figure resistance in the failed form of a traditional, aging (and dying) woman—an obsolete type, romantically strong yet unable to endure in a dynamic, many-cultured world. It is therefore a distinct scholarly enterprise to account for the ways that women acted collectively in the Era of Assimilation and for the ways they construed themselves as engaged in uniquely feminine and feminist projects.

Resistance to assimilation—by women and men, American Indians and non-Indians—can and does take the form of assertions of Indian sovereignty and legitimacy, and I will devote a considerable portion of this project to highlighting those assertions. But those assertions exist in the women's work, as Batker suggests, alongside moments that seem to advocate or accept assimilation, or at least to accept non-Indian values and practices. We might say, then, that if resistance to allotment and assimilation seems hard to uncover—if it is not easy to find textual traces of what Warrior calls forms of "nationalism" to "counter" the "dominant ideology of integration"—this difficulty exists at least partly because these women envisioned such resistance not exactly as *oppositional*, but as dynamic and mobile, able to meet new cultural challenges.

Jackson, Winnemucca, and Howard will thus help us rewrite the history of the period to account for dynamic, communally based alternatives to individualizing, nationalizing norms. Additionally, they will help us rewrite the period's literary history generically. Our picture of American literary realism has now moved far beyond the old triumvirate of Henry James, Mark Twain, and William Dean Howells to include white women writers like Kate Chopin and writers of color like Charles Chesnutt. Nevertheless, our understanding of this literary history has remained more or less focused on models that are privatized and psychological—stories of individuals finding their individual selves, their voices, and so on. Thus, the classic *bildungsroman* of Huck Finn now sits alongside narratives about the "possibilities for and impediments to, female self-development and autonomy," as the popular and multicultural *Heath Anthology of American Literature* describes them.[39] And yet artists like Howard and Winnemucca, and to a lesser degree Helen Hunt Jackson, illustrate that the literary output of the period was even more diverse.

In particular, Winnemucca and Howard mark the emergence of indigenous literary forms, which continue to challenge scholars. Despite all of the calls for inclusivity in literary canons today, many teachers and scholars still shy away from certain American Indian works, especially transcribed oral stories and written narratives produced by more than one person. In her groundbreaking *Conflicting Stories*, for example, Elizabeth Ammons has trouble making the Salish writer Mourning Dove "fit" into even her capacious paradigm of diverse women writers; she concludes that Lucullus McWhorter's heavy editing of Mourning Dove's novel *Cogewea* (1927) "muffled" her voice, "perhaps even hopelessly buried" it, and that therefore "we simply cannot talk about this text as we can those of the other women writers in this book, no matter how constrained or compromised they were."[40]

And yet heavily edited texts were a fact of American Indian women's literacy in the late nineteenth and early twentieth centuries; many Indian women wrote and told stories at the invitation or initiative of reformers and anthropologists and depended on such interventions to get into print at all. Their writings are by no means unproblematic, but they can illuminate the constraints and compromises on all kinds of writers if we can find ways of reckoning with multiple and dispersed authorship. As Warrior asserts, "a maturing American Indian criticism must be self-consciously open-ended and prepared for the unexpected in order to take into account the plethora of genres and styles of historical, contemporary and emerging American Indian writing and cultural expression."[41]

The importance—and difficulty—of such an enterprise cannot be understated, especially as we consider a period so driven by talk of and policies geared toward assimilation. American Indians in the late nineteenth century were coming into literacy in large numbers for the first time. They were thus seizing a technology that had the power both to help assimilate them and to help them resist or challenge that assimilation; and they seized this technology while maintaining and adapting their traditional forms of verbal art.

Even knottier is the ethical question—who has license to read and interpret what, in what manner, and for what purpose? As writers like Leslie Marmon Silko, Dennis Tedlock, and Greg Sarris have pointed out, the problems with transcribed oral narratives are legion, particularly those collected around the turn of the century by institutions like the Bureau of American Ethnology (BAE). When the texts weren't actually coerced out of people or printed without tribal permission, they were often "edited" beyond recognition, or collected by people who already had—and imposed— some pretty firm ideas of what they wanted before talking to Indian people.[42] Thus, such collections remain anathema to many in American Indian studies who feel that, at best, these works simply have nothing to do with indigenous storytelling tradition as Indian people experience that tradition.

But we could turn to those BAE volumes not as part of the genuine tradition of storytelling, but as a different kind of literary production. For better or worse, those anthropological works comprised a large part of American Indians' literary output at the turn of the last century. What if we read them, not as the unmediated voices of oral storytellers (which they are emphatically not), but as the traces of conversations between at least two people, two cultures? What if we read them not as one culture transmitting information to another, but as complex dramatizations of cross-cultural communication?

Transcribed oral narratives can, if well done, help us rethink the literature of the period as literature of contact. These narratives do require non-Indian (and sometimes Indian) readers to do a little extra contextualizing legwork; in this, they also ask readers to consider the context of the reading encounter itself, and to read accurately and ethically, rather than as passive consumers of cultural information. Reading Victoria Howard's stories, for example, not simply as Howard telling stories, but as Howard talking to Melville Jacobs, as a woman talking to a man, and as a Clackamas Chinook talking to a white person, we find that she is not simply responding to his requests for information about an ostensibly exotic and vanishing culture. She is, rather, redirecting those requests. She is asking him, and by extension future readers, to reconsider what makes them ask for certain kinds of information, and she invites them to hear the kinds of information she is more eager to give.

To write an oral story down, to dictate it for others and for another culture, is ostensibly to make visible the unheard and unseen. But Howard ironically uses the literate medium to gesture back toward this unheard and unseen, to underscore the impossibility of textual "mastery" and of transparent communication. She points back always to resistances that readers can't fully see, can't incorporate and assimilate. She thus moves between evading the outsider's questions and telling stories her own way, between "sharing" her culture and concealing it.

DISSEMBLANCE AND RETICENCE: RESTRUCTURING RELATIONS WITH READERS

Reasonable people have asked me: What is the point of such revealing and concealing? Why create texts at all, particularly cross-cultural texts, if not to share information about one's culture, if not to make outsiders understand? To this I would reply that there are different kinds of understanding and different kinds of audiences; no single text (including this book) seeks to communicate with *everyone*. The kinds of understanding that Jackson, Winnemucca, and Howard offer do not merely fill the desire for empirical knowledge, but instead work to prompt readers, listeners, and cultural tourists to think about that desire, about what it means, and about how it might be changed for the better. This is not, incidentally, to assume that their audiences, intended and actual, included *only* non-Indians. Indigenous audiences would usually not need the kinds of mediation I am saying these women did not provide, which would partly account for the absence of such explanatory gestures. But Jackson, Winnemucca, and Howard spoke quite directly, if not primarily, to white readers, and those readers are my focus here. Today, their audiences would obviously include a much higher proportion of Indian readers.

We can think of it this way: assimilation asks a "minority" culture to move toward the "dominant" culture, to become more like the dominant culture, to explain itself for the benefit of the majority that is trying to annex it. The women I read in this project seek to change that dynamic. In moving always between concealing and revealing indigenous lives, between inviting non-Indians in and holding them at arm's length, these women make the relationships between reader and writer, Indian and non-Indian, much more nuanced.

In this argument, I follow another strand in contemporary criticism. Many scholars have fruitfully emphasized strategies of indirection and self-concealment in women's and minority narratives, proposing that even as they claim what Edward Said calls the "power to narrate," the creators of such works avoid overexposing their identities and cultures in order to preserve those identities and cultures. Such a thesis takes various forms. It has been articulated by scholars of ethnic literature, as in Henry Louis Gates's well-known concept of "masking" in the African-American tradition, and it has been powerfully taken up by a range of feminist scholars. Darlene Clark Hine, for example, uses the phrase "culture of dissemblance" to describe female slave narratives, and Nancy K. Miller has written famously of "italicization" as an indication of feminine resistance.[43] Closer to the aims of my project, Zora Neale Hurston scholar Carla Kaplan suggests that selfrevelation isn't always self-empowerment; sometimes narrators face listeners who cannot or will not hear what they have to say, who will misread their words or even use their words against them. Much women's and African-American fiction, Kaplan says, therefore dramatizes not only the need for "but also the lack of competent—let alone ideal—interlocutors."[44]

Such arguments point us to what scholars in the ethnography of communication have long known—that narrative is first and foremost a communicative encounter, one with distinct political consequences. Along these lines, Greg Sarris has written powerfully on the verbal art of his relative, the California Pomo basketweaver and healer Mabel McKay. He finds that her speech, far from simply "revealing" Pomo culture, often points expressly to the positions of speaker and listener, to the gap between their varying cultural understandings. For instance, to a question from a non-Pomo medical student about how McKay treated poison oak, McKay's terse and witty reply was, "Calamine lotion." McKay thus uses the exchange to show that Indian practices are neither so "past" nor so unadaptable as many people might think; in so doing, she manages, as Sarris puts it, to make "the interlocutor immediately aware of the present context and of the ways the interlocutor may be framing her world."[45] I have found such readings incredibly helpful for thinking about nineteenth-century women's writings and narratives about American Indians. For they help us see that the apparent inconsistencies in stance and narrative voice in these works needn't be signs of artistic failure but are rather evidence that these women saw their readers and listeners as entities to be constantly sized up, renegotiated, sometimes even temporarily bypassed.

As they did in the Era of Assimilation, non-Indian readers today expect certain kinds of things from American Indian literatures. They want, generally, to learn about different cultures, to have some kind of access to those cultures. In their collection of essays, *Cultural Institutions of the Novel*, Diedre Lynch and William Warner observe that "novels exploit the claim to offer a detailed and inclusive representation of everyday life."[46] I would hasten to add that novels are hardly the only genre to exploit this claim, and that poetry, autobiography, and certainly ethnography have also, at various times and in various contexts, "been privileged as a window opening onto the characters of nations and peoples."[47] Moreover, it need not be the text itself, or the author herself, that actively exploits the claim to be "representative." Most ethnic writers are acutely conscious of their potential status as representative, and many actively chafe against such status. Nevertheless, *readers* continue to look to those writers' works to fulfill their desire for information about other cultures, about other ways of life.

Not all of that desire, by the way, is innately colonizing or self-invested; the desire to know an "other" can certainly be honest and constructive. But it can also be tangled up in less constructive cultural practices even as it seeks to transcend those, and the artists I discuss in this study were quite aware of those conflicted and conflicting desires. Progressive reformers in the Era of Assimilation hoped, perhaps, that by sharing information about other cultures, we could arrive at a better cross-cultural understanding. But the women in my study suggest that information about other cultures is not enough, and sometimes not even desirable, because giving people information about yourself can also give them control. Speaking to this same dynamic in the work of contemporary diversity theorists, Sherene Razack has called for a politics of accountability; in her book *Looking White People in the Eye*, she challenges the idea that with a little more information about each other, we can be innocent of history and systems of social injustice:

> Tracing our complicity in these systems requires that we shed notions of mastering differences, abandoning the idea that differences are pre-given, knowable, and existing in a social and historical vacuum. Instead, we invest our energies in exploring the histories, social relations, and conditions that structure groups unequally to one another and *that shape what can be known, thought, and said*. This does not mean that we abandon sensitivity. . . . Instead, we need to direct our efforts to the conditions of communication and knowledge production that prevail, calculating not only who can speak and how they are likely to be heard but also how we know what we know and the interest we protect through our knowing (italics in original).[48]

The "conditions of communication and knowledge" are a central theme in the works of Jackson, Winnemucca, and Howard. All are intensely concerned with what it means to be a woman speaking—speaking for and as those who have little power, speaking to those who have a great deal. Jackson created a furor by firing off vituperative letters to public officials; throughout *Ramona*, women characters similarly round up the courage to criticize men in power. Sarah Winnemucca incurred scandal and censure by critiquing powerful and corrupt male agents; her harried attempts to tell the truth and be heard form a motif in her autobiography. Victoria Howard, talking to Melville Jacobs, loaded her stories with episodes of female figures verbally jousting with males. In Howard's citation, one woman triumphantly finishes telling how she dismissed a male shaman's diagnosis: "That is what I said to him."

"That is what I said to him"—this simple statement tells of the need to speak out, to tell of the successes and failures of having spoken out. For these women, resistance to assimilation could never be as simple as merely speaking (open protest) or not speaking (silent self-preservation). Rather, that resistance became deeply intertwined with the question of how to speak, whether to speak, and how one might—or might not—be understood.

CHAPTER ONE

HELEN HUNT JACKSON, THE WOMEN REFORMERS, AND DAWES ACT DISCOURSE

Listening to Standing Bear's 1879 speech in Boston, Helen Hunt Jackson not only "discovered" American Indians as subject matter but was inspired to make a literary about-face. She had enjoyed a healthy career as what we might think of as a classic nineteenth-century woman writer, carving out power within gendered constraints: she published under pseudonyms, she made a great deal of money, she traveled widely in the United States and abroad and wrote about foreign places, and she produced poetry and novels that critics today label "sentimental" or "domestic" for their concern with subjects traditionally considered female, such as mothering, romance, and home life.

As of 1879, however, Jackson adopted a much more public stance as crusader for the oppressed. She made herself known for antagonizing men like Carl Schurz, then secretary of the interior, and she fashioned her voice as that of the national conscience, giving her pieces titles like "The Indian Problem: Questions for the People." She secured assignments from *Century* magazine to travel to southern California and visit the Mission Indians there; she got herself appointed to a commission to survey those Indians' lands and make recommendations to the Interior Department for preserving the lands. Of this period in her career, she famously remarked, "I have become what I have said a thousand times was the most odious thing in the world, 'a woman with a hobby.'"[1]

Only four years later, Jackson announced another change. Expressing dissatisfaction with the response to her nonfiction work, namely her letter-writing campaigns and *A Century of Dishonor*, she declared, "I have sugared my pill, and it remains to be seen if it will go down."[2] She was returning to the romance novel with what would become a massive best-seller, *Ramona*.

Jackson's two self-characterizations—reluctant reformer and subversive pill-sweetener—both widely quoted in past and present writings about her, reveal how the desire for self-authorization erupted into the political projects of white women reformers who claimed to speak for Indians. On the face of it, Jackson seems to say that she tried her hand at "public" (and overtly political) writing, with plenty of anxious irony about how that made her look, only to be burned back into a "private" or "women's" mode. But the circumstances surrounding her authorship were a good deal more complicated than that. Throughout her career, Jackson was a savvy self-marketer who fostered connections and friendships with influential men like Ralph Waldo Emerson and Oliver Wendell Holmes. When she used pseudonyms, she crafted them carefully for effect, acknowledging or denying them as it suited her.[3] She did arguably adopt a more public persona after 1879, but it wasn't entirely new, and it can't simply be concluded that she had previously written under different names out of timidity in the face of an inhospitable literary climate.

Part of what is at stake here are the material constraints on late-nineteenth-century women writers like Jackson—those circumstances that "forced" them to adopt pseudonyms or "forced" them to write romances. But even more compellingly, Jackson's career illuminates the narratives that women authors told about themselves as writers, the ways they envisioned and constructed their work as at once constrained, harmless, or subversive. Underlying those stories is what the literary critic Mark Seltzer calls *personation*—

Helen Hunt Jackson. (Courtesy of Tutt Library, Colorado College)

the ways a subject is called into being, or calls herself into being, as a relatively autonomous agent. Seltzer posits a recognition in late-nineteenth-century America "that bodies and persons are things that can be made."[4] Quoting Henry James, he observes that "'the happy development' of the subject—the way 'things grow up and are formed'—is also an intensity of possession and the possession of another person (or of oneself) as living property."[5]

As we will see, Jackson's conception of persons—of her characters, of American Indians, and of herself as a writer—has everything to do with the "intensity of possession" and, especially, with the ideology of possessive individualism. Her remarks on Indian policy, made to influential men and appearing in prominent newspapers and journals, underscore her public influence and illustrate some of the benefits and limitations that accrued to women when they took up Indians as their subject matter. Victoria Howard and Sarah Winnemucca capitalized on the "sympathy" of white people who wanted to "document" indigenous voices, who wanted to help American Indians be heard. Helen Hunt Jackson, somewhat differently, fashioned her own authorship and authorization around the position of "spokeswoman for" Indians. Taking such a position meant being branded with that most feminized of terms, *sentimental*. But to speak for Indians in the 1880s was also to make oneself a person, an authorized citizen, and to find oneself deeply embedded within a culture of land usurpation and assimilation, even as one set oneself against that culture.

A scene that comes relatively late in *Ramona* both dramatizes and interrogates this complex position. The Indian hero Alessandro returns momentarily to the house he has been forced out of. Through a cracked window, he hears and sees its new inhabitants: a racist and "brutish" white settler and his wife and two children. Through the gaze of the noble savage, the woman appears "weary and worn. Her face was a sensitive one, and her voice kindly." When the settler growls that "those dogs of Indians" have left the house bare, "The woman looked at him reproachfully, but did not speak for a moment. Then her cheeks flushed, and seeming unable to repress the speech, she exclaimed, "Well, I'm thankful enough . . . the poor things [took] their furniture. I'd never have slept a wink on that bedstead, I know, if it had ha' been left here. It's bad enough to take their houses this way!"[6]

Does one read this scene as pernicious or poignant? On the one hand, it seems to capitalize on the marginal status of one who must hesitate before speaking, then who *cannot* hold her tongue, who *must* have her say. The settler's wife emerges morally victorious without having to sacrifice much material comfort or stability. Moreover, a woman's speech, in this scenario, counts for a great deal. It presumably mitigates the Indian's situation: at least she feels bad about taking his lands, at least she has spoken on his behalf. On the other hand, the passage does figure this noble woman as ultimately constrained; it takes for granted her lack of options for more radical rejection of Indian removal. She does and must, after all, continue to occupy the house; she can hardly be expected to refuse to move with her husband, or to move out on him.

This text thus plays on competing senses of "possession": first, possession in the mode of Harriet Beecher Stowe, as a preternatural force that takes hold of women and makes their just and singular speech "irrepressible"[7]; second, possession of Indian property by whites, a possession in which the wives of settlers (possessions in themselves) are made complicit. Wives, who cannot possess property in the family arena, nevertheless become possessors and usurpers of indigenous lands. They speak out against a hierarchical and materialistic world but remain, in the novel's vision, complicit in the system they critique.[8]

The woman in Alessandro's house—a figure who appears again and again, in different guise, throughout the book—provides a paradigm for Jackson's authorial, self-making moves as well as for her novelistic strategies. In this chapter, I will argue that *Ramona* deploys the figure of the speaking woman to critique possessive individualism and to gesture toward more interconnected relations among citizens—that the novel is perhaps even "communitist," in Jace Weaver's sense of a literature that is committed to a sense of indigenous community that is in turn connected with the larger community. Specifically, at a time when national debate on "the Indian question" was almost uniform in its agreement that Indians must be incorporated into an Anglo-Saxon ideal based on individual acquisition of property, this novel dares not only to question that ideal but also to suggest the legitimacy of tribal ways of life and of American Indians as a collective body. In such suggestions, it yields ironic connections to the communitist discourse that I will locate in turn-of-the-century Indian work like Sarah Winnemucca's autobiography and Victoria Howard's storytelling. *Ramona* does not actually produce this discourse, which marks reservation-based American Indians as a political and cultural force. It does, however, acknowledge and respect the existence of a such a discourse.

I call *Ramona*'s connections to communitist discourse "ironic" because the book seems to have acted as such a willing participant in the cult of the noble savage and in all of that cult's assimilative baggage. The book unleashed a flood of new tourism in southern California, where it is set; a wave of Ramona-trackers, many of them famous figures like General Custer's widow, Elizabeth, wrote and spoke of their visits to the novel's "real" scenes and characters.[9] Frequently, this reportage expressed disappointment that neither the living conditions of Mission Indians nor "Ramona" herself were quite so picturesque as Jackson had painted them. But no matter. Hollywood went on to produce at least three film versions of the story, including a 1936 Loretta Young vehicle that blithely overrides the novel's angry critiques of white settlers in favor of soft focus and slapstick humor. Meanwhile, the town of Hemet, California, still stages an annual Ramona pageant, which reportedly once featured a young Raquel Welch as the heroine.[10]

Even more dangerously and materially, *Ramona* remains firmly tied to the Dawes Act and thus to the breakup of Indian lands and communities. Indeed, the act was passed only three years after the novel was published, and readers have long drawn a straight line from the one to the other. Allan Nevins writes that "the general agitation in which [Jackson] played so prominent a part was largely responsible for [the Dawes Act's] enactment"; Michael Dorris reports that Ramona "was meant to have a political as well as a literary impact, and it succeeded on both fronts," adding, "It contributed to the sentiment that swept such reforms as the Dawes Act through Congress."[11] For better or worse, *Ramona* has done significant cultural work. Indeed, in the directness of its linkage, real or imagined, to historical events and to widespread cultural attitudes, Jackson's novel ranks with *Uncle Tom's Cabin* or *The Jungle*.

The concept of cultural work has been of central importance for literary historians trying to rethink and expand traditional canons because, in Jane Tompkins's influential definition, it involves reading texts "not as works of art embodying enduring themes in complex forms, but as attempts to redefine the social order."[12] As Tompkins has demonstrated, attention to novels' social and political effects—the "designs" that books have on their readers—rather than to aesthetics alone or to supposed transhistorical universals can give us new ways of reckoning literary value. But as critics investigating cultural work know, the concept also opens up a series of difficult and provocative questions about how to determine literary meaning. Cultural work, for instance, may be unintended as well as intended: Upton Sinclair didn't necessarily envision a new Food and Drug Administration when he wrote his novel, though he did surely hope to incite public outrage over labor conditions in the meat-packing industry. Similarly, cultural work can be covert as well as overt: *Uncle Tom's Cabin* unfortunately can do as much to promote racism as it did to challenge nineteenth-century attitudes toward black slaves.

From my point of view, what is most interesting here is that cultural work is not merely a recent literary-critical coinage. Readers have always made claims for and argued about the effects of texts, be they Puritan psalm books or Arnold Schwarzenegger movies. When Abraham Lincoln called Harriet Beecher Stowe "the little lady who started the big war," he was not, of course, describing what Stowe "really" did; he was making a case for her book's cultural impact. When people since the 1850s have cited Lincoln's famous characterization, they are likewise working to establish—or sometimes to raise questions about—the ability of *Uncle Tom's Cabin* to reshape American attitudes and institutions. Similarly, when readers and reformers hail *Ramona* as somehow responsible for the passage of the Dawes Act, they are not merely reporting the book's actual effects, which are, in the final analysis, extremely difficult to pin down. Rather, they are creating a new narrative, telling us a story about what this book does and how it does it. Jackson, as we will see, participated enthusiastically in the creation of such narratives.

Assessing a text's cultural work is therefore complicated business. It involves looking at how that text has been circulated, deployed, and received, and to what ends. It involves, moreover, a re-examination of what that the text actually says, or—perhaps more provocatively—what it might be *made* to say. In what follows, I would like to tell a different story about *Ramona*'s cultural work and thus make a new case for its value. In short, I would like to stir up the common association between Jackson and the Dawes Act. I will present evidence that her texts, including *Ramona*, are sometimes ambivalent about and even openly critical of allotment and assimilation. Severing the novel from that highly devastating piece of legislation can help us better see how women in the Era of Assimilation thought about their own political agency and storytelling, as well as help us recover alternative histories of national identities.

RAMONA'S CIVILIZED SAVAGES

It is not difficult to see why readers, in Jackson's day and since, might associate *Ramona* with allotment and assimilation. The novel uses a romance plot between two eminently civilized savages—the mixed-blood heroine of its title and the American Indian hero Alessandro—to advance its protest against white encroachment and brutality. The lovely Ramona, knowing nothing of her Indian mother and Scots father, lives in the care of Señora Moreno, the widow of a wealthy landed Mexican army general.[13] The Señora, an embittered and zealously Catholic woman who lavishes affection on her delicate son Felipe, despises the miscegenated Ramona but dutifully keeps her. Into this household comes the handsome Alessandro, an Indian from Temecula, to help with sheep-shearing.

The first half of the novel culminates in Alessandro's elopement with Ramona; the second, in his death. The couple are pushed out of village after village by encroaching whites. They build and re-build homes and strive to live peacefully and self-sufficiently, while nevertheless connecting again and again with new communities as they move. Finally, Alessandro is murdered by an especially malicious settler who blames him for stealing his horse. The despondent Ramona, with her daughter by Alessandro, is rescued by Felipe, who takes her to Mexico and marries her.

As this cursory plot summary illustrates, the book turns on a series of "removals"—Ramona's removal from her mother; her flights with Alessandro, first from Señora Moreno and then from wherever they attempt to settle; and finally, Alessandro's removal through murder and Ramona's flight to Mexico. Such removals could be read in the tradition of James Fenimore Cooper's vanishing races, reassuring readers that, for better or worse, Indians are indeed disappearing.[14] The "advanced" racial state of the protagonists further reassures. Tacitly acknowledging the savage-barbaric-civilized spectrum, Jackson begins from the premise that civilization will provide the clearest case for American Indian entitlement. It is surely this premise that explains her choice of the Mission Indians of southern California as her subjects, rather than the nomadic Cheyennes or the resistant Utes about whom she herself had written in earlier letters to the press.

Mission Indians, long under Spanish and Christian influence, were like many other indigenous peoples already living a hybrid, agrarian lifestyle in the 1880s; they "had concepts that included individual and family ownership and inheritance of specific resources as well as the undivided ownership of others and inter-band use of still other resources."[15] Add to this the popular fascination in the 1880s with California missions as evocative of some twilight arcadia,[16] and the novel bolsters the view that Indians are safely vanishing through incorporation, even as its litany of cruelties strives to incite outrage over those more overt "vanishings"— Alessandro's death, the removals of his people, the death of his and Ramona's first child.

Further, Alessandro and Ramona, as some of the contemporary reviews and many later critics have observed, aren't presented as very "Indian." Alessandro, a full-blood, is so light-skinned that almost everyone, including Ramona, keeps forgetting his race (p. 75).[17] Ramona, thanks to her Scottish father, has "steel-blue" eyes that almost no character who meets her fails to note, even though they're always properly hooded by her long black lashes. Her face has "just enough of olive tint in her complexion to underlie and enrich her skin without making it swarthy" (p. 38). Her physical descriptions, like the hybrid conditions of the Mission Indians, offer a blend of exotic indigenous features and phenotypic difference easily assimilated to the Anglo-American norm.

Similarly, white and Indian blend robustly in the homes that Ramona and Alessandro make. Everything in the text seems geared toward the very Western and romantic literary goal of this couple's happily-ever-after. The narrator speaks of "the sense of home" as "the strongest passion Alessandro possessed" (p. 289). By "home" the book means *not* necessarily a return to the land on which he and his people always lived (although that clearly is important to him) but *building a house* for himself and his wife. It doesn't seem to matter *where* these Indians live; wherever they settle, they create their own felicitous domiciles. Thus, "progressive races" might be agrarian but at the same time, and in an apparent contradiction, they are also highly mobile. Andrew Jackson once asserted that while it might be "painful" for Indians to leave their homelands, they should, just as European immigrants had always done, "leave the land of their birth to seek new homes in distant regions"— hence, the Trail of Tears.[18] Indeed, Americans in the 1880s would insist, along with Charles Painter of the Indians Rights Association, that Indians be "given" lands, precisely so that they could be fixed, not so that they could "roam."[19] Thus, Ramona and Alessandro's ability—and need—to make homes literally anywhere accommodates the urgent mobility of an expanding nation as well as its agrarian imperative.

So, even on the run, Alessandro makes a soft, scented bed of ferns for his bride (p. 204). And the first time the couple builds their own house,

> It looked like a palace to the San Pasquale people, after Ramona had arranged their little possessions in it; and she herself felt rich as she looked around her two small rooms. The old San Luis Rey chairs and the raw-hide bedstead were there, and, most precious of all, the statuette of the Madonna. For this Alessandro had built a niche in the wall, between the head of the bed and the one window. The niche was deep enough to hold small pots in front of the statuette; and Ramona kept constantly growing there wild-cucumber plants, which wreathed and re-wreathed the niche till it looked like a bower. Below it hung her gold rosary and the ivory Christ; and many a woman of the village, when she came to see Ramona, asked permission to go into the bedroom and say her

prayers there; so that it finally came to be a sort of shrine for the whole village. A broad veranda, as broad as the Señora's, ran across the front of the little house. This was the only thing for which Ramona had asked. She could not quite fancy life without a veranda, and linnets in the thatch (p. 250).

These domesticating and domesticated protagonists here prove amply acquisitive, satisfied with their own "little possessions," even as they are ennobled in their poverty. They show themselves pious and hardworking citizens, all the more charming for their firm ensconcing in nature, with their thatch designed to attract birds.

The happy and literal intertwining of wild-cucumber plants and religious objects demonstrates how successfully the growing nation, for its part, will absorb the Indian: like the "olive tint" that just "enriches" Ramona's skin, the couple's "primitive" raw-hide furniture will coexist with, even enrich, this self-sufficient domicile without ever threatening its Christian ideals. I use the term *absorb* here purposefully, for it was part of Dawes's own rhetoric—a marked *stage* in the inexorable path to incorporation: "the State can only bring the Indian into the environment of civilization, and he is 'absorbed' wherever and whenever that occurs. . . . Assimilation is another and a better thing, but it is the step that follows absorption."[20] Underscoring the success of that final step, Ramona proves an indefatigable homemaker and domestic worker. She is ever on display: "feverishly" repairing a damaged lace altar-cloth, setting out flowers, beautifying everything she touches. Her only apparent wish, besides running away with Alessandro, is to go among Alessandro's people and "teach" them (p. 122). And true to that missionizing vision, her shared home becomes "a sort of shrine for the whole village" (p. 250). It resembles the residence of a field matron, whose job it was to open her house to Indians as a model.[21]

In many ways, then, *Ramona* could satisfy the desires of 1880s reformers: it offers domestic and agrarian Indians who can smoothly "fit . . . among us," in the words of educator and onetime Indian Commissioner Merrill Gates.[22] In the context of swelling immigration, rapid industrialization, and massive labor strikes—in short, of all those elements of late-nineteenth-century life that are so often cited as signs of great national unease and anxiety—the novel's ultimate vision of incorporated Indians is reassuring. Moreover, as Ramona's spectacular homemaking illustrates, the novel makes this reassurance at least partly by deploying the same kind of domestic ideology on which Stowe's famous novel predicates its own revolution. But in Jackson's novel, and in the context of the movement for general allotment, Ramona's homemaking arguably reinforces that central image of allotment discourse: individual Indian families safely maintained in their individual homes.

RESISTING ALLOTMENT DISCOURSE: JACKSON'S INDIAN NONFICTION

Just the same, it is less than clear that Jackson would have been happy with the way that allotment and Indian reform continued after her death. Valerie Sherer Mathes suggests just this in *Helen Hunt Jackson and Her Indian Reform Legacy*, by far the best book on Jackson's work. Mathes shows that while Jackson did have several short, favorable meetings with groups like the Women's National Indian Association, and while these women praised her writings, they also went far beyond the author's own goals. Avidly pursuing the goal of civilization by refueling domestic ideology, women reformers began by collecting funds and building houses for Indians, but they moved quickly to aggressive missionizing and to teaching Indian women "proper" ways. In some cases, as I discuss below, these groups even wound up fighting with American Indians over particular properties. Jackson, for her part, mainly confined her agenda to preservation of the indigenous land base: surveying lands, setting them aside as reservations, and keeping whites off them.

Historians have made much of the differences between "gradualists," like Schurz, who believed that Indians should slowly be allowed to acculturate to "civilized ways" at their own pace, and fanatics like the clergyman Lyman Abbott, who used metaphors of flooding and militarism to suggest the urgency of assimilation: "[T]hree hundred thousand people have no right to hold a continent and keep at bay a race able to people it and provide the happy homes of civilization."[23] But despite these disagreements, as we have seen, the Dawes Era was characterized by a remarkable uniformity of views. The historian Loring Priest sees this as a matter of pragmatics; widely differing groups of people—whites who wanted more land, reformers who advocated "advancement" for the "lower races," settlers who sought war prevention—found in allotment the means to their own diverse ends.[24] Yet underlying all those disparate "schools" was the assumption that anglocentric norms, based especially on the individual ownership of property, were the superior and inevitable bases of civilization.

For example, even white settlers, who, stereotypically, were categorically hostile to Indians, and Eastern reformers, who, stereotypically, were sympathetic to Indians, found a common point of interest in the enormous land cession that was one end result of the Dawes Act. Indeed, the "freeing up" of "surplus" lands after American Indians had received their allotments was not simply a shifty side effect of the legislation, nor was it a concession to disaffected white settlers. On the contrary, reformers and "sympathizers," like Secretary Schurz in his last annual report (1880), promoted the act unabashedly as a way to "open to settlement by white men the large tracts of land now belonging to the reservations, but not used by the Indians."[25] The report, which carries the implicit and then-popular assumption that Indians would "learn" from whites when the two races lived in greater proximity, holds that people who aren't situated on a fixed plot of land—farming it, improving it, using it to *produce*—aren't really "using" it anyway.[26]

Proposals to open more Indian land to whites, on the one hand, and rhetoric about assimilation and moral uplift, on the other, may look different on the face of it, but those differences are really quite superficial. No one in the 1880s was seeing or talking about American Indian communalism or communities as viable.[27] Instead, all permissible ways of talking about allotment were deeply rooted in the model of agrarian cultivation and possessive individualism.

> The study I have given to the Indian question in its various aspects, past and present, has produced in my mind the firm conviction that the only certain way to secure the Indians in their possessions, and to prevent them from becoming forever a race of homeless paupers and vagabonds, is to transform their tribal title into individual title, inalienable for a certain period; in other words, to settle them in severalty, and give them by a patent an individual fee-simple in their lands. Then they will hold their lands by the same title by which white men hold theirs, and they will, as a matter of course, have the same standing in the courts, and the same legal protection of their property.[28]

Along with almost everyone involved in allotment debates—activists, government officials, and so on—Schurz assumed that the government was powerless to take action against whites who encroached on reservation lands. But as Wilcomb Washburn points out, there *were* alternatives to allotment, one of which was to uphold and enforce the legal rights of Indians, *collectively*, to their lands.[29]

Indian sovereignty was precisely the issue in the Standing Bear case. Prompted by the visit of Standing Bear, the LaFlesches, and Suzette's husband, Thomas Tibbles, Jackson and several other prominent figures (including Henry Dawes and Henry Wadsworth Longfellow) organized the Boston Citizenship Committee. The rights for which this group was organizing bore directly on Indian self-determination. In her preface to William Justin Harsha's dreadfully dull 1881 "Indian" novel, *Ploughed Under*, for instance, Suzette LaFlesche commanded readers to "[a]llow an Indian to suggest that the solution of the vexed "Indian Question" is *Citizenship*, with all its attending duties and responsibilities, as well as the privileges of protection under the law, by which the Indian could appeal to the courts, when deprived of life, liberty, or property, as every citizen can, and would be allowed the opportunity to make something of himself, in common with every other citizen."[30] LaFlesche some-times uses the rhetoric of possessive individualism—"recognize the Indian as a person and a citizen, give him a title to his lands, and place him within the jurisdiction of the courts, *as an indi-vidual*."[31] Yet to her, and to the other members of the committee in 1879, citizenship meant something very different than it did to other activists. Most white reformers wanted Indian citizenship as a way of civilizing the savages; they thought of it as incorporating Indians into, and thus validating, already operable systems of ownership, citizenship, and political redress. LaFlesche and the Boston Indian Citizenship Committee, however, wanted citizen-ship as an *extension* of liberties to indigenous peoples, as a way of securing legal protection for tribal lands.

Clearly, then, allotment and citizenship struck to the heart of conceptions of national identity, which explains why, as Wilcomb Washburn reports, most humanitarians embraced the idea of forced allotment by 1884, the very year *Ramona* came out. In its initial form, allotment was supposed to be subject to approval by two-thirds of a given tribe, but activists quickly determined that it should be implemented by force.[32] Ruling out tribal approval as too threatening to U.S. sovereignty, reformers asserted repeatedly that an Indian nation could not be "imperium et imperio"—a government within a government.

It is possible that *Ramona*, published in 1884, contributed to such sentiment. However, it's more likely that the Elk-Wilkins decision of that year had a greater impact. In this case, brought by a nonreservation Indian who was refused the right to vote in a local election, the Supreme Court ruled that American Indians were not in fact citizens under the Fourteenth Amendment, but that Congress could make them citizens. In Priest's assessment, "most Americans were deeply shocked to learn that citizenship was possible only after naturalization."[33] This shock might best be explained by a model offered by Priscilla Wald: using Freud's notion of the uncanny, she suggests that while U.S. nation formation has historically worked by excluding certain subjects (black slaves, American Indians) from social and legal representation, that exclusion ironically makes visible, in the most unsettling ways, the constructed and contingent nature of citizenship itself.[34] This compelling explanation of the threat posed to the anxious nation by peoples whom the law deems non-representable shows how a case like *Elk v. Wilkins* could seal the push for Indian citizenship. As Hoxie puts it, the case threatened to "embarrass those who saw total assimilation as a vindication of the universality of American institutions."[35] Indian citizenship and "civilization" turn out to be not just an "Indian question," but a question about the shape of U.S. national identity overall.

Given the greed for "surplus" lands, the assertion that the government could protect only individual and not collective rights, and the press for forced allotment, Helen Hunt Jackson's relation to Dawes Act discourse begins to look much more tenuous. We may compare her, for instance, to the anthropologist and self-proclaimed "friend of the Indians" Alice Cunningham Fletcher, who once rhapsodized that "the Mission Indians are the bequest of Helen Hunt Jackson," adding, "if we love her and honor her let us be faithful, and complete what she has left us to do."[36] Fletcher took issue with an early version of the allotment bill on the grounds that 160 acres might not be a realistic amount of land for every person in every region, and that some Indians might not in fact want to be farmers but traders or other professionals.[37] She not only came around to the General Allotment Act; she also became one of its most zealous implementers. Appointed special agent by the Commissioner of Indian Affairs, she sold off lands belonging to the Omahas despite tribal resistance. A strong proponent of speedy and forced allotment, Fletcher repeatedly advertised the land-cession benefits of severalty. She felt, indeed, that Indians had far more land than they needed, and she even urged the breaking of treaties.[38]

Jackson, however, was adamantly pro-treaty, and she never alluded to the benefits that would accrue to whites from "surplus" Indian lands. On the contrary, in *Ramona* and elsewhere, she attacked white settlers as the root of the problem. In her brief tenure as Indian commissioner in southern California, for instance, she worked mainly to survey and demarcate tribal lands for their protection, not for their dissolution. In her various "Indian" writings, too, while she hardly disputed the allegedly "uplifting" benefits of allotment, she held to the idea that American Indians deserved self-determination. This is perhaps most pointed in her interventions in the Ponca dispute. Secretary Schurz's position was that it would be useless for Standing Bear to sue for recovery of his lands or for a writ of *habeas corpus*, since no court would allow Indians to sue the government. In the *New York Tribune*, "H. H." took him to task for suggesting that

> "the Department has done all that was in its power to indemnify them for the wrong done them," and that it is an open question whether it is worth while to make any effort to restore to them the lands of which they were robbed, because it would be "a mere vindication of a right to a piece of land."
>
> Yes; that is all it would be. But a great many men have laid down their lives for just such a "mere vindication." . . . No race . . . has ever shown a stronger love of "mere" "land" than the race to which the Honorable Secretary of the Interior belongs. . . . It was a strange phrase for a German to use. . . . Official though it may be, however, it stands for nothing more than the Secretary's private opinion, the Secretary's

individual standard, the Secretary's peculiar estimate of the relative significance and importance of ownership and possession.[39]

This article, commonly cited as a "flaying" of Schurz that propelled him to respond,[40] is remarkable both for its acidity—the glee it takes in assaulting this important man, especially by racially "othering" him, making him a foreigner, as he does the Indians—and for its particular articulation of indigenous land rights. It is an entirely different assertion of the value of *place* than we find in most allotment discourse, including *Ramona*. Most of this discourse, by including Indians among the progressive races who could live "anywhere," were able to shift that "anywhere" according to time and need: in Andrew Jackson's day, anywhere was "anywhere but here," west and out of reach; in Helen Hunt Jackson's day it became an anywhere "among us." Somewhat differently, without asserting that Indians should live in fixed places, Jackson's *Tribune* article suggests that the "significance and importance of ownership and possession" varies across cultures and must be respected as such.

Early on, Jackson opposed allotment more explicitly. Washburn reports that she wrote in 1881 to Oliver Wendell Holmes criticizing the severalty proposal, accusing its proponents of having land speculation as their ulterior motive.[41] In that same year, she wrote to Longfellow that Schurz's "infamous severalty bill . . . would have, as White Eagle said of it, 'plucked the Indian like a bird.'"[42] Robert Mardock argues that she "never forgave" Schurz until the end of her life, implying that she also never gave in on the allotment issue.[43] That is perhaps overstating the case, for some of her later writings do begin to endorse allotment. Like other reformers, Jackson seems to have become progressively pro-allotment through the 1880s, with one important exception: she insisted on the primacy of American Indian self-determination.

In one letter to Schurz (far more "polite" and contained in tone than the *Tribune* piece), Jackson simply asks whether she could believe that Schurz "would be in favor of the Poncas recovering their lands by process of law, provided it were practicable?" Additionally, she raises the problem of whether allotment will so "naturally" guarantee Indians' rights, asking simply if the severalty bill has actually been brought before Congress and whether it is "so worded as to secure" the rights Schurz argues it will bring.[44] Jackson quotes an anonymous *New York Times* editorial to get more starkly to the point: "it is to be regretted that the Secretary did not pause here long enough to show how the giving to an Indian of 160 acres of land can clothe him with civil rights which he does not now possess, and which the Secretary thinks the courts cannot give him."[45]

Jackson's 1881 report on the status of the California Mission Indians, written jointly with Abbot Kinney during their appointments as Indian commissioners, contains more favorable references to severalty. The report focuses mainly on preserving a tribal land base, though its eleven recommendations also include provisions for Indian education. Its fourth recommendation suggests that "all these Indians' reservations, those already set off by Executive order, and all new ones made for them, whether of Government lands now in their occupation, or of lands which may be hereafter by legal process reclaimed for them from the grant lands on which they are now living, be patented to the several bands occupying them; the United States to hold the patent in trust for the period of twenty-five years."[46] The report develops this reference to severalty further down the page: "The best way and time of allotting these Indians' lands to them in severalty must be left to the decision of the Government . . . agents and commissioners being instructed to keep the advantages of this system constantly before the Indians' minds."[47] In these lines we find the same paternalism we find everywhere else in Dawes Act discourse: Indians must be made to see that allotment is the best thing for them.

However, the document also goes on to say of the Indians that

> Some of them are fit for [allotment] now, and earnestly desire it, but the majority are not ready for it. The communal system, on which those now living in villages use their lands, satisfies them, and is apparently administered without difficulty. It is precisely the same system as that on which the pueblo lands were cultivated by the early Spanish settlers in Southern California. They agree among themselves to respect each other's right of occupancy; a man's right to a field this year depending on his having cultivated it last year, and so on. It seems not to occur to these Indians that land is a thing to be quarrelled over.[48]

I want to underline this gesture toward the validity of "the communal system," however grossly this passage seems to misconstrue that system and to subsume it under the values of earlier colonizers. The last line, arguably condescending in its reference to "these Indians" (who are "not ready" for indisputable progress), sounds ironic and critical of Euro-American values based on "quarreling over" property. It thus positions itself somewhere against a prevailing discourse about the inevitable link between property and the "cultivation" of civilized values—a discourse exemplified by Ezra Hayt, Indian commissioner in 1877 and an early proponent of general allotment, who could write, with no evident self-awareness, that "the system of title in common has also been pernicious to [the Indians], in that it has prevented individual advancement and repressed that spirit of rivalry and the desire to accumulate property for personal use or comfort which is the source of success and advancement in all white communities."[49] The Jackson-Kinney report entertains the possibility that there may be different "successes," different systems and communities that might coexist. At a time when so much in the United States was pressing toward incorporation, that suggestion remained an unsettling one.

RE-READING *RAMONA* FOR
COMMUNITIST DISCOURSE

However much we want to make the case for *Ramona*'s cultural importance, painting its author as "the little lady who started this big legislation" turns out to be an unappealing route, partly because of the Dawes Act's horrific effects and, more importantly, because Jackson's nonfiction writings show such ambivalence about and even hostility toward allotment. In contrast to the nonfiction, *Ramona*'s specific intervention is somewhat elusive; the book's message cannot be immediately pinned down to much more than "justice for the American Indian." The novel is surely plastic enough to permit Dawes Act reformers to have loved and cited it for their purposes; I am not, therefore, arguing that *Ramona*, nor indeed Helen Hunt Jackson, was "actually" anti-Dawes Act. Rather, I want to point to Jackson's writings as one of the very few recorded places where we can recognize the slightest resistance to or skepticism about the assumptions underlying the policy of allotment and assimilation.[50]

Jackson was fascinated with the California missions, an interest that converged with a national obsession with "local color" as part of American identity. But while Jackson's focus on the missions was implicitly sympathetic to an imperialist heritage, it also supported a more benevolent investment in communal landholding. *Ramona* is regionalist writing; it emerged at a time of intense fascination with southern California in particular and charming localities in general. As the literary critic Richard Brodhead has explained, "nineteenth-century regional writing produced a real-sounding yet deeply fictitious America that was not homogenous yet not heterogeneous either and whose diversities were ranged under one group's normative sway."[51] Brodhead and others have argued that regionalism provides a narrative of supercession; with the local being supplanted by national brands, national corporations, and transcontinental railroads, it provides something all Americans can cherish. Similarly, *Ramona* uses its representation of residual Catholicism to endorse the consolidating nation. On the face of it, its love affair with Franciscans and Madonna statuettes might seem a departure from the bulk of Indian reform discourse, which was generally Protestant. Nonetheless, as Kevin Starr argues in his fascinating literary/historical study of southern California as an emergent regional identity, Jackson's novel offers a site where "a representative Protestant sensibility, deracinated from place and dogma, feels the comforts of a local Catholic tradition."[52] Catholics, like Indians, are made less frightening and less other in this formula—quaint relics of the past available for touristic consumption.

To say, as does the report on the Mission Indians, that the indigenous communal system is "precisely the same system as that on which the pueblo lands were cultivated by the early Spanish settlers" is not only to occlude the real differences between indigenous and Spanish systems, but also to elide that earlier, troubling history of colonization. The Mission Indian way of life in the 1880s was already a palimpsest on which was written the painful colonial history of *congregación/reducción*—the process by which Indians were brought together to centralized locations where they could be worked, taxed, and acculturated.[53] Indigenous peoples often lived in the missions under coercion, producing labor and goods for the Spanish military, and they were subject to horrific discipline, something Jackson's travel writings seem blandly to approve: "The rule of the friars was in the main a kindly one. The vice of drunkenness was severely punished by flogging. Quarrelling between husbands and wives was also dealt with summarily, the offending parties being chained together by the leg till they were glad to promise to keep peace."[54]

Nevertheless, Jackson also flirts with the possibility of alternative norms and communally held property. It is on these grounds that she emerges as a radical voice in the 1880s, when, as we have seen, it was imperative precisely that Indians cease to exist as a collective entity. In a key scene, for example, the naive Ramona and the still-pure but more-worldly-wise Alessandro explicitly discuss the role of the missions. The passage represents the novel's curious mix of romanticizing colonialism and chafing against it.

Alessandro has just finished recounting a spectacle that Jackson also uses in her travel texts: the fantastic (or better, phantasmic) scene in which the beloved Father Peyri must leave his mission.[55] As he boards his boat for Spain, the Indians jump into the sea and swim after him, crying. And yet, Alessandro must admit, there were bad men at some of the other missions. One, he remembers, who just happened to have been a converted Indian, cut off the ears of some neophytes who escaped the mission. Alessandro concludes,

> "The Indians did not all want to come to the Missions; some of them preferred to stay in the woods, and live as they always had lived; and I think they had a right to do that if they preferred, Majella [his pet name for Ramona, an hispanicized, feminized and diminutive version of the term for "Wood-Dove"]. It was stupid of them to stay and be like beasts, and not know anything; but do you not think they had the right?"
>
> "It is the command to preach the gospel to every creature," replied the pious Ramona. "That is what Father Salvierderra said was the reason the Franciscans came here" (p. 231).

This highly elliptical passage, despite its rosy view of a terrible period in the colonization of indigenous peoples, at least drops the hint that mission life wasn't always so rosy. It contains that suggestion, of course, by making the "one" bad missionary an Indian and by Alessandro's admission that "it was stupid of them to stay and be like beasts." But this containment seems subverted by his eloquent declaration that the Indians had the *right* to live as they chose, an assertion that echoes the Jackson-Kinney report's statement that the communal land system appeared to work well enough for the Indians who chose to continue it.

Moreover, the narrative voice here proves remarkably elusive. In one tight gesture—"the pious Ramona"—it both elevates *and* questions its heroine's reply. Unlike the white women in the novel who speak in defiance of powerful men, Ramona acts as a mere mouthpiece for the Franciscan father she so loved, almost as though she can't be expected to know any better. She's ostensibly the heroine of this novel, but her authority is undercut in this passage. No didactic narrator intervenes to assure that we take her side in this discussion. Like many places in the novel, this passage pulls back from its best critique just when it is poised to deliver it. At the same time, it shows how the polyvocality of a novel can open up critical possibilities not available in more monologic texts like Jackson's travel writings, a point I address in the final section of this chapter.

To be sure, one of the disappointing things about the book for many contemporary readers and especially for feminists is its saccharine and voiceless heroine. "Ramona herself is lifeless," Dorris avers, "so uncomplex in her goodness, loyalty, piety, and brave endurance that she exists more as a cipher than as flesh and blood. . . . She does not grow, since she begins as perfect."[56] In some ways *Ramona* reads like a step backward from other women's novels of its day: Louisa May Alcott, Frances E. W. Harper, and Kate Chopin were creating heroines who show dissatisfaction with the status of women, who discover meaningful work and artistic creation in processes of self-determination, who have sexual desire. Jackson's own *Mercy Philbrick's Choice*, which she wrote eight years before *Ramona*, features a character who, pursued by and in love with two men, finally leaves both to live on her own and write poetry.

Ramona, meanwhile, exists to be looked at. Thus chapter 3 introduces her in contrast to her Mexican guardian: "For the one eye that could see the significant, at times solemn, beauty of the Señora's pale and shadowed countenance, there were a hundred that flashed with eager pleasure at the barest glimpse of Ramona's face" (p. 23). Constantly on display yet of course completely oblivious to her own charms, Ramona is a model of womanly virtue—kind, loving, and selfless. One of her few articulated desires seems to be to marry Alessandro and live happily ever after. And while Alessandro frequently serves to condemn U.S. policy and treatment of Indians, Ramona speaks far less; in fact, the narrative points just as much to her *silence* as to her words.

This silence is of course racially inflected. American writers are famously enamored of silent noble savages; James Fenimore Cooper springs first to mind. Eventually, we find, Ramona comes to understand Alessandro, whose "silence was more than silent; it was taciturn" (p. 209). And when Alessandro is killed, Ramona retreats into complete muteness, or at least into the unintelligible speech produced by fever and delirium. Though the kindly local judge postpones the murderer's trial for a week in the hope that she will recover, she is unable to testify. The killer is finally discharged on grounds of justifiable homicide.

But in this instance, Ramona's refusal to speak is not mere stereotype, for it critically dramatizes a statute that prevented Indians from testifying in court.[57] The community, in short, would not likely accept Ramona's testimony anyway, and the narrative—filtered through the judge—reflects that "the word 'justice' had lost its meaning, if indeed it ever had any" (p. 321). So while Ramona's silence has roots both in stereotypes of noble savages and in ideals of proper womanhood, it also protests a culture that legally and socially denies her a voice. It works as a comment on injustice, a way of pointing to profound imbalances in the social conversation and a refusal to participate on such terms.

Indeed, after a white settler tries to steal some beef from her family, Ramona says to Alessandro, "Take me where I need never see a white face again!" (p. 306). Such a withdrawal is not so much a failure of the heroine as a failure of the culture to accommodate and hear her. While *Ramona* may look like a far cry from some other late-nineteenth-century texts that feminist scholars have praised and revived, Jackson's still-neglected book does share some things with those texts. I am thinking here of the well-known "suicide" novels, like *The Awakening* and *The House of Mirth*. Like Ramona, Edna Pontellier and Lily Bart can be—and indeed have been—criticized for failing to exercise enough agency, for capitulating to ideologies of ideal womanhood. And yet each of these texts has been read—much more satisfactorily, in my view—as an indictment of a social order that simply has no *place* for the kinds of women their protagonists are.[58] We might think, too, of the nameless narrator's retreat into madness in "The Yellow Wallpaper," a reaction to the pressure of a domestic ideology that refuses her right to write and to define herself and to form alliances with others besides her physician husband.

The comparison to madness is instructive, for madness is Alessandro's fate as well. He predicts his impending condition himself when he has to sell his home at San Pasquale; when he returns home with money in his pocket from the sale, he throws the money on the table and begins laughing. Ramona asks if he has gone mad, and he replies, "No, I am not mad; but I think I shall soon be! What is that gold? The price of this house . . . and of the fields,—of all that was ours in San Pasquale! Tomorrow we will go out into the world again. I will see if I can find a place the Americans do not want!" (p. 263). To grant Alessandro madness is to grant him that most coveted of late-nineteenth-century staples of identity—an interiority: "Speech, complaint, active antagonism might have saved him; but all these were foreign to his self-contained, reticent, repressed nature," and his "brain gave way" (p. 312).[59]

More dramatically still, even as Alessandro appears devastated by madness he manages to use self-destruction as a means of control: when a white settler shows up with papers entitling him to Alessandro's house and field, asking what can hinder him from taking the harvest as well, since the Indian has no "rights here, whatever, according to law," Alessandro replies, "I shall hinder. . . . I shall burn down the sheds and corrals, tear down the house; and before a blade of the wheat is reaped, I will burn that" (p. 265). The novel's use of madness, hints of self-immolation, and finally death for Alessandro are not strategies for getting rid of the Indian in the tradition of James Fenimore Cooper—any more than Gilman's narrator retreats into madness because the story needs to eliminate her. Rather Alessandro's fate is a strategy for critiquing a world that cannot accommodate him. This is not to say that the book cannot have been adapted to different kinds of cultural work, but to point out that it contains other, under-read possibilities.

However contained the novel's critiques of white settlers may seem to us today, it is worth remembering that Teddy Roosevelt, that white settler extraordinaire, hated Helen Hunt Jackson's work, criticizing it as sentimental and unrealistic.[60] In Dawes Act discourse, whether articulated by strong pro-settler voices like Roosevelt's or by sympathetic reformers, "the problem" as Hoxie says, "was not how to keep whites away from tribal lands, but how to manage Indians so that 'progress' could continue."[61] In this context, one of *Ramona*'s greatest successes is its contrary depiction of the problem—managing greedy *whites* so that Indians can get on with their lives. The Indians would be just fine, the book suggests repeatedly, if whites would only leave them alone.

Ramona and Felipe finally move to Mexico, sickened by "the methods, aims, standards of the fast incoming Americans . . . [t]heir boasted successes, the crowding of colonies, schemes of settlement and development . . . [t]he passion for money and the reckless spending of it, the great fortunes made in one hour, thrown away in another" (p. 359). Ramona's silence, Alessandro's madness and death, and Felipe's plan to move hardly comprise a ringing endorsement of the new American way of life. On the contrary, these actions mirror what recent theorists of nation, including Benedict Anderson and Homi Bhabha, have spoken of as the *estrangement* of community and kin that is the truth of the modern nation-state. Felipe, for example, "found himself more and more alone in the country. Even the Spanish tongue was less and less spoken" (p. 359).

In place of that estrangement, *Ramona* supplies model commun-ities as refuge from and as alternatives to the consolidating nation. Put simply, the novel shows the good things that can happen when citizens—especially women citizens and indigenous citizens—get together for linguistic and cultural exchange. The novel often shows such exchanges to be both the product of and resistance to displace-ment and movement. One night, for example, Ramona and Ales-sandro interrupt their flight so that Alessandro can visit a white shopkeeper friend to borrow money; despite the dispossession of his home he maintains alliances and connections with such friends. For safety's sake, Ramona stays behind in a graveyard with Carmena, an Indian woman who spends her time near her infant's and husband's graves, afraid to return to the village the Americans have taken. Carmena and Ramona share no language, but the two manage to achieve profound communication through much melodramatic hand-clasping and pressing of hands to breasts. Ramona tells Alessandro, "Was it not a strange thing? . . . she spoke in your tongue, but I thought I understood her" (p. 224). The interaction, like Ramona's silence, helps essentialize her as Indian (as though the language is magically in her blood), but it also pro-vides a model of community *replacement*, one built not on any metaphor of homogeneous identity but on alliances across borders.

Similarly, in chapter 22, Ramona, Alessandro, and their new baby are rescued during a snowstorm by the Hyers, a poor Tennessee family who have moved to the Southwest for their son Jos's health. At first they mistake the young couple for "no-'count Mexicans," as the husband Jeff calls them, although Aunt Ri, his wife and the emotional center of the family, replies, "Naow, Jeff, yer know yer wouldn't let enny-thin' in shape ev a human creetur go perishin' past aour fire sech weather's this" (p. 282). When Ramona makes their racial identity clear, Aunt Ri (who has just been admiring the baby's blue eyes) responds, "Injuns! . . . Lord save us, Jos! Hev we reelly took in Injuns? What on airth—well, well, she's fond uv her baby's enny white woman!" (p. 283). Aunt

Ri's education and conversion are almost immediate; she may be poor and uneducated, but two minutes with the refined Ramona and Alessandro make her an ardent champion of their cause. "The experience to was, to her, almost incredible. Her ideas of Indians had been drawn from newspapers, and from a book or two of narratives of massacres, and from an occasional sight of vagabond bands or families they had encountered in their journey across the plains. Here she found herself sitting side by side in friendly intercourse with an Indian man and Indian woman, whose appearance and behavior were attractive; towards whom she felt herself singularly drawn" (p. 287).

In Bhabha's and Anderson's formulations, the estrangement of nation-state-making is supplanted by metaphor: "the nation fills the void left in the uprooting of communities and kin, and turns that loss into the language of metaphor," the metaphor of the "imagined community," in Anderson's phrase.[62] And as a regionalist caricature, Aunt Ri arguably consolidates a notion of American identity and exceptionalism. She declares, after all, "I'm an Ummeriken! . . . we're Ummerikens! 'n' we wouldn't cheat nobody, not ef we knowed it, nor out er a doller . . . an' I tell you, naow, the Ummeriken people don't want any o' this cheatin' done . . . Why, it's a burnin' shame to any country!" (p. 291). But this exceptionalism looks much more like an ironic italicizing of "Christian" norms than like Teddy Roosevelt's strenuous imperializing. The images of nationhood and community inherent in Jackson's notion of American-ness are more generous than those based on "cheatin'" and usurpation. For Jackson, the American nation-state is founded not only or necessarily on the incorporation of racial others to a homogeneous ideal but on the extension of rights and privileges to all. In her formulation, human contact and community lead to empathy, which will lead to social change and activism.

However, the basis for *collective* action is less clear. The book remains mired, as I discuss in greater depth below, in a model of individual women duking it out with men in power.

WOMEN, INDIANS, AND
POSSESSIVE INDIVIDUALISM

If Dawes Act discourse was virtually monolithic in its obsession with an ideology of possessive individualism and of domesticating racial others, then against this backdrop Helen Hunt Jackson's great Indian protest novel looks less like a book that made severalty happen than like a book that questions that legislation and its assumptions. I don't really propose to have uncovered some hitherto hidden meaning here, but I do want to ask why the book's resistance—and indeed, most other resistance—to allotment ideology has been so difficult to recover.

In the case of *Ramona*, one answer seems to lie in the Indian reform movement and its attending ideology of personation. Allotment was based on an ideology of personation; Dawes himself spoke of severalty as a way of "bidding [the Indian] to be a man."[63] Dividing up tribal lands became inextricably linked not only to conferring citizenship but to *making men* of Indians, to personation—and a gendered personation at that. Meanwhile, Jackson and other white women involved in Indian reform held to an ideology whereby, isolated from others and from sources of power, they could "negotiate" and "infiltrate" patriarchal structures in the attempt to become autonomous citizens and agents. In other words, for Jackson and her contemporaries, writing about Indians was not first and foremost about collectivity; rather, it was about validating oneself as an author, a citizen, and a person.

Like other high-minded reform activities (temperance and settlement houses come to mind), Indian reform gave women access to power within the system.[64] For instance, aided by increased access to railways, they now could travel much more freely. Jackson and members of the Women's National Indian Association (WNIA) conducted "investigative tours" to the various reservations and missions and wrote up reports of their findings. On one such trip, Jackson wrote with outrage of an Indian family pushed off their lands, and then—a mere two pages later—unself-consciously described her own request that the wife of the family "sell me the lace-trimmed pillow-case and sheet from her bed": "[H]er cheeks flushed at first, and she looked away haughtily before replying. But, after a moment, she consented. They needed the money."[65]

That the naked power of economic purchase can masquerade as the marginal status of the radical out to expose injustice suggests, in turn, that women like Jackson weren't just covertly insinuating their way into the public sphere. Rather, they already had remarkable power to participate in public discourses about Indian policy.[66] Far from being utterly marginalized and subversive, Jackson, the women reformers, and their activities and publications bore directly on legislation; indeed, lawmakers made a show of welcoming reformers' input on the grounds that the reformers were better informed than government officials. Thus, women's work in Indian reform was not merely reacting against misogyny, no matter how much Jackson and others may have painted it that way; to at least an equal degree, women reformers influenced policies that had supported the status quo.[67]

To be sure, as *Ramona*'s depictions of indigenous homemaking suggest, the subversion of domestic ideology was hardly the issue. Both white and American Indian women entered into missionary and field matron work in the 1880s with newfound zeal.[68] As Helen Bannan proffers, they may have done so partly out of a sense of adventure, or because it was lucrative, or because their options for self-fulfillment and work remained limited.[69] But they also filled the urgent need to produce civilized homes run by civilized mothers, who would in turn produce more civilized citizens.[70] The rhetoric surrounding field matron work, like much nineteenth-century philanthropic discourse, focuses on the exotic Other, offering Christian mothers as corrective agents of nation-formation. One Indian commissioner wrote, drawing on the old stereotype of Indian women as drudges, that indigenous women remained "in ignorance and rags . . . their homes and home-life riveted to their ancient barbaric habits and customs. Here, within our own borders, are women whose degradation can hardly be matched by the Zenarias in Oriental lands for whose welfare so much of Christian sympathy and effort have been deservedly evoked."[71] White women in this view are not tangential to the superior culture but representatives and agents of it; they fend off the disturbing barbarism "here, within our own borders."

Women's Indian reform writings and Indian reform work thus have a two-part agenda: Christianizing the Indian woman and legitimating the white woman. Both had to be validated as citizens on anglocentric, patriarchal terms. Field matron work thus harnessed both Indian and white women to the labor needs of the expanding nation. As *The Southern Workman* reports, Miss Webb, a woman missionary at Santee, Nebraska, starts her day

> at half past five and ends at ten, often later. It is crowded with constant supervision of the girls in their work and play. The every day wants and decencies of life call for constant, systematic thought and labor. There are great difficulties to be overcome in the nature of the material itself.
>
> Yet, Miss Webb is really happy *in her work* as well as in her success. "I often wonder," she says, "if there is something wrong about me or my field that I do not feel it to be more of a sacrifice" (italics in original).[72]

Not unlike Helen Hunt Jackson in her remark about the "woman with a hobby," Miss Webb reasserts and re-authorizes herself in her very assertion of selflessness. The intense labor of producing better Indian citizens is so profoundly rewarding that it doesn't *feel* like work or like self-sacrifice. And indeed it isn't self-sacrifice, for it is precisely through this "constant, systematic thought and labor" that Miss Webb both produces other persons (the improved Indian girls) and produces and possesses her *self*.

So Indian reform did not become simply a route to public advancement for nineteenth-century women; it also provided the occasions for narratives of self-possession. Both Jackson and her sister activist Alice Cunningham Fletcher reportedly experienced epiphanies at Standing Bear's talk: Jackson turned to writing about Indians; Fletcher moved from archaeology to ethnology.[73] The "Indian problem" thus provided the basis of rebirth, the impetus for new selves and new self-possession. Joan Mark observes in her biography of the anthropologist that Fletcher repeatedly described her work as "struggle" and herself as "alone in the world." Mark reads this as a parallel between Fletcher's personal situation as a professional woman and the experience of immigrants in their "rootlessness," but I think we can more cogently read it as symptomatic of the way women reformers deliberately figured themselves in opposition to a dominant culture. They envisioned themselves as loners, making their way in a hostile world and trying to exert some small benevolent influence on that world. Yet Fletcher was easily one of the most influential—and dangerous—people in the history of allotment. While we can hardly say that she never suffered from sexism or abuse from men—she certainly did—it's also hardly the case that she was a thoroughly dispossessed subject who had to "struggle" to be heard by men.

Similarly, when Jackson first heard of Schurz's response to being "flayed" by her letter to the *New York Tribune*, she wrote to her editor that she was "about wild with delight" and asked if the "blockhead" had offered an answer that "helped his cause."[74] Such a response suggests that painting herself as opposing the great man was a genuine boon to her work and her public profile. This is not to say that Jackson didn't have some good reasons to see herself as marginalized, or that she was never opposed or frustrated. Indeed, a San Luis Rey *Star* editorial on her tenure in Indian Affairs exemplifies the vituperative, distinctly gendered attacks such women could suffer: it called her a "busybody" and a "meddlesome feminine pet of the Hon. Secretary," concluding that "no woman should occupy the position of Indian Commissioner; it is no place for any member of the feminine gender."[75] But we must still ponder the ways that women reformers' insistent self-narrations as oppositional figures may have thwarted their goals of "helping" the Indians.

For example, in the early 1890s the WNIA got embroiled in a fight over land at Cahuilla—at or near the very setting of *Ramona* (indeed, the field matron there even claimed, as did many reformers, to have met "the real Ramona").[76] At Cahuilla the organization built a small field matron's cottage for teaching Indian women housekeeping skills. Without their approval, however, an Indian agent in southern California had agreed with some Indians that the cottage be moved, and that the cottage and the land it was on would revert to the Indians after five years. A long and bitter dispute over the land ensued. Eventually the Indians demanded that the field matron be removed from the land, and the land grant to the WNIA was denied.[77] The women reformers undoubtedly felt that they had the Indians' best interests at heart, but clearly they were also accustomed to pitting themselves against male agents, especially through letter-writing campaigns. In this case, such oppositional tactics threatened to keep a valuable piece of land—reportedly containing all the springs and hot springs for Cahuilla—out of the hands of indigenous people so that missionary women could continue their own work.

In Fletcher's case, a determination to go it alone resulted in profoundly tragic consequences for the Omahas. As Mark puts it, "she did her philanthropy with the special claims of a woman," and despite public ridicule for her "sentimental way of calling the Omahas her children," she told and re-told herself as a kind of mother to the tribe, a rescuer who found the Omahas poor and waiting, childlike, only for her.[78] Fletcher saw the disastrous effects of her allotment work when she revisited the tribe in 1897 and found them impoverished and demoralized, but she never admitted her failure publicly.[79] Moreover, she started having conflicts with

Francis LaFlesche, whom she saw as her research "assistant" and who was in fact an important ethnographer in his own right. Fletcher was altogether willing to capitalize on LaFlesche as an imprimatur to her own work and writings, but when he suggested they share their scientific reputation more equally, the two butted heads.[80] And Fletcher's presence created a rift between Francis and his sister Suzette, who was such a strong and eloquent proponent of Indian self-determination. We can trace many tragedies—for one man, Francis LaFlesche, for his family, and for his people on a larger scale—to Alice Cunningham Fletcher's self-declared "struggle." It is not enough, then, to say that reform gave women a foot in the door; we must examine the particular uses and consequences of that leverage.

FEMALE AUTHORSHIP AND THE CULTURAL WORK OF GENRES

Helen Hunt Jackson's own construction of herself as an embattled female speaker going up against men in power was tightly bound, I have suggested, to her conception of genre and the kinds of cultural work that different genres can do. In her writings about American Indians she straddled several forms—the sentimental protest novel, realist or local color fiction, and touristic reportage—a straddling that partly disables her most potentially radical critiques of assimilation but also generates alternative meanings that scholars today can draw on and re-read to recover such protests.

In depicting her own return to romance-writing as "pill-sugaring," Jackson deliberately aligned herself with the sentimental protest novelists of the mid-nineteenth century. Even more explicitly, she said, "If I could write a story that would do for the Indian a thousandth part what Uncle Tom's Cabin did for the negro, I would be thankful the rest of my life."[81] This meant not only writing a novel that could shake up the way her contemporaries saw racial others;

it also meant writing a work that would have broad appeal, the better to infiltrate mass culture and thus mainstream beliefs.

We are familiar by now with readings of women's fiction in general, and of the sentimental novel in particular, as working underground, as adopting the occasional racist stereotype or paternalistic ideal in the interests of funneling through more progressive messages. In her famous reading of Jackson's precursor, for instance, Tompkins suggests that "Stowe's very conservatism— her reliance on established patterns of living and traditional beliefs— is precisely what gives her novel its revolutionary potential. . . . The brilliance of the strategy," she concludes, "is that it puts the central affirmations of a culture into the service of a vision that would destroy the present economic and social institutions."[82] She could just as well be talking about *Ramona*. Jackson scholars have reasonably followed her critical path, as Dorris does when he argues that "as a novel that cashed in on every positive stereotype in the cultural repertoire, *Ramona* neutralized some historic aspects of American hostility toward Indians."[83]

For the women who wrote sentimental novels in the nineteenth century and the feminist scholars who recovered those novels in the 1970s and 1980s, it wasn't just that the personal was political. The political, we might also say, was personal. Personal incursions against, say, one's husband could constitute a viable form of female resistance. And personal *feeling*—the empathy that drove characters and readers to weep for Little Eva, or for Ramona and Alessandro, the empathy that motivated these personal incursions— could be a promising basis for social change. As I suggested at the beginning of this chapter in my reading of the woman who finds herself and her family having usurped Alessandro's house, there is much to admire in such a view. Materially disenfranchised people must work with what their culture and material circumstances make available to them. So, that the settler's wife goes no further in her assault on the dispossession of Indian lands than speaking up against her husband, or that Ramona's own resistance to land theft finally does not amount to much more than a flight to Mexico, is not so much a *personal* failure as it is the symptom and scourge of a culture that offers women and Indians few options, really, for more radical change.

Still, the sentimental protest was limited in what it could do against allotment, not least because it was predicated on a brand of domesticity that ultimately underwrote the attempted assimilation of American Indians in this period. Moreover, it was predicated on the ideology of personation of which I have been speaking in this chapter; it depends on the image of an individual (female) author who must slyly insinuate herself into the dominant culture, and on isolated (female) characters who must single-handedly subvert the male power around them. On some level, *Ramona* actually seems content with just such minor incursions, with the vicarious thrill offered by women who speak out but who finally do little more.

For example, one of the book's most entertaining examples of covert resistance comes from Señora Moreno, who ingeniously uses her speech—and, specifically, the ideals of speech deemed appropriate to her gender, race, age, and class—to manipulate those around her.

> She looked simply like a sad, spiritual-minded old lady, amiable and indolent, like her race, but sweeter and more thoughtful than their wont. Her voice heightened this mistaken impression. She was never heard to speak either loud or fast. There was at times even a curious hesitancy in her speech. . . . It often made her appear as if she did not know her own mind: at which people sometimes took heart; when, if they had only known the truth, they would have known that the speech hesitated solely because the Señora knew her own mind so exactly that she was finding it hard to make the words convey it as she desired, or in a way best to attain her ends (p. 2).

The Señora plays off familiar expectations that, as an elder widow and an exotic Spanish Catholic, she will be "sad" and "spiritual-minded"; that, as a member of the landed gentry, she never talks "loud or fast"; that, as a woman, she never appears too assertive.[84] It is a classic act of tricksterish masking, for the Señora is indeed a powerful character.

Meanwhile, Aunt Ri, a horse-sense figure in the tradition of Mark Twain, Marietta Holley, and other local colorists, uses her speech, rendered in a thick dialect, to challenge people in power more directly. In the book's very final chapter, for instance, she spars with the Indian agent:

> "But ef yeow've got power ter git a man put in jail for sellin' whiskey t' 'n' Injun, 'n' hain't got power to git him punished ef he goes 'n' kills thet Injun, 't sems ter me thar's suthin' cur'us abaout thet."
>
> "That is just the trouble I have in my position here, Aunt Ri," he said. "I have no real power over my Indians, as I ought to have."
>
> "What makes yer call 'em *yeour* Injuns?" broke in Aunt Ri.
>
> The Agent colored. Aunt Ri was a privileged character, but her logical method of questioning was inconvenient (p. 351).

Aunt Ri's translation of his possessive adjective ("my" to "*yeour*") generates one of the novel's powerful challenges to the government's "management" of Indian nations and the ideology of ownership on which that management is predicated.[85] Together, then, she and the Señora serve as vivid critics of andro- and anglo-centric norms. Both are at least partly motivated by the estrangement of their community and kin; Aunt Ri is "heartily tired of being on the move" (p. 287), and the Señora, who lost her husband in the Mexican-American war, is embittered by the encroachment of whites into southern California. The passages featuring these two women's voices constitute some of the novel's most powerful attacks on allotment era thinking.

For all this useful critique, however, neither the Señora nor Aunt Ri are able to do much more than make themselves *individually* "inconvenient." Aunt Ri's comedic dialect and isolation limit the power of her new interpersonal ties across familial, geographic, and cultural borders. And the Señora's power is ultimately power won for herself—over her son, over her household, over those who work for her. It never leads to any kind of meaningful resistance to colonization (in which she, as a Spanish landholder, has already been implicated), despite her vitriol for American "hounds." What readers get from the scenes involving the Señora, Aunt Ri, and other similar women characters, then, is an opportunity to cheer these women on for having overstepped their bounds, and for having spoken out against injustice. What they don't get is any real drive toward more culturally developed strategies of resistance, or gestures toward organized collective action against government officials or land-grabbing settlers.

These are, however, hallmarks of the sentimental protest—what Tompkins characterizes as a savvy strategy for using cultural norms to subtly turn them over. But while *Ramona* may seem like the quintessential sentimental novel, its author also took decisive steps to distance herself from that distinctly feminized form. She published, for example, a piece called "Hysteria in Literature," where she condemned overabundant emotion and those readers who "thrill and weep in sympathetic unison with ridiculous joys and sorrows, grotesque sentiments, and preposterous adventures."[86] Indeed, the literary realist elites like William Dean Howells and Richard Watson Gilder, for example, welcomed Jackson. Two prestigious realist journals—*Harper's* and *Century*—competed for her California travel pieces.[87] *Ramona* was serialized in Henry Ward Beecher's *Christian Union* and was favorably reviewed in the *Atlantic* and the *North American Review*, where Albion Tourgée, far from decrying the book as "preposterous," applauded its author for avoiding the pitfall of "the modern American novelist," who, "in his desire to avoid unreal sentimentality . . . has gone to the other extreme of a far more unreal and unnatural cynicism." *Ramona* succeeds, in his view, because it remembers that "American gentlemen are honest wooers, and American women tender sweethearts still."[88]

As Tourgée's review illustrates, elite American journals harbored differing and competing senses of the real. And while Jackson did talk about *Ramona* as "sugared," it is far from clear that she envisioned the book as primarily "sentimental" rather than realistic. On the contrary, she was famously disappointed in the reception of the book: "I am sick of hearing that the flight of Alessandro & Ramona is an 'exquisite ideal,' & not even an allusion to the eject-ment of the Temecula band from their homes."[89] One of *Ramona*'s selling points was precisely its basis in fact; Jackson had written, for example, of the murder of an Indian man (on which she modeled the murder of Alessandro) in an article for the *Independent*.[90] While it's true, then, that Jackson portrayed herself as somehow "giving in" when she wrote this romance, she was also clearly proud of the book, primarily because it was "real." And saccharine as her Indian novel may look to us today, it also helps us continue to break down the notion that women continued writing "sentimental" books while male writers like James and Howells produced "realist" texts.

Ramona departs again from sentimental form in its narrative voice. Sentimental novels typically deploy didactic narrators: *Uncle Tom's Cabin* directly addresses its readers to tell them how to respond to characters and interpret events, and Jackson's own *Mercy Philbrick's Choice* uses long narrative disquisitions on love and independence. *Ramona* obviously does not avoid didacticism, but it does generally eschew direct address to readers—something we tend to associate more with literary realism and local color.[91]

In the passage above where Aunt Ri confronts the Indian agent, for example, the narrative voice firmly supports her, not directly, but by way of an ironic filtering through the agent; we can reasonably expect that "privileged character," "logical method," and "inconvenient" are all words that go through his head at this moment, words that attempt to distance him from the obvious discomfort Aunt Ri puts him in. Similarly, in the passage about the Señora's techniques of manipulation, while it is admittedly the narrator who describes the Mexican "race" as "amiable and indolent," it is the Señora who builds her persona, actively and carefully, around her knowledge of exactly this stereotype. In fact, we can read the narrative voice here as engaged in its own unique form of subversion. The narrator repeats these stereotypical descriptions in a way that might validate the racist reader but which is arguably filtered through the consciousness of the Señora, who capitalizes on precisely these racist and sexist stereotypes to achieve her ends. After all, it is the Señora's *voice* that "heightens this mistaken impression," just as the cagey and opportunistic narrative voice plays on racist tropes. Both these voices require constant vigilance and modulation, highlighting the performed nature of female and narrative identities in this novel.

Now, most literary critics can find polyvocality in a text when they decide to look for it.[92] But I do want to press the multi-voiced nature of *Ramona* as a distinct departure from some of Jackson's other writings, most notably her nonfiction "Indian" texts and her travel pieces. As a point of contrast, let us examine a recurrent fascination in Jackson's California essays—the image of a band of Indians about to attack a mission when, "on the unfurling of a banner with a life-size picture of the Virgin painted on it, they flung away their bows and arrows, came running toward the banner with gestures of reverence and delight, and threw their beads and other ornaments on the ground before it, as at the feet of a suddenly recognized queen."[93] There aren't too many ways to read this, I think. It is pure touristic spectacle—the threatening Other rendered docile and impotent. The appeal of such a spectacle to Indian reformers is obvious—the savages can be converted and safely assimilated, in the blink of an eye and without bloodshed or cost.

Jackson's enthusiasm, by the mid-1880s, for narratives of such spectacular and highly improbable events complicates any attempts to read *Ramona* as deliberately anti-allotment or otherwise revolutionary. Still, the polyvocality of the *form* she chooses in the novel makes more resistant meanings available—meanings that do not appear in her travel writings, with their consuming tourism. To take an example of Native conversion as it gets treated in the novel, the book's very first scene features the Señora trying to forestall her ranch's annual sheep-shearing for the visit of her favorite priest, Father Salvierderra, so that when he arrives he will have a large group of Indian workers at his disposal. She envisions "the chapel full of them kneeling, and more than can get in the door" (p. 5).

The Señora's motivations are somewhat veiled and a bit complicated. For instance, she says that "the spirit of unbelief is spreading in the country since the Americans are running up and down everywhere seeking money" (p. 10). This suggests a sincere desire to use religion as a bulwark against U.S. land-grabbing, a desire to which the novel seems wholly sympathetic. But it also suggests a religious/ nationalist fervor of which the novel is a bit more skeptical. The Señora's head shepherd, another local-color figure named Juan Canito, provides a running comic commentary that calls into question his employer's incomprehensible interruption of his work.[94] Not even the benign Father Salvierderra, aging and demoralized by the ruin of Spanish mission lands as they have reverted to white settlers, shares the Señora's zealous drive to convert the Indians. The scene has the same effect then, as Alessandro's recounting of the Father Peyri incident for Ramona—assuredly colonizing, yet undercut. Casting the image of the Indians at Mass in the shadow of the Señora's own nationalism and providing these multiple vantage points on her ideal calls the spectacle into question, ironizes it in a way that Jackson's more monologic travel writings simply do not—and, perhaps, even in ways she did not intend.

It is not necessarily in Jackson's intentions, then, that I wish to locate *Ramona*'s chafing against allotment-era ideologies, though given the paucity of written protest in that period, her documented history of reactions against allotment certainly does matter. It is rather in the kind of polyvocal text that she produced by virtue of her movement between two major periods and genres—that of the mid-nineteenth-century sentimental protest novel and late-nine-teenth-century realism. When Jackson says she "sugared her pill," I take her to refer at least partly to such multi-generic maneuvers, like the staging of debates between characters, particularly male and female characters, and the (rather unsentimental) tamping down of the didactic narrator. These maneuvers produce dialogues around and dissents against assimilation that appear not to have been registered in many other arenas, political or cultural, in the 1880s. While literary critics have learned to be duly cautious of claims that "values" inhere in texts, I believe it is still possible to argue that certain texts, like Helen Hunt Jackson's, Sarah Winne-mucca's, and Victoria Howard's, warrant our attention not only for the work they "actually" performed but also for those textual features that allow us, more than a century later, to re-read history and nation.

As a dyed-in-the-wool cultural tourist, Jackson could not, per-haps, enact the complex representational strategies we will now encounter in the works of the American Indian storytellers Sarah Winnemucca and Victoria Howard. She does not, in other words, point to the viability and continuation of certain tribal practices in ways that really ask non-Indian readers to reconsider their con-suming relationship to these materials. She shares with these two women, however, a sense of the inherent legitimacy and sovereignty of American Indian nations—a sense that was profoundly threat-ening and greatly silenced in the United States in the 1880s. Like them, she struggles with various ways of thinking about Indian and female resistance, about indigenous and cross-cultural com-munity. Winnemucca and Howard can offer Jackson some more refined theorizing of these questions.

CHAPTER TWO

SARAH WINNEMUCCA'S
INDIAN AGENCIES

Sarah Winnemucca makes one of her earliest written appearances in, of all places, the appendix to Helen Hunt Jackson's *A Century of Dishonor*. Reprinted there is a letter from "an educated Paiute woman," dated April 4, 1870, and addressed to Major Henry Douglass, then Indian superintendent to Nevada.[1] At issue was an attempt to send the Paiutes back to the Pyramid Lake Reservation, which they had left for the army fort of Camp McDermitt amid mounting tension with the Indian agent in charge of the reservation, as well as with other whites living there.

In Winnemucca's view, living under army protection had proved better than living under government agents, who often withheld or even sold food and clothing intended for issue to Indian people, allowed whites to use or move onto reservation lands, and used other harsh methods to "discipline" Indian people.[2] As Winnemucca puts it,

> It is enough to say that we were confined to the reserve, and had to live on what fish we might be able to catch in the river. If this is the kind of civilization awaiting us on the reserves, God grant that we may never be compelled to go on one, as it is much preferable to live in the mountains and drag out

an existence in our native manner. . . . [I]f the Indians have
any guarantee that they can secure a permanent home on
their own native soil, and that our white neighbors can be
kept from encroaching on our rights, after having a reasonable share of ground allotted to us as our own, and giving us
the required advantages of learning, I warrant that the savage
(as he is called to-day) will be a thrifty and law-abiding
member of the community fifteen or twenty years hence.

This letter typifies Winnemucca's dramatically oscillating rhetorical strategies. On the one hand, produced about a decade before
the greatest burst of assimilative effort, it gives the nod to stereotypes
of American Indians (especially those who, like the Paiutes, lived
nomadically) as base and primitive, while at the same time reassuring readers that those peoples can, in time, be safely incorporated
into the national "community." On the other hand, it also italicizes
those terms—"the savage (as he is called)," and "if this is the kind of
civilization"—calling into question the very language with which
Winnemucca must communicate. The letter reads like a promise of
racial progress, with its picture of Indians in a "permanent home";
yet it insistently locates that permanent home on Paiutes' "own
native soil," not (if we recall Andrew Jackson's mandate for a mobile
populace) anywhere the expanding United States sees fit.

Winnemucca radically asserts that the Paiutes, too, have their
own ways of survival, ways other than Euro-Americans' beloved
agenda of allotment, acculturation, and farming. To say that "drag-
ging out an existence in the native manner" is "preferable" to the
reservation system is of course a critique of that system, which
allotment was partly designed to eliminate; yet it also firmly
asserts the legitimacy and viability of tribal ways. In juxtaposing
the word *allotted* and the pronoun *us* (a possibly deliberate choice,
since the pronoun shifts to the third person in the next sentence),
the passage maintains a vision of collective, indigenous sovereignty: "*ground allotted to us as our own.*" *Allotment* is here recast to

protect tribal ways of life, not eliminate them—hence, the pointed demand for an end to white encroachment.

This letter looks like it should have mollified late-nineteenth-century audiences invested in assimilation, including readers of *A Century of Dishonor*. But it also sounds very like the one alternative to allotment and assimilation that historian Wilcomb Washburn has said U.S. citizens were not willing to entertain: to "maintain the status quo; support existing treaty guarantees, tribal integrity, and the right of tribes to hold land in common; protect the individual Indian against white aggression."[3]

Sarah Winnemucca's work contains powerful critiques of allotment and assimilation and a powerful communitism, an activist commitment to indigenous community. One critic has suggested that "the very fact that [Winnemucca] was not perceived as threatening enabled her to be very assertive in advocating for the Northern Paiutes,"[4] but it is quite possible that she *was* profoundly threatening. This would explain why her popularity was finally dwarfed by that of her contemporary, Jackson, and why, during her life, she came under considerable attack by powerful white people. During her first trip to Washington, D.C., Jackson's old nemesis, Interior Secretary Carl Schurz, requested that Winnemucca refrain from lecturing in that city.[5] But despite the way she seems to have troubled white Americans, Winnemucca has often been read as catering to whites and endorsing assimilation. The circumstances of her life, as well as the rhetorical complexity of her writings and performances, might help explain why.

MEDIATION, ASSIMILATION, RESISTANCE

Compared to Jackson's heady popularity, the attention bestowed on Winnemucca was brief and mixed. She shot into the public eye in 1879, the same year that Jackson had her reported epiphany at Standing Bear's speech, and had fallen out of favor by 1884, perhaps replaced in the public imagination by the fictional Ramona. Born around 1844, Winnemucca came from what is now western Nevada, from loosely related groups of indigenous peoples who came to be known as the Paiutes. Her family's relations with whites were conflicted. Her mother's father, called Captain Truckee, was known as a guide to emigrant parties and fought with General John Fremont during the Bear Flag Rebellion in California. Her parents, however, were warier of whites. Her father, Old Winnemucca, spent much of his life fleeing reservations, with Sarah often enlisted to bring him back. Her mother and maternal grandmother fed the children frightening stories about white settlers, and Sarah recalls being terrified of whites as a child. Her own feelings, as she describes them in her writings, changed somewhat after she lived several years with white friends, worked as a domestic, and learned to read and write in school. In 1864, Winnemucca and her family earned money traveling around Nevada and California in tableaux presenting the Pocahontas story and other popular myths. In the years following, she worked as a scout and interpreter for the U.S. Army.

In 1879, Winnemucca went on her own east coast tour to lecture about the Paiutes' hardships on their reservations. She dressed for these talks in a stereotypical Indian Princess costume of her own making—upright feathered headdress or, sometimes, a tiara; tasseled and fringed cloth dress; beaded bag and sequined belt; stockings decorated with metal studs. She posed for studio portraits in such costumes, sometimes in "natural" settings (among rocks and trees) with her hair loose around her shoulders. One such photograph appeared as the frontispiece for Winnemucca's popular autobiography, *Life Among the Piutes*, published in 1881; others were sold at her lectures.[6]

This was probably the height of Winnemucca's popularity; newspapers and magazines (including the children's magazine *St. Nicholas*, which published Suzette LaFlesche's fiction) carried stories and pictures of Winnemucca and her family. She also befriended

Sarah Winnemucca as Princess, the frontispiece for Winnemucca's *Life Among the Paiutes*. (Courtesy of Nevada Historical Society)

Sarah Winnemucca in "natural" setting, a popular photo from her lecture tour. (Courtesy of Nevada Historical Society)

many influential white women, notably the education reformer and historian Elizabeth Peabody and her sister Mary Mann (widow of the educator Horace Mann). In the 1880s, Indian women could gain a relatively wide hearing, especially with a little help from a well-placed sympathetic white friend.[7] Thus Peabody, determined "to multiply occasions for [Winnemucca] to *speak*,"[8] secured engagements for Winnemucca around Boston and elsewhere in the East; Mann edited *Life Among the Piutes*, which was received well, thanks in part to a new thirst for stories of individual Indian lives.

After the book's publication, Winnemucca returned to Nevada and, with support from Peabody, set up a bilingual school for Paiute children near Lovelock, one of the only schools of its kind. During her life she married at least three times, the last time to a white Army lieutenant named Lewis Hopkins; little is known about him and the other husbands. After Hopkins's death and the closure of her school Winnemucca moved to her sister's home in Idaho, where she died in 1891, having weathered a great many attacks on her personal character by people associated with the Indian Bureau. Partly in response to Winnemucca's many articulate assaults on the corruption of white officials, the bureau kept a file on her "character," including slanderous "affidavits" by white settlers, all of them men.[9] Thus, *Life Among the Piutes* concludes with its own dossier of letters attesting to Winnemucca's character—documents that try to instruct us how to read her, for she was acutely conscious of being read and re-read.

As this brief biography suggests, Winnemucca was a performer and a mediator—someone who sought to articulate American Indian problems to non-Indians (and, in turn, to bring elements of non-Indian culture home) and who carefully crafted her public image to fit what her audiences might have expected. For these reasons, perhaps, many critics emphasize her accommodations, reading her either as pleading for the assimilation of the Paiutes or as trying to bring Indian and non-Indian together. LaVonne Ruoff, for example, has written that "both in her lectures and in

her book, Winnemucca staunchly supported the General Allotment Act," even though *Life Among the Piutes* includes no explicit
endorsement of that legislation.[10] Other scholars, presumably
thinking of those places in the autobiography where Winnemucca
appears to plead with white readers for patience as the Paiutes
learn civilized ways, simply assume that she favored assimilation.

But, as in the case of Helen Hunt Jackson, there is buried evidence that Winnemucca may actually have spoken out *against*
allotment and assimilation. Elizabeth Peabody, who had befriended
Winnemucca and accompanied her on a visit to Henry Dawes,
once wrote that the senator "was interested in her [Winnemucca]
by a letter she wrote to him, *criticising* the Senatorial bill."[11] The
bill in question, passed in July of 1884, moved two bands of Paiutes
to the Pyramid Lake Reservation, assigning 160 acres of basically
nonarable land to each head of family. Winnemucca had been
pressing for the passage of an earlier bill, sponsored by Dawes, to
move the Paiutes instead to the Camp McDermit area in Oregon—
land the U.S. military ultimately insisted on keeping for its own
uses.[12] According to Peabody scholar Bruce Ronda, Winnemucca's
activism on this issue is telling: It suggests that she apprehended
the measure as an approach that universalized hugely variable
local and tribal realities and that she recognized its failure to guarantee Indians land they could actually use for the government's
much-vaunted plan of transition to agrarian, "civilized" living.[13]
In his important biographical study of Peabody, Ronda observes
that Peabody's and Winnemucca's commitments to bilingual education would have made them further skeptical of the Allotment
Act itself. He also claims, even more dramatically, that "*Life Among
the Piutes* made clear the radical stance that Winnemucca was
taking in resisting calls for the assimilation of indigenous peoples
into the cultural mainstream."

Even when scholars haven't overlooked Winnemucca's disagreements with allotment and assimilation, they have tended to promote
her "mediations" at the expense of her cultural traditionalism and

protectiveness. In a chapter titled "Sarah Winnemucca's Mediations," Cheryl Walker argues that Winnemucca wanted "to bring peoples together and allow passage of ideas from one group to another."[14] Noreen Groover Lape similarly sees Winnemucca as "redefin[ing] assimilation to preserve the frontier by sustaining contact between cultures."[15] Maggie Montesinos Sale describes *Life Among the Piutes* and other ethnic women writers' works of the period as hybrid, "literate not only in English, but also in the codes, assumptions, and expectations of the broader society" yet seeking to "communicate understandings and information that differed from or were at odds with these various codes, assumptions, and expectations";[16] such hybridity, Sale concludes, "made [Winnemucca's] story comprehensible."[17] Exploring Winnemucca's strategic uses of literate conventions, Margo Lukens observes that Winnemucca writes "to create links between Paiutes and white Americans."[18] And Eric Gary Anderson writes that "Winnemucca's traveling across regions and cultures is a personal and tribal survival tactic with which she positions herself as a highly flexible cultural mediator";[19] he adds that she "upholds a strong sense of Paiute culture while adapting and making that culture and her experiences accessible to a larger American culture."[20]

Mediation can be a useful concept when it describes a two-way movement among cultures, with all that such movement entails, including conflict and unintelligibility. For scholars trying to understand Sarah Winnemucca, the concept is historically apt; she really *did* devote much of her life and work to rendering Indian and non-Indian cultures mutually intelligible. Moreover, there is something ethical about reading for mediation, for it is helpful to our own historical moment—when cultures inside and outside the United States compete for resources and power—to see how someone like Winnemucca reckoned with such struggles and how she thought about human mutuality and cultural co-existence in the context of those struggles. The best of the recent Winnemucca criticism works in this vein, exploring not only the ways she smooths over cultural differences but also how she confronts and preserves them: Lape, for example, shows that Winnemucca eschewed radical assimilationism while advocating cultural contact; and Walker finally argues that, in Winnemucca's brand of mediation, "the *value* of the two peoples is equal."[21]

However, I have strategically culled phrases from this scholarship both to illustrate the current fascination with mediation as healing and to show how "cultural mixing" can sometimes bleed into "cultural absorption." In these cases, the supposedly two-way process of mediation suddenly goes one way, with Indian culture now "accessible," "comprehensible," and available to whites. In the end, this brand of "mediation" is not terribly unlike what happened during the Era of Assimilation, when "liminality," "border movements," and "sustained contact between cultures" (or some versions of those terms) were not just material realities and survival tactics but also the very tools of incorporation. The promotion of cultural contact, indeed, was not meant to acknowledge the human mutuality and coexistence of different groups but rather to assimilate the Indian into the non-Indian. Hence, reformers spoke often of "intermingling" "red and white races" so that the latter would improve and absorb the former. Thus did the hapless Schurz rationalize the breakup of communally held Indian lands: "On most of the Indian reservations [the Indian] lives only among his own kind, excepting the teachers and the few white agency people. He may feel the necessity of changing his mode of life ever so strongly; he may hear of civilization ever so much; but as long as he has not with his own eyes seen civilization at work, it will remain to him only a vague, shadowy idea. . . . In order to learn to live like the white man, he should see and observe how the white man lives in his own surroundings, what he is doing, and what he is doing it for."[22]

Like many American Indian people, Winnemucca successfully learned and adopted elements of Euro-American culture. She learned to read and write, she spoke favorably of non-Paiute agricultural practices, she wore Victorian dress and espoused ideals of Victorian womanhood as well as other recognizable Anglo virtues (as in the promised "thrifty" and "law-abiding" Indian of her letter, above). But such cultural mixing does not seem to have meant, for her, that "white" values replaced "Indian" ones. More importantly, it does not seem to have necessitated the eradication of Paiute traditions nor of collectively owned land. Indeed, Winnemucca's work often protects traditional practices by concealing and obscuring them from the gaze of the non-Indian reader.

In what follows, then, I want to approach Winnemucca's mediations cautiously. The cross-cultural movement in her texts—the hyper-vocality that the letter to Major Douglass only begins to illustrate—is the product of several forces. It is a response to an audience with multiple and contradictory demands. It is also a result of the *production* of her writings, which were edited by white people, possibly heavily. But Winnemucca's mediations and multi-vocality are also finally the products of a struggle with mediation, cultural contact, and cross-cultural representation themselves. Winnemucca tries to figure out how to mediate without simply assimilating, how to live with the changing shape of nations (both the Paiute nation and the United States) while preserving for indigenous peoples that "reasonable share of ground," both literal and figurative. She ponders how at least two Euro-American structures—the reservation and written self-representation—might give the Paiutes space for self-governance, collective ownership, and the continuance of traditional ways of life.

Winnemucca's resistance can be hard to hear because of the complexity of her communitism. On the one hand, like Jackson's, her communitism coexists with traits that may have made American Indians appear more easily assimilable, like Victorian womanhood and agrarian living. On the other hand, unlike Jackson's, Winnemucca's communitism is dispersed among sometimes competing voices, and it is not as finally dependent on a notion of the individual woman as strategic infiltrator. But I posit that we can serve her best by actively highlighting those moments of resistance and by attending to the ways that she finally evades or reworks cross-cultural representation. At the same moment that Winnemucca seems eager to show that Paiutes are, or can someday be, "just like" whites, she also shows that they are *not* like whites, forcing readers to acknowledge and make a space for cultural difference even as she forces them to acknowledge a common humanity. Winnemucca does not simply satisfy her readers' thirst for spectacles of exotic and supposedly vanishing ways of life; rather, she challenges them to question their own positions of power in this inter-cultural conversation.

SUSPICIOUS SPECTACLES: THE POCAHONTAS TABLEAUX

Poststructural critics are fond of what they call the "free play of signification," that is, the way that meaning can seem to proliferate once we put pressure on a given word, image, or text. Meaning, we may observe, is not inherent in texts, but rather depends heavily on their context; thus, readers, listeners, and viewers can re-read, misread, and use texts in ways the author never expected, ways that might be productive or dismaying beyond what the author imagined or intended. The conflicted responses to the Winnemucca family's tableaux will help explain why, in her writings, Winnemucca herself chose such mobile and apparently contradictory rhetorical strategies, in a possible attempt to control her meaning. At the same time, the responses to the tableaux illustrate that, while audiences can indeed quarrel over meaning, the play of signification is hardly infinite when it comes to representations of Indian peoples. The quarrels of non-Paiute viewers who read the Winnemuccas ranged from mild disagreement to open opposition, but their readings all tended to serve American nationalist ends.

Performed in San Francisco and in Virginia City in the early 1860s, the tableaux included Winnemucca, her father ("Old Winnemucca"), her sister, and some other Paiutes. As described in Gae Whitney Canfield's scrupulously researched biography, the shows featured the following components: "The Indian Camp," "The War Dance," "Grand Scalp Dance," and "The Coyote Dance." Images of Pocahontas saving John Smith followed. One reporter praised the tableaux because the performers appeared to "possess the power to maintain an inanimate position as if carved of bronze."[23] Yet the crowd also proved spellbound by living, mobile Indians—a fascination the Winnemuccas traded on by riding through the streets in open carriages, wearing buckskins, war paint, and feather headdresses. Before the shows, Old Winnemucca addressed crowds with Sarah interpreting for her father; her "very good English" seems to have impressed audiences wherever she went. In these speeches, the Winnemuccas reported that other tribes invited them to join attacks on whites, but that the Paiutes refused such overtures. The performers thus appeared to demonize other Indian peoples in order to position themselves as "good Indians"; their Virginia City appearances included scenes illustrating the "Scalping of an Emmigrant Girl by a Bannock Scout" and "The Capture of a Bannock Spy," capitalizing on the Paiutes' conflict with a neighboring Nevada tribe.

Winnemucca never wrote about this period in her life, nor indeed about any of her public appearances, even though her autobiography was surely marketed to people who were familiar with her popular image. So we have no record, honest or otherwise, of her of her family's intentions during the early 1860s. As Canfield points out, it seems ironic that Winnemucca's father, with his strong youthful resistance to white settlers, finally "sold out"—or, put differently, that he profited from parading in front of the very people he hated. Canfield attributes the apparent change in his behavior to the underlying "pomp and circumstance in his nature."[24] Whatever Old Winnemucca's personality, though, his appearances at Virginia City and San Francisco mark a complex response to highly malleable and confusing circumstances.

In current critical theory, such performances are considered compromised. Indeed, scholars generally agree about displays of American Indians, from James Fenimore Cooper's novels to Smithsonian-mounted exhibits at World Fairs: these spectacles, they argue, bolster narratives of U.S. national progress; provide visual justification for economic expansion, for imperialist interventions, and for so-called Anglo-Saxon advancement; and assure "mainstream" citizens that the changes happening before them— changes at once exhilarating and troubling—are the logical results of the ascension of a superior race.[25]

The Winnemuccas' performances did generate some mixed responses. Even as they seemed to unify predominantly white audiences by race, *convening* them as one public, the events also divided residents by class. Audiences tossed money into a hat after Old Winnemucca's talks; San Franciscans attending the Indian performances could pay a dollar for the orchestra and dress circle at the Metropolitan Theatre, 50 cents for the "parquette," or 25 cents for the gallery.[26] The appeal of the shows also seems to have been mixed. News reports describe "rapturous applause" from the "ladies" and "the Pi-Ute war whoop from the boys."[27] Margaret Watson, author of a history of early Nevada theater, confirms that such displays were highly popular.[28] At the same time, those with enough cultural capital to write about the shows met them with either ridicule or pity. The same reporter who praised the performers' "lifelessness" also horribly derided Old Winnemucca's speech ("rub-a-dub, dub! Ho-daddy, hi-daddy; wo-hup, gee-haw") and flippantly defended the crowd's crass thirst for such "novelties" as "aboriginal entertainment" and "Chinese theatrical troupes."[29]

Precisely *as* a commercial venture, therefore, the tableaux provided a vehicle for those trying to craft themselves as positioned outside (and perhaps above) a mainstream culture. In the comments of the reporter, at once enthralled and repelled by the performances, we can hear early grumblings about a rapidly changing nation and increasing commodification. We also get a glimpse of the overlap and competition among the many people who exhibited the Paiutes—capitalist venue owners trying to make money, cultural critics trying to morally inculcate a nation, and the Winnemuccas themselves.

But despite such complications and nuances, the tableaux consistently helped constitute a "white" public satisfied—and legitimated—by the spectacle of inferior racial others, even when observers tried to challenge that public more directly. One sympathetic white woman, for instance, approached the Winnemuccas after one of their Virginia City performances and "asked the chief why he had taken the white man's ways to show himself?" In a letter to a local newspaper, she described her conversation with Old Winnemucca, passionately decrying the injustice of seeing the aging chief "stooping from his dignity to become a common actor."[30]

This letter illustrates the tensions as well as the fruitful alliances between white women reformers and Indians. The woman describes her backstage visit as a literal struggle over who gets to speak: "Well, as soon as I could hear myself speak (for their chatter was not unlike that of a flock of magpies in springtime) I asked the chief. . . ." She *invites* Old Winnemucca to speak about his motives and engages him in dialogue, suggesting some mutuality, and yet a certain cultural capital undeniably accrues to her when she writes and speaks for him. She seems worried that the Winnemuccas are franchising themselves instead of relying on charity ("the 1st thing to be done is to rescue the Chief, his daughters and his native attenders from the present degrading exhibitions, and provide for their immediate wants").[31] Alongside these investments, however, the woman also disturbs such paternalism by speaking as a cultural conscience, pointing to the material conditions driving the family's performances: "The fact is that Winnemucca's tribe is starving because of our usurping of their right." Like Jackson, this letter-writer both capitalizes on the power invested in her as a white woman and willingly begins to interrogate that power. Her power and her critique of that power are mutually self-consuming. Winnemucca herself would eventually begin working with such women—women whose status was not unproblematic but who nevertheless provided an opportunity for the opening of cross-cultural dialogue.

The Winnemuccas' tableaux were available for a wide range of uses and identifications, uses and identifications to which Winnemucca would variously try to articulate her writings; but even progressive responses to the tableaux were deeply implicated in white power. As much as responses to the tableaux shifted over place and time, they usually confirmed the moral and material supremacy of Euro-Americans. Thus, audiences in 1864 reportedly laughed at and rebuffed the Winnemuccas' "warnings" about impending Indian attacks, feeling confident in their superior firepower and indeed in their superior race.[32] By 1882, conversely, Americans would be much enamored of Sarah's narrations of her adventures crossing Bannock enemy lines in 1878 and of her attempts to save her people from that allegedly bloodthirsty tribe. Sympathetic white women and non-Indians eager for ethnographic details, both emergent audiences in Virginia City and San Francisco in 1864, helped make Winnemucca infinitely more visible and popular by the late 1870s and early 1880s. By that time, many Americans found in Indians no longer a force to be disparaged but a cause to embrace—something to distinguish oneself *with* rather than *against*, though such alliances hardly elevated Indians to the status of equals. In such a climate, Winnemucca would devise ever-more mobile strategies and find ever-more highbrow acceptance.

LIFE AMONG THE PIUTES: BICULTURALISM, INDIVIDUALISM, COMMUNITISM

Life Among the Piutes has been aptly described as a bicultural text. In *For Those Who Come After*, his excellent introduction to the genre,

Arnold Krupat defines American Indian autobiography as "original bicultural composite composition." Noting that such texts didn't come into being until Euro-American people decided to initiate such projects, he shows that on some level, written indigenous autobiographies are always collaborative, often involving at least two people and always involving at least two cultures.[33] True to this form, Winnemucca's book has certain features we would associate with the Western autobiographical tradition: it is more or less linear and it foregrounds her as an active agent in history. Other features of this book might be traceable to Paiute oral tradition: she quotes other Paiutes at considerable length and makes the book as much the story of a people as the story of an individual. Thus, she begins: "I was born somewhere near 1844, but am not sure of the precise time. I was a very small child when the first white people came into our country. They came like a lion, yes, like a roaring lion, and have continued so ever since, and I have never forgotten their first coming. My people were scattered at that time over nearly all the territory now known as Nevada" (p. 5).

The first chapter, "First Meeting of Piutes and Whites," continues to merge individual, cultural, and cross-cultural lives. The second chapter, "Domestic and Social Moralities," is a short ethnography geared toward Victorian ladies; indeed, one of Mann's editorial footnotes asserts that the "refinements and manners that the Indian mother teaches her children" are "worthy the imitation of whites" (p. 45). Other short chapters cover the death of Winnemucca's grandfather, Captain Truckee; the conflict at Pyramid Lake (referred to in the above letter to Major Douglass); and a brief period of happiness on the Malheur reservation under the benevolent Agent Samuel Parrish. After increased hostilities between whites and Indians in the area, the Paiutes were removed from the Malheur reservation, some being exiled to the Yakima Reservation in Washington. In 1866, the army hired Sarah and her brother Natchez as translators and couriers during these hostilities. Most of the remainder of *Life Among the Piutes* is devoted to this time, to

Winnemucca's struggles with dishonest reservation agents and her work with the military, including her assistance to General Oliver Howard during the Bannock War of 1878.

Based on these highly adventurous elements, it is easy to see why the book would have been appealing to late-nineteenth-century readers, especially the white women reformers who befriended Winnemucca. As a character in her own story, Winnemucca is mobile and active. She races across the mountains to send messages from whites to Indians; she evades a rape by jumping up and punching her attacker in the face (p. 231); at night, she sneaks into the Bannock enemy camp to rescue her father and other Paiutes. Winnemucca sometimes presents these episodes as remarkable for a woman, perhaps playing to white women's sense of themselves as disempowered; at other times, she makes her activity seem quite natural, playing to that same audience's sense of Indian cultures as more egalitarian. As Brigitte Georgi-Findlay points out, Winnemucca's adventurous yet eminently refined persona speaks to at least two contexts: a tribal context and, "possibly with a view to a female audience, . . . the context of feminine respectability."[34]

There is no mention of the school at Lovelock in the book, and barely any mention of Winnemucca's husbands. The autobiography concludes with a short dossier of letters attesting to her character and a petition to Congress to restore the Paiutes to the Malheur reservation.[35] Mary Mann's introduction to the latter document reads: "Whoever shall be interested in this little book or by Mrs. Hopkins's [Sarah Winnemucca's] living word, will help to the end by copying the petition and getting signatures to it, and sending the lists before the first of December to my care. . . . Several hundred names have already been sent in" (p. 247). With its emphasis on Winnemucca's "living word," this plea suggests a good deal of confidence, as do Jackson's writings, that women's speech and the texts women produce can lead directly and materially to social change.

Given the hugely varying responses to Indian speakers we saw manifested at the Winnemuccas' tableaux, it is little wonder that

Winnemucca shifts dramatically in her address to audience. At times, Winnemucca generously mediates. For example, in describing her relatives cutting their hair and making gashes in their own skin, she notes, "this is the way we mourn for our dead" (p. 21). Such mediations arise out of a desire to explain cultural difference, but they also bear the influence of literate convention, particularly that of the sentimental novel, as in sentences like, "Now, my dear reader, there is no word so endearing as the word father, and that is why we call all good people father or mother" (p. 39). This kind and didactic address to the non-Indian reader sometimes reaches a pitch that might encourage readers to take this text as pro-assimilationist: "Oh, my dear good Christian people, how long are you going to stand by and see us suffer at your hands? Oh, dear friends, you are wrong when you say it will take two or three generations to civilize my people" (p. 89).

At other times, though, Winnemucca chastises this reader. Some-times, as in her letter to Major Douglass, she does this by ironizing certain terms: she often refers to "that praying agent" or that "*Christian* agent's doings." Elsewhere, her critiques of the dominant culture are much more direct:

> Oh, for shame! You who are educated by a Christian govern-ment in the art of war; the practice of whose profession makes you natural enemies of the savages, so called by you. Yes, you, who call yourselves the great civilization; you who have knelt upon Plymouth Rock, covenanting with God to make this land the home of the free and the brave. Ah, then you rise from your bended knees and seizing the welcoming hands of those who are the owners of this land, which you are not, your carbines rise upon the bleak shore, and your so-called civilization sweeps inland from the ocean wave; but, oh, my God! leaving its pathway marked by crimson lines of blood, and strewed by the bones of two races, the inheritor and the invader (p. 207).

Winnemucca shows American colonial identity to be made, not given or natural, and she targets the central myths by which it is so made. Further, she reveals that U.S. national identity is built on the erasure and destruction of other nations, thus refusing to let the conquerors (here her interlocutors) mask their own power and violence.[36]

In a wonderful article on Harriet Jacobs's *Incidents in the Life of a Slave Girl*, Franny Nudelman finds a similar kind of restless narrative voice in this narrative that, like Winnemucca's, was edited by a white activist, Lydia Maria Child. Nudelman finds Jacobs strategically deploying a "rhetoric of contrast" that "figure[s] the opacity rather than the transparency of the slave woman's experience."[37] Jacobs's slave narrative thus intervenes in the politics of sentimentalism, which assumes that *feeling* and experience are ultimately communicable. In this emotional economy, Nudelman says, "slave suffering only becomes visible through the articulate reaction of an empathic white spectator."[38] We might recall here the scene in *Ramona* where Alessandro revisits his old house; the white settler's compassionate wife renders the Indians' dispossession *real* by *feeling* for them. To call out the uglier side of this dynamic: Indian "feeling" is one more possession to be colonized.

Conversely, Winnemucca's text, like Jacobs's, is not necessarily invested in revealing the experience of one culture to someone from another culture. Rather, it also seeks to alter the politics of cross-cultural communication itself. Considering Mann's own experience with and investment in this sentimental politics (especially pronounced in abolitionism, with which she had been heavily involved), it is worth considering Winnemucca's autobiography as a similar kind of intervention—one that refutes the notion that experience (like so much property) can, or should, be effortlessly transferred from Indian to non-Indian.

Some of the shifts and apparent contradictions in *Life Among the Piutes* can thus make readers question their relationship to Winnemucca's material, unsettling them the same way Suzette

LaFlesche's use of oral narrative can unsettle her young readers. These shifts are also, of course, the products of Winnemucca's own struggles with literacy and with the book's collaborative nature and its editing. About this Mary Mann writes in her preface: "My editing has consisted in copying the original manuscript in correct orthography and punctuation, with occasional emendations by the author, of a book which is an heroic act on the part of the writer. . . . In fighting with her literary deficiencies she loses some of the fervid eloquence which her extraordinary colloquial command of the English language enables her to utter, but I am confident that no one would desire that her own original words should be altered" (p. 2). Here Mann expresses some confidence in her fidelity to Winnemucca's "own original words"—even as she worries about the potential loss of voice—and in her own role as quiet facilitator. In a private letter, however, Mann's tone is markedly different: .

> I wish you could see her manuscript as a matter of curiosity. I don't think the English language has ever got such a treatment before. I have to recur to her sometimes to know what a word is, as spelling is an unknown quantity to her, as you mathematicians would express it. She often takes syllables off of words & adds them or rather prefixes them to other words, but the story is heart-breaking, and told with a simplicity & eloquence that cannot be described, for it is not high-faluting eloquence, tho' sometimes it lapses into verse (and quite poetical verse too). I was always considered fanatical about Indians, but I have a wholly new conception of them now, and we civilized people may well stand abashed before their purity of life & their truthfulness.[39]

Based on these comments, most scholars conclude that Mann's editing was indeed minimal in its impact.[40] That consensus is remarkable, given the absence of an extant manuscript. Patricia Stewart claims that Mann "co-edited or ghost-wrote" the book, absurdly asserting that much in the book is "not possible for an Indian, such as the continual harping on whether or not a white person is automatically a 'Christian' and a number of contrived references to Negroes (who certainly did not abound on the frontier)."[41] Louise Tharp proposes (also without offering evidence) that Mann wrote the book and gave Winnemucca credit.[42] Ultimately, we can't know for sure what is really "Winnemucca's" and what is "Mann's" or anyone else's.

Much criticism of this book has nevertheless been preoccupied with separating its different voices and techniques. Scholars have debated, for example, whether certain features come from "literate" or "oral" traditions and, by extension, whether the book reflects individualism or communalism. Ruoff, maintaining the commonplace that autobiography "represents a break with oral tradition because personal narrative is not part of American Indian oral literatures," traces Winnemucca's narrative strategies—mixing personal experience with ethnographic information, including the final dossier of letters from white friends to "legitimate" her story— to literate traditions followed by earlier Indian writers. Ruoff points out that slave narratives also frequently use such authenticating devices.[43] David Brumble tries to counter the suggestion that we must work from literate models; he roots certain features of Indian autobiography in oral tradition—such as coup tales and stories of the acquisition of powers. Brumble thus sets elements of Winnemucca's and other Indian autobiographies, even those elements that appear "self-centered," in the oral tradition of self-vindication.

Here we have an interesting predicament, with each critic trying to claim a somewhat ill-defined feature—"personal experience"— for his or her respective side. In Ruoff's view self-narration is antithetical to indigenous tradition; in Brumble's, it is an integral part of that tradition. It is worth remembering that the autobiographical model of personhood—a model that is heavily psychologized, that "develops" in a linear, temporal fashion, and that is an active agent in history—is historically and culturally contingent; it is true, too, that many indigenous autobiographies (as well as many women's, ethnic, and even white men's autobiographies) reject such a model. But it is untenable to suggest that American Indians never self-narrated until whites came along to help them, or that self-narration is somehow essentially "un-Indian."

Winnemucca's periodic self-justification and insistence on her individual agency may be a feature of Western autobiography, attributable to her education and so-called acculturation, but as Brumble aptly points out, her moments of self-vindication also speak to a Paiute audience, since Paiutes as well as whites criticized her.[44] Indeed, contrary to Brigitte Georgi-Findlay's claims that Winnemucca is "uninterested in self-definition," that she emphasizes "actions" more than "feelings," self-vindication in *Life Among the Piutes* sometimes means an insistence on highly individual feelings and emotions, precisely because the book addresses a Euro-American audience inclined to deny psychological complexity to nonwhites. Thus, Winnemucca includes an anecdote about a Colonel Wilkinson, who tells her he is surprised that she can cry because she is "only an Indian woman." Of this incident Winnemucca says, "I tell you the world is full of such people. I see that all who say they are working for Indians are against me" (p. 243). Self-vindication, then, proves a useful concept for understanding *Life Among the Piutes* exactly in its intercultural context.

Krupat, Ruoff, and Brumble have advanced a critical tradition that usefully reminds us that texts are multiculturally produced and shaped and that American Indian texts in particular may owe much to oral tradition. Yet it is reductive to siphon off textual features as essentially Indian or non-Indian, as Stewart's preposterous claims about what is "not possible for an Indian" make clear. What we must say, rather, is that the text was created by two cultures and two people—if not by Mann and Winnemucca equally, then certainly by Winnemucca with Mann's help, and by Winnemucca with an acute consciousness of what women like Mann would have expected. A more fruitful approach is suggested by Eric Lott, who writes in his well-known study of blackface minstrelsy that

> Black performance itself . . . was precisely "performative," a cultural invention, not some precious essence installed in black bodies; and for better or worse it was often a product of self-commodification, a way of getting along in a constricted world. Black people, that is to say, not only exercised a certain amount of control over such practices but perforce sometimes developed them in tandem with white spectators. Moreover, practices sometimes taken as black were occasionally interracial creations whose commodification on white stages attested only to whites' greater access to public distribution (and profit).[45]

Life Among the Piutes was produced by at least two women—one an American Indian who capitalized on a widespread fascination with "vanishing races," probably for her own gain as well as to help her tribe, and the other a white who had certain investments in white values and institutions but who also was willing to question those values and the very power they gave non-Indians over Indians. The result is a book that, like blackface minstrelsy, is an interracial creation. Winnemucca developed it in concert with her white interlocutors. Thus, when we encounter in it features that appear either individualistic or communitist, far from reading them as "white" or "tribal" essences, we can read them as performances. In performing them, though, Winnemucca does sometimes mark certain features as distinctly "Paiute" or "non-Indian," and so we can now ask what such marked performances accomplish politically.

THE MALHEUR AGENCY

The petition that concludes *Life Among the Piutes* demands the restoration of the Malheur Agency, a reservation in Oregon set aside for the Paiutes in 1867 but from which they had been forcibly removed. In the petition, Winnemucca asks "the Honorable Congress of the United States to restore to them said Malheur Reservation, which is well watered and timbered, and large enough to afford homes and support for them all, where they can enjoy lands in severalty without losing their tribal relations, so essential to their happiness and good character, and where their citizenship, implied in this distribution of land, will defend them from the encroachments of the white settlers, so detrimental to their interests and their virtues" (p. 247).

As in her letter reprinted in *A Century of Dishonor*, here Winnemucca makes it clear that protection from white usurpation is the primary issue. Again she rejects the definition of allotment as an agenda that will break up tribal lives and landholding, describing it instead as 'severalty without losing their tribal relations.' This reconfigures allotment as something that will protect Indian lands (whether communally owned or not) as a basis for Indian community, rather than simply protecting those lands against white encroachment, as some reformers hoped, or breaking up the basis for Indian community. Winnemucca thus expresses a communitist ethos over and against, though not in strict opposition to, Anglo-American institutions and presence.

In chapter 6, "The Malheur Agency," Winnemucca similarly begins to articulate a model for an Indian republic within the rapidly changing United States. The chapter describes a happy year (1875–1876) under Agent Parrish, when food and supplies were finally distributed as legally required and the Paiutes could think of the reservation as their own (previous and subsequent agents treated the Paiutes as mere tenants and would even evict them from the reservation as punishment). According to Winnemucca, "My people, who had been under the other agent's care, did not know how to work" (p. 105)—meaning work by Euro-American, agrarian principles. Yet, as she describes it, Parrish taught them how to work: the Paiutes built an irrigation ditch, grew crops that they could keep, learned trades including carpentry and blacksmithing, and built a schoolhouse. She quotes Parrish at length:

> Now you are my children. I have come here to do you good. I have not come here to do nothing; I have no time to throw away. I have come to show you how to work, and work we must. . . . We must work while the government is helping us, and learn to help ourselves. The first thing I want you to do is to make a dam and then dig a ditch. That is to irrigate the land. Some of you can dig the ditch, some can build the dam, some can go to the woods and cut rails to build fences. I want you all to work while the government is helping us, for the government is not always going to help us. Do all you can until you get helped, and all you raise is your own to do with as you like. The reservation is all yours. The government has given it to you and your children. . . . I want to teach you all to do like white people (p. 107).

The paternalism exhibited here suffuses the chapter. Parrish refers to the Paiutes repeatedly as his "children." He praises them in terms that emphasize not the work itself but how it pleases him: "I am glad that you have been so obedient" (p. 111). While "allowing" them to continue some traditional practices, in true fatherly fashion, he even tells them not to "stay too long" at the hunt (p. 112). His brother's wife, the schoolteacher Mrs. Parrish, becomes "our lily white mother" (p. 117). And yet in Winnemucca's account the Paiutes are as happy as they have been for most of her lifetime; Parrish protects older people from hard physical labor, he builds a school for the children, he confers with the Paiutes to ask whether they approve of his plans, he staves off further white encroachment (other agents actually facilitated it), and some traditional practices continue: "Oh, how happy my people were! That night we all got together and had a dance. We were not so happy before for a long time. All the young people were on the hunt, and the old staid and drew their rations right along" (p. 112).

The chapter, in short, describes an agrarian utopia. Disheartening though it may sound today, it has some important differences from the agrarian utopias envisioned by Indian Bureau officials, whose "insistence on agriculture as the sole economic activity was clearly unrealistic,"[46] for Parrish promoted a more diversified economy than they did. It also differs crucially from other literary nineteenth-century agrarian utopias. On the first pages of Cooper's *The Pioneers*, for instance, readers feast their eyes on a region both picturesque and ordered:

> The mountains are generally arable to the tops, although instances are not wanting where the sides are jutted with rocks that aid greatly in giving to the country that romantic and picturesque character which it so eminently possesses. The vales are narrow, rich, and cultivated, with a stream uniformly winding through each. Beautiful and thriving villages are found interspersed along the margins of the small lakes, or situated at those points of the streams which are favorable to manufacturing; and neat and comfortable farms, with every indication of wealth about them, are scattered profusely through the vales and to even to the mountaintops. Roads diverge in every direction, from the even and graceful passes of the hills. Academies and minor edifices of learning meet the eye of the stranger at every few miles, as he winds his way through this uneven territory; and places for the worship of God abound with that frequency which characterizes a moral and reflecting people, and with that variety of exterior and canonical government which flows from unfettered liberty of conscience. In short, the whole district is hourly exhibiting how much can be done, in even a rugged country, and with a severe climate, under the dominion of mild laws, and where every man feels a direct interest in the

prosperity of a commonwealth of which he knows himself to form a part.[47]

Every sentence here works to show how the land can be made to do what humans want, not just materially, but also aesthetically. Another example of this kind of agrarian utopia is provided by the wife of Agent Nathan Meeker, whose writings describe his decision to move the Ute reservation to a spot where the Utes had been grazing their ponies. Mrs. Meeker describes this new spot as an agrarian utopia and paints the move as a matter of convenience: "[W]e did not like the site of the old agency, as it was in a canyon. The altitude was too high for the practice of agriculture"—no farms exuberantly reaching to mountaintops here—"and the winds blew fiercely and constantly."[48] After the move, however, she and her husband were afforded "a charming spot" with a "magnificent view." Her prelapsarian agency is even more neatly mapped and divided than Cooper's Susquehanna River valley:

> Comfortable buildings were erected and fine avenues were laid out. One of these, the main street, which ran as straight as a line from the canon [sic] to the agency, was named after Chief Douglass. My husband was preparing to plant mountain evergreens on both sides of it. The agency grounds were well kept. The government Indian farm was enclosed with a neat wire fence, and it produced all kinds of crops. The Indians, until the mutiny, helped to cultivate the soil. They raised potatoes, beets, turnips and other vegetables. The white employes [sic] planted the wheat.[49]

It is, of course, simply not the case that the land so naturally suited itself to the needs of farming settlers, or that they so invariably overcame nonarable terrain. Thus, we can read Winnemucca's descriptions as counters to the agrarian utopia insofar as they refuse the picturesque and the neat cordoning off and controlling of land that goes in hand with such aestheticizing. It is in fact rather difficult to get a clear picture of what the Malheur reservation looked like; Winnemucca seems more interested in re-creating the communitist spirit that evolved there. In the landscapes and reservations limned by Cooper, Meeker, and other writers like Hamlin Garland, Indians are menial laborers or mere visitors in a greater civilized scheme. Winnemucca's account breaks this picture up by presenting Paiutes as the subjects—or, better yet, the agents—of their reservation.[50]

Indeed, images of the Paiutes obediently bending to Parrish's agenda can also suggest collectivity and communitism: "What a beautiful time we had all day long issuing clothing to all" (p. 114); and in the schoolhouse, "Oh, how happy we were! We had three hundred and five boys, twenty-three young men, sixty nine girls, and nineteen young women. They learned very fast, and were glad to come to school" (p. 116). Like Helen Hunt Jackson's fantasies of weeping and converted Indians, the Malheur scenes conjure up spectacles of large groups of Indians in the process of being assimilated. But they are also something more—illustrating the Paiutes' uses of new practices while maintaining collective and traditional ethics.

As Martha Knack and Omer Stewart explain in their ethnohistory of the Pyramid Lake Reservation, where Winnemucca and her family lived for a time, Paiutes responded to the push for agriculture with "overt disinterest, surreptitious evasion, and clandestine modification."[51] Historically forced to adapt to a harsh and unpredictable environment, Paiutes drew ably on white traditions as new resources while refusing to give up traditional beliefs and practices. In farming, they usually worked in groups when clearing land and digging ditches. This practice was ardently discouraged by the agents, but it was continuous with their earlier practices of harvesting crops like pine nuts in groups.[52]

Winnemucca seems to confirm this picture. She shows not uncomplicated or uncontested assimilation but canny adaptation. The Paiutes she depicts, while embracing Parrish, are also adamant that they want control and ownership of the reservation. They are articulate about these demands, and they always speak plurally. As two men, quoted directly by Winnemucca, tell Parrish, "[W]e don't want to give up any of our reservation. We want it all. . . . There are a great many of our people, and we do not want to give up any of our land. Another thing, we do not want to have white people near us. We do not want to go where they are, and we don't want them to come near us" (p. 116).

This assertion, an historically contingent response to the realities of white encroachment, explores the political uses and limitations of opposition but is not reducible to static separatism or facile identity politics. The Paiutes tried every imaginable form of resistance: they adapted to white presence and practices, they attempted to get redress for their grievances through legal means including the white courts, they took up arms. White settlers, they knew, would not stop at having the Paiutes take up "civilized" ways and would not stop at having pushed indigenous peoples onto reservations; they wanted the land, and all of it. When Winnemucca and the Paiutes seem to advocate separatism, therefore, they are not so much saying that different races cannot live together (*Life Among the Piutes* says almost everything but that) but that white people have failed to acknowledge Paiutes' humanity and legitimate claims to their land. To reassert that humanity and those claims, as the Paiutes do when they speak to Parrish, was radical in 1883.

Winnemucca does represent the viewpoint we might call more nationalist, or traditional and conservative, even if she doesn't finally promote it. This viewpoint is given voice in the man, Oytes, who prefers to hunt rather than to "work" (the book sets up these two terms as opposites). Parrish trounces him rather easily by pitting Euro-American money and rationality against Paiute superstition and fraud: "Oytes, I have three hundred dollars. If you will let me shoot at you, if my bolt won't go through your body the money is yours. You say bolts cannot kill you." Instantly (and astoundingly) Oytes crumples, "Oh, my good father, don't kill me.

Oh, I am so bad. Oh, I will do everything you say" (p. 115). This scene, along with another in which Winnemucca herself chastises the recalcitrant Oytes, makes him a childlike, ultimately harmless figure; these scenes together must have worked to make at least some readers relieved that civilization, in the end, always wins. But there is nonetheless a certain pathos about Oytes's position. After all, when Winnemucca lectures him, her main point is that the whites "are people who are very kind to any one who is ready to do whatever they wish," hardly an unconditional endorsement of Parrish's position (p. 113). Likewise, the subchief Egan, upon meeting the new agent, remarks that the farming plan sounds kind, but concludes "we have no other way only to do what we are told to do" (p. 107). While the book does finally silence and recuperate Oytes, it nevertheless allows him to speak; it gives several pages of this short chapter on the Malheur Agency to a voice seldom heard in the literature of the period.[53]

In so doing, *Life Among the Piutes* moves toward a more dispersed notion of agency than that achieved in Jackson's works. Unlike Jackson, Winnemucca does not seem to subordinate her concern for communitism to individualistic conceptions of female or Indian agency. This does not mean she is never individualistic, for we have seen that she most emphatically can be; nor is it to romanticize her, as an Indian, as somehow essentially more communal than her white contemporary. It is, however, to observe that she characteristically allows other viewpoints to speak through her writing, including those of radically conservative Paiutes. This multivocality may be a feature of Paiute oral tradition; Catherine Fowler suggests that, in this tradition, Winnemucca's viewpoints "would be balanced by those of other narrators—a context that it loses in print."[54] But we could still read Winnemucca's use of extensive direct quotation as a recreation or an active continuation of that tradition into writing.

We could also note that, in contrast to Jackson's beloved image of the disempowered woman who garners power by speaking out,

Winnemucca raises serious questions about the connections between speech and power, possibly because of her complicated position as interpreter for the U.S. government. Government promises often turned out to be false, as when Carl Schurz finally agreed to let the Paiutes return to Nevada after they were banished to Yakima, but the agent there refused to accept a copy of the secretary's letter.[55] Thus, Winnemucca says of her employment in the military, "words have been put into my mouth which have turned out to be nothing but idle wind" (p. 258). Sometimes she quotes herself in ways that explain the frustration that many Paiutes must have felt as they listened to her repeated reports of white officials' promises that never panned out: "I tell you, my dear children, I have never told you my own words; they were the words of the white people, not mine" (p. 236). At still other times, though, Winnemucca constructs her own speech as politically radical and dangerous, as when she remarks toward the end of the book, "[M]y work at Vancouver for the military government may be my last work, as I am talking against the government officials" (p. 242). She oscillates between wanting to claim agency as a speaker and wanting to divest herself of that agency, between wanting to assert the power of cross-cultural speech and sketching out its dangers and misuses.

Life Among the Piutes is predicated on the hope that to speak is to be heard and understood, and thus to effect change. Yet it also shows the connections between speech and political agency to be troubled and complicated. Sometimes, speaking for oneself is neither possible nor desirable. Winnemucca's autobiography thus tells at least two stories—a thrilling story of a remarkable woman who spoke out and made things happen, but also a story of loss. It shows a world in which, no matter how truthfully or eloquently a good man like the subchief Egan speaks, in some sense he cannot be heard. In some sense, to tell the story of Indians speaking to whites in the nineteenth century is necessarily to tell a story of failure, the failure of audience. It is thus that Winnemucca tells us that the Paiutes sometimes retreat into silence, refusing to self-represent; they "are the most sociable people in the world in their own camps; but they are shut up to white people, because they are so often wronged by them" (p. 93). Winnemucca points to the limits of a model in which the woman simply speaks and constitutes herself as an empowered subject. Those limits, she shows us, persist because speech and self-creation do not arise in a vacuum, but rather in dynamic, communicative encounters where the interlocutor has a defining role to play. And sometimes that interlocutor is less than amenable.

WINNEMUCCA'S ETHNOGRAPHIES

And yet Winnemucca begins with ethnography, which assumes amenable interlocutors and the seamless passage of information from one culture to another. She wrote two pieces we could call ethnographies. One is chapter 2 of *Life Among the Piutes*, "Domestic and Social Moralities," which is devoted to descriptions of Paiute traditions: the Flower Festival, presented as a rite of passage for young girls; marriage customs; young men and their rites of passage; tribal governance, including the role of women therein; antelope charmers. The other is a little-discussed article, "The Pah-Utes," published in 1882 in a magazine called *The Californian*. Similar in format to "Domestic and Social Moralities," with paragraphs on different cultural topics, "The Pah-Utes" discusses some additional elements of Paiute culture—war signals, medicine men, and oral tradition—not covered in the other piece. Fowler surmises that this article may have been based on one of Winnemucca's speeches.[56]

Ethnography, with its systematic descriptions of different elements of a culture, presents itself as cultural preservation and mapping. It invests in what Clifford calls the "allegory" of "cultural loss and textual rescue."[57] Readers in 1883—observing, requiring, and perhaps even lamenting the assimilation of indigenous peoples—could feel Paiute culture preserved between the covers of Winnemucca's book. Thus, an apparent digression from that second chapter's cultural description—"My people have been so unhappy for a long time they wish now to *disincrease* instead of multiply" (p. 48)—is in keeping with ethnography's premise that the passing of primitive cultures is sad but inevitable.

Further, ethnography reflects what Curtis Hinsley has described as the Victorian search for order amidst social chaos, a yearning for "solace as well as aesthetic pleasure in the vision of a progressively evolving humanity."[58] Hence, Winnemucca sticks to customs that are not too strange and that will appeal especially to her high-minded women readers, like the Flower Festival, with its picture of young Indian girls who "all go marching along, each girl in turn singing of herself; but she is not a girl anymore,—she is a flower singing" (p. 47). Aesthetic pleasure and solace are also offered in this chapter's emphasis on manners: the first sentence reads, "Our children are very carefully taught to be good" (p. 45). Ethnography puts a culture under glass, satisfying readers' desire for exotic spectacle, assuring them that the object under scrutiny is a thing of the past, and reaffirming the values and institutions most familiar to them.

Conventionally, ethnography employs what Johannes Fabian has famously called "the ethnographic present"—that is, the generic use of the present tense when describing other cultures and societies, as when Winnemucca writes, "Indian girls are not allowed to mingle freely with the braves." Among other ills, Fabian notes, this convention "unduly magnifies the claim of a statement to general validity" and "project[s] a categorical view" on a culture. Moreover, it works to establish a "scientific" dialogue between writer and reader that contrasts with the object being spoken about; it "presupposes the givenness of the object of anthropology as something to be *observed. The present tense is a signal identifying a discourse as an observer's language.* Such a language provides glosses on the world as *seen*" (italics in original).[59]

But Winnemucca's ethnographic writing breaks up this triangulation of reader and writer over object, because she speaks both *about* Paiutes and *as* a Paiute, positioned both within and outside of indigenous culture. "The Pah-Utes," for example, begins: "My Indian name is Somit-tone, meaning Shell-Flower. I was educated at the St. Mary's Convent in San Jose."[60] This hybrid and mutable position contravenes both the subject and object of conventional ethnographic study; it moves between an autobiographical "I" ("In 1867 I was interpreter for my people") and a collective "we" ("Our culture is not a written one, but oral"). Winnemucca thus makes herself and the Paiutes not only objects but subjects of this article; her ethnographic present is not just an "observer's language."[61]

This is not so much a world seen, either. Just as Winnemucca tells us about the Malheur reservation without really giving us the tools to visualize it spatially, so she also describes the Paiute people without much physical detail. The article is not accompanied by any photographs or illustrations (though neighboring articles in *The Californian* have plenty, many of them quite stereotypical); and despite the aesthetic idea of practices like the Flower Festival, these pieces are not terribly visual. Most notable is the absence of any physical description of the Indians. Whereas many white ethnographers and tourists remark such characteristics at length,[62] Winnemucca tells us nothing about skin color, stature, physiognomy, or any of the other features used to exoticize a people as well as their customs.

So we might say that Winnemucca "does" ethnography in part to challenge it. But I want to qualify this argument first. Like the rest of *Life Among the Piutes* and her other performances, Winnemucca's ethnographies are bicultural texts, produced in conversation with a dominant culture or set of ideologies. Ethnography itself remains a dialogue; despite its most notorious elisions of informant voices, lives, or desires, it still arises from and is based on some kind of intercultural exchange, though the terms of that exchange have historically been—to put it bluntly—asymmetrical. So ethnography itself is not a purely "white" discourse, against which Winnemucca could or would write a purely "Indian" or resistant one. Therefore, to read or set up "The Pah-Utes" or "Domestic and Social Moralities" as "native" ethnographies that directly countermand a tradition of "white" ethnography would be an oversimplification. It would also be impractical; since no manuscript exists for either of these texts, it is, once again, impossible to know how much is "Winnemucca's" and how much "the editor's." And it is, again, so difficult to account for these textual effects—are they Winnemucca defying ethnographic convention? Struggling to write in an unfamiliar mode? Struggling to write from a Paiute aesthetic? Or some complicated combination of all of these?

We can nevertheless make some useful observations about these two pieces and their apparent editing. In "Domestic and Social Moralities," for starters, Mann is a good bit more intrusive than she is elsewhere in the autobiography: not only do the title and tone of this chapter suddenly trumpet Victorian feminine manners, but a particularly long editorial footnote makes Mann's presence palpable. In this footnote, Mann extols the virtues that Paiutes teach their children, notably their "self-respect, and respect for each other" (p. 51). She praises Indians' education of their children "in heart and mind" and advocates for the education of Indian children in English. She cites a William B. Ogden, railroad executive, and first mayor of Chicago, "who has always maintained that the Indians ought to have citizens' rights, and be represented in Congress, founding his opinion on his life-long knowledge of the high-toned morality of Indians who wore blankets. [He] said to my sister in 1853, that it was the stereotyped lie of the fur-traders (whose interest it was) that they could not be civilized" (p. 52). Finally, she quotes Helen Hunt Jackson, saying that "we know from H.H.'s "Century of Dishonor" that from the beginning the Christian bigots who peopled America looked upon the Indians as heathen. . . . Thus Christendom missed the moral reformation it might have had, if they had become acquainted with the noble Five Nations, and others whom they have exterminated" (p. 52).

This commentary repeats and refines the many contradictory identifications and dis-identifications we have seen throughout the works of Jackson, Winnemucca, and the white women reformers. Amidst all this intercultural empathy, the role of white women is clear and powerful: they will be the agents of the new civilization. As Gail Landsman has shown, white women suffragists had a long history of invoking images of politically empowered Indian women "simultaneously as a symbol of women's past power and natural rights, on the one hand, and as a validation of women's special 'civilizing' qualities, necessary to the contemporary goals of reform and American expansion, on the other."[63] Along these lines, Mann's footnote testifies both to white women's struggles for power and to the power that they already had in the public sphere.

On the opposite page from this footnote and thus in visible, immediate dialogue with it, Winnemucca's text describes Paiute governance as more egalitarian than white: "[I]f the women are interested they can share in the talks. . . . The women know as much as the men do, and their advice is often asked . . . if women could go into your Congress I think justice would soon be done to the Indians" (pp. 52–53). These words are strikingly similar to an emphatic line from Elizabeth Peabody's letter in 1885 to Grover Cleveland's sister Rose: "Woman's *wit* is needed in *administra-tion*."[64] Winnemucca's words point to the complex dialogues among women reformers and Indian activists and the many complications in the relationships between the two groups: they appeal to white women's sense of themselves as marginal yet essential; at the same time, in asserting women's equality as a specifically Paiute attribute, they reassert the value of indigenous community and tradition to the very audience that might wish to absorb such traditions.

A single, knotty phrase from Mann's footnote—the reference to "the high-toned morality of Indians who wore blankets"—further spins out these complications. Perhaps such "moral" Indians are to be "saved" precisely because they seem to conform so well already to white values, to "Christendom." And yet they are not Indians in petticoats, but Indians in blankets—the stereotypical reference to a custom that is backward and strange. Is this phrase erasing or subsuming cultural difference by suggesting that what looks strange may after all be "just like us"? Is it reversing the terms of savagery and civilization—what appears to be "savage" is in fact more "civilized" than Euro-American culture? Does the phrase cunningly assert Indians' rights to wear those blankets—to maintain their own traditions—if they wish? Does it, finally, make Indians more intelligible, assimilating them in a sense, or does it avow their difference and thus point toward their rights to cultural self-determination?

It is not likely, I think, that such questions jarred readers in 1883. But this biculturally produced piece of writing opens up all of these above possibilities, whether intended or not. It would, therefore, be reductive to read *Life Among the Piutes* either as silenced and determined by Mary Mann or as evidence of Winnemucca trying to use white cultural assumptions to go undercover and say what she really wants to say about indigenous sovereignty. If we are to assume that Winnemucca crafts her writing in dialogue with Mann and others—that her interactions with white culture shape her work—it is only sound to assume that Mann also undergoes some changes, though not necessarily the same kinds of changes, because of her position of relative power. Mann's footnote creates powerful new identifications for white women through *dis-identification*. Against Christian bigots, fur-traders, self-invested male agents and (elsewhere in the footnote) women teachers who sit in classrooms only to read dime novels, Mann creates a more civilized kind of civilized person.[65] As we have seen, that new civilized person often unwittingly shored up the very culture she purported to contest. But in the same gesture she shows a willingness to begin examining the conditions of her and culture's power.

Mann insists, for instance, on human mutuality and exchange: "It is not unlikely that when something like a human communication is established between the Indians and whites, it may prove a fair exchange, and the knowledge of nature which has accumulated, for we know not how long, may enrich our early education as much as reading and writing will enrich theirs" (p. 52). In this, Mann echoes Jackson and the other white women reformers, who moved, often uncomfortably, between claiming power for themselves at the expense of Indian peoples and seeking a genuine recognition of those peoples' humanity. "Domestic and Social Moralities" thus suggests compromises as well as mutual dialogues and possibilities.

"The Pah-Utes," though, reads quite differently. It is much less geared to women's equality; indeed, it was published in an entirely different forum. Where *Life Among the Piutes* was published in New York, under the guidance of a sympathetic eastern audience eager to take up the case of Indians, this article appears in a western magazine that juxtaposes articles on Spencerism and rail travel with vignettes of Chinese immigrants and Franciscan missions. With this presumably more hostile audience, "The Pah-Utes" points much more aggressively at its readers, asking them to scrutinize their own positions.

The article opens with Winnemucca's briefest personal history, followed by one paragraph about Paiute food, with a few gently mediating remarks like, "*Kouse* root . . . tastes a little like hard bread" (p. 108). Immediately, though, Winnemucca turns on her reader:

> Now you must not suppose that my people are weak or uncourageous. They are not what you call "slouches." . . . We helped the Bannacks and the Umatillas in the war, because we were kindred of theirs. They are our cousins; therefore we helped them. Now you say, Why did they make war? I will tell you: Your white men are too greedy (p. 109).

Not much collusion between reader and writer here. The object under scrutiny has reared its head to speak, to become a subject, making the reader the object instead. It is as if Winnemucca knows what her audiences want; she draws them in with the promise of privileged information and then implicates them in the act of usurping Paiute lands and Paiute stories. These readers are similarly under scrutiny in *Life Among the Piutes*, where the concluding dossier of letters includes this one from a C. E. S. Wood:

> My Dear Sarah—What are you doing now, and how are you getting on? I write to ask you as a favor to me to please to write me out a description of the way the Indian young men and women do their "courting," and the marriage ceremony, and also the burial of the dead. You told me at one time, but I have forgotten. If not too much trouble, please also write me a description of that flower festival you say the Piutes have in the spring-time. Please ask Mr. Symons to give you the paper, pen, and ink. All here are very well (p. 265).

Perhaps Winnemucca's way of telling about her people, without really dissecting and picturing them, was what made it so hard for Wood to remember the desired objects. Perhaps, too, we are looking here at Euro-American culture's demand to have things written down and not told, the better to master and possess them. Readers of *Life Among the Piutes*, having perused pretty much the contents Wood asks for, thus find themselves oddly mirrored in this letter.

Winnemucca's ethnographies were surely written first for non-Paiute audiences. This is not to say that Paiutes could not and never have read and used them; it is to say, though, that the politics of cross-cultural communication are of dramatic concern here. It is thus that Weaver can write, of the earliest American Indian writers, that while "they could not hope to reach a wide Native audience, their work nevertheless served Native purposes and reflected communitist values as they sought not only to preserve and defend their cultures but also to assert their own and their fellow Natives' humanity."[66]

The emphasis in both "The Pah-Utes" and "Domestic and Social Moralities" is therefore not really on the spectacle of culture but on cultural parity. Winnemucca does throw her reader some brief descriptions of Paiute customs, and these may in fact be what readers mainly take away, but she is also instructing those readers in the terms of the intercultural conversation. At times this means chastising them, as above. At other times it means insisting on the fundamental equality of Paiute and Euro-American cultures—or even, as Walker has observed, on the superiority of Paiute culture. In "Domestic and Social Moralities," Winnemucca asserts, "We have a republic as well as you" (p. 53)—a direct assertion that Paiute culture cannot simply be absorbed into U.S. culture. In "The Pah-Utes," noting that Paiute warriors wear eagle feathers in battle, she remarks, "The eagle is our national bird; the Americans taking that emblematic notion from the Indians in the early days of their nation" (p. 111). As Werner Sollors has pointed out, the eagle "is not just the classical emblem of republics but also the biblical eagle of Exodus [19:4] and Revelation [12:14], an image of escape and emigration."[67] Consequently, it "may indicate the Americanization of people who use it. Yet it can, alternately or at the same time, serve to define a new ethnic peoplehood in contradistinction to a general American identity. The rhetoric in support of American group cohesion and consensus can also be used to forge divergent and dissenting ethnic groupings."[68]

While one could point out that indigenous peoples pre-existed "Americans" in the United States, Winnemucca is in fact defining a "new" ethnic peoplehood; she appropriates "Paiutes," a non-indigenous designation to refer to a range of culturally similar but not theretofore especially united peoples in the Great Basin era, as a way of asserting a viable and visible ethnic identity.[69] While mainstream discourse in the Era of Assimilation construes American Indians as vanishing, Winnemucca constructs them as emergent—as a new cultural and political force to be reckoned with. As we have seen her do so many times, she deploys images and typologies that can be read as buttressing U.S. national identity, but that in her hands bolster indigenous self-determination, community, and viability.

On the question of intercultural contact, Winnemucca has no single theoretical position; she does not consistently advocate separatism or assimilation or unlimited exchange. Her approach, rather, is contingent and conflicting, suggesting that how we judge contact between Indian and white depends on the material effects of such contact. Of medicine men's increased tendency to charge money for their services, she says simply, "Thus we follow your customs as our association grows with you" (p. 112); she hardly praises such commodification but, herself a self-franchiser, also does not overtly condemn it. On the matter of changing marriage practices she is more acerbic, remarking that "One of the latest evidences of civilization is divorce—an indulgence taken advantage of to abandon an old wife and secure a young one" (p. 113). Winnemucca, multiply divorced, sometimes by white men, surely had personal stakes here, resurfacing in her characteristic ironic use of *civilization*.

Earlier in the article, however, Winnemucca tells a story about the Paiutes' conflict with another tribe, the Side-okahs, "which means man-eaters, or cannibals" (p. 109). The Side-okahs fight the more numerous Paiutes, terrorizing them, until the Paiutes finally conquer them and win all their land. The story concludes:

> After the Side-okahs were exterminated we lived peaceably, now and then only having a little fight with other tribes—no tribes being allowed to settle among us. If they came on very important business they could stay a while; or if they came for a visit, they would be entertained by feasts and plays and dancing: amusing them all the time they were with us. They always brought presents to our chiefs, and they gave them presents to take back; but they were never allowed to settle with us or marry with us, each tribe maintaining its own

individuality very pronounced; every nation speaking a different language (p. 110).

This story, which readers could pass over as a quaint "myth" about remote tribal infighting, has everything to do with Paiute nationalism, self-determination, and land ownership—and also everything to do with Indian-white contact.

For the Paiutes, cannibalism had strong associations with white people; in *Life Among the Piutes* Winnemucca reports, "Our mothers told us that the whites were killing everybody and eating them" (p. 11). She adds that, as a child, she eventually came to "love the white people" (p. 33), suggesting that in believing whites to be cannibals, she and the other Paiutes were primitive and naive. But Winnemucca was born around 1844, only two years before the notorious Donner party got stranded in western Nevada and resorted to cannibalism to survive. The story of became part of indigenous oral history in the region.[70] The story of the Side-okahs thus resonates with Paiute experience of whites, not only as it registers indigenous fears of barbaric behavior but also as it enacts the struggle over land. It is a national narrative, explaining the Paiutes' right to that territory.

This narrative of the Side-okahs has further implications for disrupting ethnography. Winnemucca's references to oral tradition, though few, are crucial. She says, "our language is not a written one, but oral" (p. 110) and alludes to some of the visual signals the Pah-Utes use to communicate. In *Life Among the Piutes*, Winnemucca refers to the oral tradition in her description of Truckee telling an origin story. These stories can have the effect of revealing indigenous practice, of giving the non-Indian reader glimpses into a different culture. And yet they are also oddly devoid of context or explanation. Their inclusion thus points beyond the particular story to the Paiutes' broader traditions, traditions that precede and exceed Winnemucca's writing about them. Clifford has pointed out, following the implications of Jacques Derrida's redefinition of writing, that all human groups "write" their world in ritual acts. Such a recognition shakes up the image of the ethnographer as the one who brings the culture into being through writing.[71] Retold by Winnemucca as something that preceded her writing and will continue thereafter, her short summaries of oral stories also light up the Paiutes' *own* "writing" of their culture, quite apart from the gaze, presence, and "assistance" of non-Paiutes.

SIGNS TAKEN FOR WONDERS: NATIONAL ANTHEMS, NATIONAL AESTHETICS

Sarah Winnemucca was thus not as clear a voice for assimilation as she has sometimes been read. Her resistance has been hard to register. This is partly because her writings were so complex— sometimes fiercely oppositional, sometimes reticent and protective, and always working somewhere between Euro-American conventions and Paiute aesthetics. Her resistance is also hard to register because, no matter what form of resistance Winnemucca tried, Americans seemed nevertheless to annex her to their own nationalizing purposes. Winnemucca has been hugely biographized, usually in ways that show how much she accomplished for the United States. One of her many biographers, Carolyn Foreman, focuses largely on Winnemucca's years as a paid employee of the American government. She responds to debates over whether Winnemucca could aptly be called a "princess"—the "daughter of a chief, as she claims"—by concluding that "she well deserved a title if her services to the United States and her own people are considered."[72] Winnemucca turns out to have been serving the United States all along, even before she served the Paiutes.

I would like to conclude with a look at one specific co-opted Paiute resistance strategy. In the first chapter of *Life Among the Piutes*, Winnemucca recalls how her grandfather Captain Truckee, who had his own complicated position as a self-dubbed Paiute "chief" and aide to General Fremont during the Mexican War, taught the Paiutes "The Star-Spangled Banner." As she does so often, Winnemucca seems to play many hands at once. She sets the incident in an apparently assimilationist context: it is one of the many "wonderful" things her grandfather has seen and learned during his travels in "the mighty nation" of his "white brothers" (p. 18). But in describing the national anthem, she undercuts melodrama; she says simply that "the funniest thing was that he would sing some of the soldier's roll-calls, and the air to the Star-Spangled Banner, which everybody learned during the winter" (p. 18). Later, when she hears some whites sing the anthem under the direction of a major she remarks, "It was not a bit like the way my grandfather used to sing it" (p. 60).

In this, there is a humorous suggestion that Paiutes sang the song but sang it "wrong," that they sang it their own way, that they were even making a mockery of it. Whatever their intentions, their repetition of the anthem produces what Homi Bhabha would call an ambivalent colonial presence: "[T]hrough an act of repetition [as in the Paiutes learning the U.S. national anthem], the colonial text emerges uncertainly."[73] Winnemucca's elliptical account of the anthem-singing opens all kinds of possibilities—possibilities for the assumed authority of the Euro-American nation but also possibilities for resistance to that authority.

American readers have nevertheless consistently shut those possibilities down. Elinor Richey, another biographer using only the autobiography as a source, says that Sarah "well remembered her little grandfather's quavering rendition of the Yankee anthem."[74] Katherine Gehm paints the incident as one of Truckee's many sincere efforts to get Paiutes to accept and understand whites.[75] The image of Truckee and the Paiutes singing the anthem thus becomes something like Helen Hunt Jackson's favorite story of the Mission Indians praying en masse—a spectacle of primitives collectively and reverentially making their solemn tribute to the superior race.

Indeed, Truckee was read as pure-hearted, trying to welcome whites and assuage their fears. In "Famous Indian Chiefs," which appeared in *St. Nicholas* magazine in 1908, General Howard depicts Truckee trying to fulfill a burning lifelong wish to befriend whites. Even as the trappers in his account shout and shoot at the Indians, who are all picturesquely and diminutively riding "little ponies adorned with cedar sprigs and some bright flowers fastened to their manes and tails," Truckee "got down from his saddle fifty or sixty yards away, put his strong bow and quiver of arrows on the ground, and spread out his arms as a sign of peace."[76] The accompanying illustration shows trappers behind their horses, realistically rendered in the fore; in the upper left-hand corner, a tiny and ethereal Indian stretches his arms toward them, half-dressed, a lone feather sticking up from his head. Like the "Star-Spangled Banner" scenario, this spectacle, whatever Truckee intended or didn't intend, confirms a non-Indian readership in its national unity and racial supremacy.

In considering Winnemucca's work and its effects, we might remember Lott's description of blackface. Key in Lott's analysis is the commodification of blackface, which "attested only to whites' greater access to public distribution (and profit)." It is not simply that Winnemucca and her family "took the white man's ways to show themselves"; rather they created a mode of representation in dialogue with their white audiences. That biographers and other readers and users of her image repeatedly translate Winnemucca's highly multivocal, multivalent performances and texts into quite flat and transparent images reveals more about the limitations of the dialogue itself than about her individual successes or failures. Her works aren't, as Lott says elsewhere, "*inherently* anything," but "given the right context, they could become transformative."[77]

And yet Winnemucca so rarely got the "right" context, the one that would allow her disagreements with acculturation and her insistence on Indian sovereignty and self-determination to be heard. It is all very well to explore the infinite play of signification, but

"He spread out his arms as a sign of peace"

Captain Truckee greeting white settlers. (Drawing from illustration in O. O. Howard, "Famous Indian Chiefs I Have Known")

the historical reception and use of Indian images—precisely *because* of Indians' *material* disenfranchisement—has been altogether narrow.[78] In the struggle over cultural meaning, nationalizing forces seemed to win, not because Winnemucca's textual strategies were too limited (as we have seen, they were hardly that), but because the material conditions of her life restricted the control she had over her own signifiers.

It is therefore understandable, and even politically acute, that some American Indian artists pull back from cross-cultural self-representation, preferring to omit information about themselves, or to obfuscate that information in order to shift the position of non-Indian readers away from one of textual "mastery." It is also politically useful to espouse an American Indian aesthetic. Such an aesthetic, which does not conform to readers' expectations of story and of the transmission of information across cultures, has at least the potential to alter those readers' preconceptions and relationships to the materials they read and consume. We will see this most vividly now as Victoria Howard talks to Melville Jacobs.

CHAPTER THREE

CAN THE CLACKAMAS WOMAN SPEAK? RECONSTRUCTING "VICTORIA HOWARD"

One of the most delightful stories that Victoria Howard told Melville Jacobs is "She deceived herself with milt."[1] A wealthy widow prepares salmon for winter storage. As she extracts the fish's milt, or male reproductive gland, she casually says, "Oh that you become a person."[2] The next morning, she wakes to find in her bed "a fine-looking man" who is "light of skin." But this man leaves her for a new wife. The two women begin harassing each other, with the first—the creator of this fickle milt-man—singing at the second, "She deceived herself with milt. / She deceived herself with milt." She sings this five times. Finally, she uses her sacred regalia to change the man back into the negligible gland from which he came.

This story hints at why Victoria Howard has intrigued scholars across disciplines, from the linguist Dell Hymes to the literary critic Jarold Ramsey, and why her work has been republished in recent anthologies of American Indian oral literature. Her stories have it all: sex, race, class, and lively telling. *Clackamas Chinook Texts* includes numerous myths in Clackamas and Molale, a handful of stories of "transitional" times (as opposed to the pre-human times of the myths), and seventy-seven ethnographic texts, in which Howard speaks of traditional practices and events in her own life.

Hymes finds in this collection a "woman's standpoint," a standpoint that the tale of a wealthy widow making a man out of milt seems to reflect. Ramsey concurs, advancing the milt story in particular as both a feminine recasting of a Chinookan oral tradition in which *men* are the active wishers and also as an ironic account of interracial sex. These readings, too, point to what Howard can contribute to a study of American women telling stories about Indians: like Helen Hunt Jackson and Sarah Winnemucca, she constructs herself, her female characters, and other women telling traditional narratives as embattled *female* subjects, subjects who struggle with, circumvent, and manipulate the power of men and white people.

Howard's work is also aesthetically compelling. Despite the constraints of the transcription process, and despite the vagaries of reading back through that process to glean what the storyteller actually said, Howard appears to have been a skilled and even dynamic performer. She fills her stories with the quoted speech of her characters (as when she sings the woman's song, above) and emphatically re-narrates key scenes (often five times, an important number in the region's indigenous culture). Many storytellers, of course, use direct discourse and repetition; direct discourse, in fact, is a prevalent feature of Chinookan languages. But the occurrence of such features in Howard's stories also reflects a special concern for women as they speak, and for the relation of female speech and storytelling to female and indigenous empowerment.

In translation, further, the stories are usefully multivocal. Jacobs includes the Clackamas and English versions on the same page, and while he doesn't regularly include information about features like intonation or pause or volume,[3] as some translators do, he does provide footnotes representing some of Howard's extranarrative remarks, or describing the mood of her telling. He also glosses the text, sometimes overmuch, with parenthetical elaborations of the literal English translation—elaborations that he worked out with Howard's help, for Jacobs didn't speak Clackamas and depended

Victoria Howard. (Courtesy of University of Washington Press)

on her for translating. The result is a collection of texts that uniquely allow us to read their *production*—that is, the conversations between storyteller and transcriber, woman and man, Indian and non-Indian. They are what Mary Louise Pratt has famously called "contact zones"—intersections of hitherto geographically and historically separated people that allow us to see how those "subjects are constituted in and by their relations to each other."[4]

To give an example, here is Howard's "A widow's mourning,"[5] in its entirety:

> The day when a person died the widow would cry. She wanted to jump into the grave (of her husband). But she just did that (in hypocrisy).

This very short and elliptical account, which Jacobs classifies as an "ethnographic text" and which thus purports to reveal something about Clackamas culture, raises more questions than it answers. What did Howard think of these widows? Would their "hypocrisy" have been obvious to all participants at burials, or only to women, or only to a few astute observers like Howard herself? Is she critical of this hypocrisy? Is she humorously suggesting the women were glad to be rid of their husbands ("But they just did that")? Is she distancing herself from or being reticent about a traditional practice she anticipates Jacobs might find strange or primitive?

Indeed, the word *hypocrisy*, a strong term with connotations of condemnation, seems to be Jacobs's, and yet because he worked through these glosses with Howard's help, we cannot be absolutely sure whether *hypocrisy* was his translation (or even mistranslation) of a subtler phenomenon she was trying to explain, or whether she herself characterized the widows' actions as disingenuous. In Jacobs's field notebooks the literal, original translation of that last sentence reads "just making believe, fooling she does."[6] Is that lighter tone closer to the Clackamas original? Does it reflect an indigenous worldview, or perhaps a lack of interest in psychologizing the widows' behavior? Or is this language the trace of Howard's fluent but non-standard English? Perhaps she was saying simply that the widows went through the motion of wanting to jump in their husbands' graves, not necessarily in any "hypo-critical" way, but not actually making the jump, either. Then again, Howard may have been dismissing an outsider's probing questions: "they just did that" . . . "just making believe."

Whatever its meaning, this piece recalls and speaks, in engaging ways, to Gayatri Chakravorty Spivak's influential thesis about silent subalterns, for it implies that widows can transform a ritual wailing into a strategy for both concealing and revealing con-flicting responses to patriarchy.[7] It shows the widows' mourning as *performative*—performative in the sense that it may be expected behavior of women upon their husbands' deaths, and also per-formative in the sense that it may be ironized even as it is enacted.

"A widow's mourning" foils efforts to distill a parenthetical, translating Jacobs from an original, narrating Howard. It matches the widows' mourning in its caginess; like the behavior it describes, it withholds and conceals even as it reveals. Howard's citation of the widows hints that the subaltern *does* speak, but that we should not assume we can hear her, though we can continue trying. In trying, very few readers will see Jacobs's field notes, and fewer still will read the Clackamas original; they will have only the published text. But that text valuably calls attention to itself as a product of cross-cultural dialogue, with all of the misapprehensions, misap-propriations, evasions, explanations, and mutual recognitions that human communication generally entails.

In calling attention to these conflicts and possibilities, the Howard-Jacobs texts challenge their own media (ethnography, transcription, and translation) by moving readers into a different kind of relationship with them—a relationship where cultural information isn't simply passed from one party to another, but where the participants examine the conditions of cross-cultural communication itself. To transcribe the oral is purportedly to make it visible, legible, accessible. And to have an American Indian woman speaking, as we have seen, is allegedly to have the ideal "mediator."

Jacobs often held Howard up as his ideal informant, and in some ways she was: she obligingly recounted traditional and exotic narratives for his recording pen, answered his eager questions about the remote past. But she didn't answer all of his questions, she didn't give intelligible explanations for many cultural differences, and she didn't talk much about herself, although Jacobs asked her to. This is surely because, as an indigenous woman, she told stories and saw the world differently than he did. But Howard's talk can at the same time be a form of resistance. She worked with Jacobs at the tail end of the Era of Assimilation, when the drive to incorporate American Indians into some imagined cohesive nation was beginning to reverse. Like her foremother Sarah Winnemucca, Howard would thus have lived much of her life in commerce with white people—with their notions about individualism and storytelling, and with their theft of her people's land and traditions. In this context, *as well as* in a Chinookan context, her stories serve female and indigenous ends: they express female and indigenous values and systems, while also rendering those systems somewhat opaque in the interest (intentional or not) of restructuring relations with readers.

This chapter is about the many discourses—ethnographic, biographical, linguistic, literary—that make up "Victoria Howard," and through which we must read her. A strong tradition of scholarship in American Indian literatures has exposed some of the politics of transcription and translation, revealing the ways—sometimes egregious, sometimes well-meant—that ethnographers have reshaped indigenous narratives to their own standards, biases, and aims. I will therefore explore Jacobs's methods as well as the material conditions under which he recorded Howard's stories.

But I will also try to hear both sides of this conversation, for of course it was not only Melville Jacobs who produced these texts, but also Victoria Howard. They are not always and everywhere equal participants, but they are both participants and authors, and Victoria Howard has as yet been little understood as an author. I will thus also approach Clackamas and Grand Ronde reservation culture, as well as the circumstances of Howard's life, so far as they can be known.

What I hope to retrieve is a richer sense of the limitations and possibilities of transcribed oral narratives for indigenous cultural expression and for feminine and indigenous resistance. Victoria Howard's cultural and historical contexts had the potential both to restrict her and to enable her, and examining these contexts will reveal a picture of her as a woman and an American Indian—a picture of her speaking *as, for* and *to* both Indian and non-Indian cultures.

ETHNOGRAPHY: RECONSTRUCTING CULTURE

Readers who for geographical, historical, or political reasons do not have ready access to the living oral tradition of an indigenous people may find themselves looking to ethnography to understand that people's verbal art. If we are to draw on ethnography in reading Victoria Howard as a "Clackamas Chinook Indian," we must do so with many cautions and qualifiers, attending to the process of looking as much as to the content we find. Like any other texts, American Indian ethnographies necessarily reflect the perspectives of the people writing them (often non-Indians), sometimes revealing even more about these authors than they do about indigenous perspectives and practices. In the case of Pacific Northwest ethnography, materials tend to be limited and dated. Anthropological research on American Indian cultures was largely concentrated in the late nineteenth century and the early half of the twentieth, when institutions like the BAE and universities made their greatest research efforts. Support for research in Oregon was even more limited.[8] Thus, while Oregon Indians are very much alive today, producing their own writings and other representations of their cultures, research into Victoria Howard's life via conventional scholarly materials will be a piecemeal, cobbling process.

The process is further troubled by *Clackamas Chinook* as a descriptor of Howard's culture and identity. "Chinook" Indians, so called by the indigenous neighbors who recognized their importance as traders, lived along a two-hundred-mile stretch of the Columbia River beginning at the mouth of the Pacific. Speakers of Clackamas lived toward the eastern end of this area and shared a dialect similar to Wasco and Wishram.[9] Jacobs sought Victoria Howard out as "the last of the Clackamas Indians."[10] But her obituary in the Portland *Oregonian* deemed her "the last of the Molalla tribe of Indians."[11] Howard's mother was indeed part Molale, but her father was Tualatin; her second husband was Santiam. While Howard knew the Clackamas language from her mother's mother, in all probability she would have grown up speaking mostly English and Chinook Jargon, a pidgin that enabled diverse peoples in the region to communicate.

It is simply not clear, then, that Howard would have identified herself as "Clackamas Chinook," since her lived experience would have been more that of a Grand Ronde Indian—nor, certainly, that she would have thought of herself as the "last Clackamas," since she had many children.[12] More precisely, as Jacobs says in his preface to the Clackamas volumes, Howard was "one of three or four remaining speakers of the Clackamas dialect of Chinook" in 1929.[13] And yet even this may not be entirely accurate, for despite anthropologists' habitual delight in finding the "last" of a particular group, remaining speakers frequently turn up later.[14] What the fervor over "last" members of tribes shows, more than indigenous reality, is the non-Indian investment in claiming to have discovered the "last," and in seeing older Indians as the "last" of *something*.

A search for print materials on Clackamas Chinook will basic-ally start and end with *Clackamas Chinook Texts*. Jacobs, with Howard's help, was one of the few people to write down informa-tion about this culture. It is important to keep in mind, though, that *Clackamas Chinook Texts* is not just a rare written record of a way of life but also the *product* of one man's search for a certain type of document. Jacobs was a linguist, and although his broader vision of his task included cultural and literary analysis, what he asked for, and got, was texts in Clackamas, thus partially occluding Howard's hybrid cultural background.[15] This practice, which Hymes calls "the ethnological habit of dissolving individual lives into processes labeled with group names," creates the illusion that collections like *Clackamas Chinook Texts* are the enduring record of a particular tribe, rather than the complex products of specific multicultural and multilayered interaction.[16] Clackamas is a dis-tinct language, but its speakers were nomadic and exogamous, and they shared cultural practices with many neighboring peoples.

We might then broaden the search into what anthropologists call culture areas, meant to derive discrete, definable, and quanti-fiable cultural traits. Most discussions of indigenous Pacific North-west cultures thus enumerate such traits as a nonhorticultural subsistence, an economy based on fishing with hunting and gath-ering, material culture involving highly developed woodworking techniques for plank houses and dugout canoes, and social organ-ization around permanent winter and summer residences. But this approach also has limits, because it occludes important differences among peoples in a region.[17] In general, then, an attempt to learn about the context of Victoria Howard's stories will mean balancing materials that appear to be "outside" with those that are "inside" her language and tribe.[18]

Having said that, we might be skeptical about whether a single collection of narratives can tell us very much at all, directly, about real women, whose status and lives have, of course, been far more complex than any single collection of narratives can suggest. Still, it is worth trying to glean something about indigenous women in western Oregon wherever we can. To be sure, despite our engaging examples of ironic mourning widows and the woman who changes a fish gland into a husband, and despite Hymes's, Ramsey's and other scholars' detection of a "woman's standpoint" in Howard's stories, those stories can also be a bit of a disappointment for feminist scholars. Most of the protagonists—if such they can be called—are in fact male, their heroism often predicated on the destruction of strikingly demonic and aggressive females, like the grizzly ogress who kills her gentle sister and eats her—all but the breasts, which she brings home to roast for her nieces and nephews.[19] Elsewhere, we find mothers who stupidly neglect their children, cannibal girls with human-finger hair combs, and wives who are punished for refusing to mourn dead husbands properly. Some of the ethnographic texts describe taboos on women. One of these texts, called "Restrictions on women," describes the isolation of widows and menstruating women.[20] Another, "Mourners' taboos," describes further restrictions on widows, including warnings to them not to touch their own faces or hair, lest they become wrinkled and grey. In that text, Howard talks of these practices with some nostalgia and approval:

> The old people would speak of all sorts of things (of that kind), long ago when they spoke to us. We believed and minded them. You see us here when we are old persons now and we are still getting about. . . . On the other hand now those of you who are since that time (you younger people), you do not believe these things, and so you are ill in various ways now.[21]

Jacobs was himself a progressive and even feminist thinker, directly interested in the question of Clackamas women's status.[22] What this interest meant for him, writing in the 1930s through the 1950s, was an attempt to critique a perceived oppression of women.

In *The Content and Style of an Oral Literature* (1959), his own literary analysis of the Howard stories, he reads those stories as directly reflecting Clackamas culture rather than as actively maintaining it or even intervening in it. He reads texts like those described above as proof that Clackamas culture demeaned women—as opposed, for instance, to reading them as evidence of Howard's communitist commitment to Clackamas values. Jacobs concludes that "patrilocal residence supported Oedipal patterns, feminine lower status, and other factors in maintaining the literature's prevailing [negative] treatment of some older females." Further, he suggests that Clackamas people idealized "feminine immobilization," valuing, "sitting it out, being vigilant, having acumen, and bracing up to a male who could take over."[23]

We need to read these arguments both in the context of Jacobs's own progressive ideas *and* in the long American tradition of interpreting indigenous women as demoralized. For while late nineteenth-century white women reformers like Mary Mann romanticized Indian women as empowered, other Americans (often men), back to founding fathers Thomas Jefferson and Benjamin Franklin, sought to justify Euro-American dispossession of Indians by showing that indigenous cultures were so barbaric as to denigrate women.[24]

Specifically, indigenous women have been stereotyped, with remarkable consistency, across scant written representations of Oregon Indians.[25] J. V. Berreman, who conducted research at the Grand Ronde reservation not long after Jacobs, thought that Indian girls were flattered by and "in trouble" with white men, who assumed them to be "approachable at will"; his contorted picture had Indian girls locked in "a typical vicious circle in keeping up the reputation and the fact of [their] loose character."[26] The lascivious Native woman also makes a gratuitous appearance in a novel from the liberal 1960s, Don Berry's *Trask*, a rare fictional treatment of Tillamooks and Clatsops in the mid-1800s. The book follows its angst-ridden Leatherstocking-like hero's thoughts thus: "[H]e had been tempted more than once by the easy availability of a squaw to keep his fire and make his meals and warm his body at night with her own. Most of them you could have for a pint of whisky that was half water; and they'd spread their legs for less than that."[27]

This is a particularly egregious example, but it should serve to remind us that, like fictional renderings, and for that matter like my readings of the women in this book, ethnographic accounts of women's status are never just factual accounts of reality, but particular *interpretations* geared toward particular *ends*. In embarking on feminist literary criticism of indigenous oral narrative, we would do well to keep in mind anthropologist Barbara Babcock's measured stance:

> Feminist anthropologists have been rightly cautioned both against projecting our own political concerns and theoretical models onto our analyses of the position of women in other cultures and against using data about women there to buttress arguments about women here. Nonetheless, if we are not attuned to gender dynamics and the politics of discourse in the cultures we are studying as well as in our own, we will perpetuate such idealistic and projective distortions as the ideas that simpler societies are not contaminated by sexual politics.[28]

More recent sources on Pacific Northwest cultures can help us reach this more measured approach. Though most mention Lower Columbian women's status only in passing and tend to draw on the older written representations (travel accounts, Hudson's Bay Company records, letters from Indian agents), the results are different. Michael Silverstein acknowledges that Chinookan culture was patrifocal, with polygamy a sign of male status.[29] Stephen Dow Beckham notes that some puberty rites isolated girls, suggesting further limitations on female status.[30] On the other hand, Jeff Zucker maintains that Chinookan women played important roles in political and social decisions, including decisions about marriage. Zucker notes that women sometimes acted as leaders or shamans, and that they were central to Indian economies.[31]

Somewhere between these two poles, Robert Ruby and John Brown's history, *The Chinook Indians*, maintains that while women were forced to work hard, were subject to specific taboos, and were generally treated as men's property, they were also known to act as chiefs or participate in village council debates.[32] In this account, Chinookan women had a history of commerce, often sexual, with white men, and while that commerce may have generated some pernicious stereotypes of the women, it also afforded women considerable power.[33] For instance, many mastered Chinook Jargon and participated in important trade transactions. "Contact with white sailors," say Ruby and Brown, "had intensified their marital infidelity and the contraction of venereal diseases, infecting their men and leaving a mark on their children. Yet through it all Chinookan women increased in importance to their people at a time when their men rose to or fell from leadership largely on the basis of their relations with ship traders."[34]

Despite the obvious sexism of these statements, Ruby and Brown point to an irrevocable complexity in Chinookan women's status. This feminine status must have been as complicated and varied as it is in any culture—irreducible to either pure disempowerment or unfettered agency. The presence of whites, particularly of white men, must have had a profound impact on women's status in indigenous culture. And yet, as we are seeing, it is difficult to separate women's material status from the perception of that status among outsiders, here mainly men. In a rather bizarre 1958 article on "The Romantic Role of Older Women" in Pacific Northwest cultures, for example, Jacobs surmises that older women's willingness to work with him had its precedent in a Tillamook tradition of liaisons between older women and young men. We can only wonder how Howard saw Jacobs's interest in working with her. But we can posit that her status as a woman, both within her native culture and within her working relationship with Jacobs, must have been a complex one affording her both obstacles and opportunities.

GRAND RONDE CULTURE:
RECONSTRUCTING HISTORY

In his own analyses of American Indian women's ethnoautobiographies, Greg Sarris offers us a further lead in the use of materials like those described above. He uses ethnographic data modestly, pointing back to the broadest strokes of history to find "rejection. Distrust. Anger. Hatred. . . . Old patterns of domination, subjugation, and exclusion by whites."[35] A history of the Grand Ronde reservation, where Howard lived most of her life, will confirm these patterns and will also begin to suggest how the people who lived there, in particular the women, responded to these old patterns of domination, subjugation, and exclusion.

Indian Agent Joel Palmer initiated the reservation's establishment in 1855, about sixty miles southwest of Portland, with the idea of "protecting" the American Indians in the region. White settlers resented even the small amount of land the Indians were allowed to keep, and some never gave up the lands they had claimed within the reservation. The Indians were, of course, devastated by the removal; two decades after the Cherokee, they had their own trail of tears as they were marched long distances, during the winter months, to Grand Ronde. The reservation thus forced together many culturally and linguistically diverse groups. Each individual group was small, having already suffered losses from disease and conflict, most notably a devastating wave of tuberculosis and smallpox in the 1830s and the Rogue River Indian Wars of the 1850s.[36] To add insult to injury, the reservation itself was short-lived. The school and agency closed in 1907, and the reservation finally fell prey to the U.S. government's "termination" program of the 1950s.

In 1983, Ronald Reagan, of all people, reinstated the reservation, restoring its corporate charter and federal recognition. The new reservation, about forty miles southwest of Portland, is much smaller than the old one. Today, the Grand Ronde Community has, among other things, a tribal council, a cultural center, a newspaper, an annual powwow, and an increasingly vibrant culture and economy. It uses revenues from its Spirit Mountain casino to boost a repatriation program and to repurchase lands.

Indeed, the people of Grand Ronde are now writing their own history; their Web site is one of the most thorough resources on the history of the reservation.[37] It fills in the history of allotment, which began there in 1872. In 1901 there was a major land cession—about 25,791 acres out of an original 69,000. Only 537 of these were repurchased through the Indian Reorganization Act, which the people of Grand Ronde accepted in 1936, only to see themselves "terminated" less than two decades later.

This history of removal, concentration, dispossession, and renewal has surely affected conceptions of tribal identity. Grand Ronde Indians have historically seemed to oscillate among a pan-Indian approach to identity and parallel, sometimes coincident tribal identities. In 1934, Berreman thought that Indian identity at the reservation was eroding. He found poverty, malnutrition, alcoholism, and intergenerational conflict among Indians, as well as substantial bitterness against whites there. Some of the elders appeared to him outwardly "assimilated," keeping pictures of Christ on their walls and priding themselves on being "whiter" or more "progressive." The Catholic Church, indeed, held considerable sway at Grand Ronde.[38] Berreman did elicit from local residents a good deal of talk about cultural loss, partly because that is what he sought. Most of the people he interviewed (about fifty altogether, Indian and non-Indian), agreed that traditional tribal practices (sweat houses, dancing, shamanism, languages) had been out of use for as long as two to three decades.[39] Many also agreed that Indians no longer had much awareness of specific tribal affiliations, so extensive was intertribal and white-Indian marriage. John Warren, a full-blood Umpqua about seventy-five years old, told Berreman, "if you stay here a while you be all mixed up too."[40]

However, Henry Zenk, a linguistic anthropologist who did research at Grand Ronde in the 1980s, suggests a different interpretation of such cultural "mixing." In the late nineteenth century, in order to communicate, the diverse groups there had to use English or Chinook Jargon. Under such circumstances, Zenk argues, the varied tribes constructed an intertribal, "Indian" identity in opposition to white identity. In this scenario, though, intertribalism or the recession of the specific tribal allegiances doesn't necessarily mean cultural loss so much as cultural *realignment*.

Indeed, a pan-Indian approach to cultural identity need not preclude a simultaneous maintenance of more specific tribal affiliations. Some of the elders I spoke to in 1995 talked about themselves as "Grand Ronde Indians" but also kept careful and extensive family trees (written and oral) and were actively conscious of the many different tribal affiliations (and non-Indian lineages) that made up their family histories. Cultural memory and multiple histories can thus coexist with emergent identities and histories. Even Berreman, who was most interested in cultural loss, found elders who actively remembered the past and its injustices. He saw a tribal council meeting in 1934 in which a copy of the 1855 treaty was held up, and resistance called for. Such scenarios show that forms of active resistance and survival can operate *alongside* forms of apparent cultural loss; more pointedly, we might say that they greatly muddy the distinction between assimilation and resistance.

Grand Ronde has thus had a complicated history of conflict, accommodation, and resistance, and it is in this, among other contexts, that we must read Victoria Howard. She, too, actively remembered past injustices. For example, she tells vividly of the arrival of whites, and the sicknesses they introduced, at the time of removal:

Right here at this place (Oregon City) they again got fever. One myth (white) shaman person lived here. When they (the Indians at Oregon City) got a sickness, they (various whites) came to get him, they took him to the house of sicknesses (a hospital or infirmary) there. They brought the sick person, they shaved him (his head hair—a terrifying and humiliating loss, to an Indian). They gave medicine to him, they gave him water. Presently then he died. That is the way the myth (white) persons' shaman (the white doctor) was doing. Many of them died (all Indians who went to the hospital died, according to Mrs. Howard, while Indians who did not go there survived).[41]

There is some evidence that, in Howard's day, storytelling itself provided a form of resistance at Grand Ronde, especially for women. For instance, although storytelling and traditional healing practices on the reservation had allegedly ceased in the early decades of this century, stories about shamanism seem to have continued to circulate.[42] As we will see below, Howard herself tells many fascinating stories about shamans.

Far from assimilating Indian ways to white, some of these stories do exactly the reverse, showing that rather than giving way to "white" norms, Indian identity is in fact able to encompass and *use* other practices. One man told Berreman that the Indians liked the local chiropractor because "he works very much like the old Indian doctors, rubbing pains to the surface and out."[43] A Mrs. Simmons gave Berreman a gloriously entertaining account of her visit, against the wishes of then-Indian Agent Andrew Kershaw, to a shaman we will also meet in Howard's stories: "Polk Scott [the shaman] said right away that she would get well and outlive Kershaw. . . . He told her she had a bad pain clear through her chest. Gradually he worked it up. She says she could feel it coming up. Finally when he got it up he put his mouth on her chest and sucked it out. He showed it to her, she said it looked like a worm, just like the pictures of T.B. germs she has seen since in books, spotted worm. . . . Then she got all well and is hale and hearty now, while Kershaw is very feeble. She thinks she will outlive him yet."[44] Indians at Grand Ronde actively disliked Kershaw, who had caused them to lose a great deal of land by getting them to run up debts at his store, or by giving choice allotments to Indians whom he knew would soon sell them. Other women also told Berreman of their encounters with him; of Mrs. Josephine Shirley he wrote, "she has a grudge against Kershaw, says she once knocked his cane out, and he fell down."[45]

It may be that, by the time Victoria Howard worked with Melville Jacobs, few people used traditional myths in traditional ways anymore, and that traditional shamanism was no longer in widespread use. Her performances are thus all the more remarkable. As Hymes has suggested, "the persistence of the tradition disclosed in performances . . . was not merely of memory from a remote past. . . . What has survived for the telling now has largely been material that has continued to be relevant to the ethos of the community, to its moral and psychological concerns."[46] Howard's stories are thus not just the record of Clackamas Chinook culture, as Jacobs may have hoped, but also dynamic, active speech events. Like Mrs. Simmons's and Mrs. Shirley's stories about their trouncing of Agent Kershaw, Howard's stories reflect personal and political concerns as well as aesthetic ones; they are informed both by contact with white culture and by indigenous systems and values.

BIOGRAPHY:
RECONSTRUCTING HOWARD'S LIFE

What was life like for this woman who laughed about ephemeral light-skinned husbands, who talked about traditional practices allegedly gone by? Like the lives of most other anthropological informants, Howard's was never written down. As I discussed in the last chapter, American Indians may not have had the resources or the impulse to write down their individual life stories. White people historically initiated the recording of those stories, partly out of their determination to capture what they believed were vanishing cultures.

But there is another side to the history of Indian autobiography and biography, which is the erasure of the lives and identities of anthropological informants. Storytellers' names were often left out of ethnographic collections, not to reflect any indigenous concern with community or privileging of collective tradition over individual innovation, but because the anthropologist or ethnographer was considered the true author of these collections.[47] As a result, many of the American Indian people who worked with ethnographers in the early twentieth century and since are lost to literary history. Anthropologists like Melville Jacobs thus deserve considerable credit and admiration for the interest they did show in informants' lives. For biography, as Ojibway scholar Gail Valaskakis has argued, plays a key role in the best ethnography; it represents a "move away from the notion of the narrative Other as an object . . . toward what native people have long incorporated as lived experience."[48] It is thanks to Jacobs that much of the following information is available.

Howard was probably born around 1865; most accounts agree that she was sixty-five when she died in September of 1930, only a few months after Jacobs finished working with her—an event that must have confirmed his sense that he had secured texts from this "last of the Clackamas" in the nick of time. Information about Howard's early life is scant. In the "ethnographic accounts" at the end of the Clackamas volumes, she describes only a few personal incidents. Among these are some elliptical accounts of receiving shamanistic healing, traveling with her family to the mountains in the summer for hunting and blackberry picking, and hearing stories from her grandmother. These stories reveal very little about Howard's thoughts or feelings, at least explicitly.

In one story, for example, she describes going to the mountains with her older female cousin to pick berries. After a while, Howard discovered that the cousin's horse had died. The cousin insisted that Howard ride on ahead. That ride is the longest part of the narration:

> I went on. Then I again waited for her. She got a (thick long) stick, she made a cane of it. She followed behind me. I waited for her a few times, she would get to me, I would look at her, her appearance was somewhat different. Her face had become reddish. She spoke to me. She had a (small) pack on her, a small one on her back. She said to me, "Do not wait for me. Go along! Hurry now! It is evening now!" I kept going, and then I waited for her again. Presently she came, she was puffing as she came. I got to thinking, "Maybe she is getting exhausted." I said to her, "Now you yourself ride the horse." She said to me, "No! I told you go along now! It will be getting night soon."
>
> So then I left her. I went on and on right to her house. I told her daughter, "Here are her things." She said to me, "Where is she?" I told her, "She is coming. She will get here presently." "Very well," she replied to me. Then I left her, I went back home.[49]

The style of this scene (drawn out, with quoting of Howard herself and her relative) and the fact that, as Jacobs reports in a footnote, Howard "pressed" him to take down this story reveal her affective connections with female relatives and suggest something of the impact this incident had on her.

From Jacobs's field notebooks, we can learn a bit more about her life among female relatives. He notes, for instance, that shortly after Howard was born, her Clackamas grandmother put her in the headboards traditionally used among some Northwest peoples to flatten the forehead as a status mark.[50] Her father took the boards

off.[51] The recounting of such an event marks the complex relationship that Howard and her women relatives had with some of
their traditions; she describes a similar scenario between herself
and her mother-in-law when her own first child was born: Howard
removed the headboard because she was afraid her baby would
be injured by the old ways of handling.[52] The picture of Howard
that emerges here is one of a woman at once very much outside a
female-centered indigenous tradition (Jacobs's footnotes often
deem her "an acculturated Indian") and deeply within it (she was
raised mainly by her grandmothers).

The written records provide little else on Howard's childhood
and youth. The Grand Ronde Registers of the Catholic Church for
the late 1800s record the marriage of Howard, there called "Victoire
Washington," to Daniel Wacheno on December 12, 1882.[53] Dan's
father, Old Wacheno, was a nominal Clackamas chief; Old
Wacheno's wife, along with Howard's Clackamas grandmother,
would provide many of the stories that Howard told Jacobs.
According to church and Grand Ronde census records, it appears
that Howard had at least eight children with Wacheno, though
only three or four lived very long.[54] By 1905, only one child, their
twenty-year-old son, Charley, was listed in the census as living
with them.

Wacheno's brother, Foster, had married Howard's mother, Sarah,
in 1878. According to Jacobs's field notes, Howard's marriage to
her stepfather's brother was "a relationship that would not have
been countenanced in earlier times"; any determinable relations,
no matter the distance, were barred from marrying in this exogamous group. Jacobs adds that Howard's maternal grandmother
"growled darkly about it," and that her mother's brother warned
her that she would have to suffer if Wacheno became abusive, or
poor, though this same uncle helped Howard when she left
Wacheno years later.[55]

When Howard left her first husband, or why, remains a mystery,
at least in written records. The 1906 Grand Ronde census marks

Dan Wacheno as "widower," still living with Charles; but Victoria, forty-one, is then living with her new husband Eustace Howard, with whom she has a daughter, Mary, age three. The written record is full of such contradictions and omissions. Two years later the Howards and Wachenos drop off the rolls altogether, as did most Indians who received fee simple patents for allotted lands.

It is hard to reconstruct, on the basis of the written records, what Howard's adult life was like. But if we can get a sense of her status within her community, especially her status as a woman, this might enrich our reading of her work. The "widower" next to Wacheno's name in the census, along with the "no determinable heirs" on his fee patent cards, seems literally to write Howard out of the family. However, whether this has a tribal or U.S.-governmental signification or is simply a family matter is hard to tell. In any case, the written record alone does not yield much evidence that Howard had very much material power or authority. Jacobs, meanwhile, thought he detected in his informant an "obvious resentment of Indian men."[56]

We can glean from the records a few more details about Howard's gendered status—either directly or by conjecture. Howard probably had some form of schooling. People of her generation went to the reservation school, while later generations went either to one of three public schools on the reservation or were sent away to Catholic or boarding schools. Berreman reports that literacy rates on the reservation were high, though among the few who could not read or write was the only Howard relation he seems to have interviewed, John Wacheno, who was about eighty then.[57] In tribal politics, women were not especially likely to be involved, though one woman was elected to tribal council in 1934, and women are a major presence in the workings of Grand Ronde today. As for work, the picture that Berreman paints of Indian life at that time is one of men working at logging, in mills or in hop yards, and women working at home, perhaps making baskets or picking berries. Howard herself made baskets, possibly for money.

One additional source of work for Howard, however short-lived, was of course Melville Jacobs's ethnography project. In 1929, she and Eustace both worked for Jacobs; she made two dollars for four hours of work each afternoon; he made two dollars for four hours each morning. Howard was thus one of many American Indian women who worked with anthropologists in the early twentieth century, taking the opportunity to earn an income, to record stories for "posterity," and to be an author and an authority of her culture.[58]

Stories like "She deceived herself with milt" suggest that Howard was an accomplished and energetic performer, and this raises provocative possibilities for her authorship and authority. Storytelling may have been an ability or talent that Howard had all along, one that she demonstrated for Jacobs. Or hers may have been a latent ability, only emerging when Jacobs approached her about doing this work. Indeed, her complicated status as a woman in her community and family, and as an Indian working with a white person, suggest that telling stories for Jacobs may also have afforded unique opportunities to create authority and express her feminine and indigenous experience.[59]

TRANSLATION:
RECONSTRUCTING A DIALOGUE

It is useful to think of the texts that Jacobs elicited from Howard, and transcribed oral texts in general, as emergent, as particular speech events. Obviously, anthropologists do not simply go into the field and record natural speech (whatever that is); their expectations, their questions, their demands, and their very presence shape what they get. The experience of dictation itself can affect the storytelling: Clara Pearson, a Nehalem Tillamook woman who worked with Jacobs's wife Elizabeth Derr Jacobs, fleshed out character motivation for her transcriber's benefit, and cut conventional repetitions because she found the slow dictations boring.[60] And researchers sometimes intervene more aggressively: Jacobs's field notebooks include lists of notes to himself to ask for certain texts in Clackamas, for example. In his introduction to *Kalapuya Texts* he indicates that he asked his informant John Hudson to repeat certain things in Santiam Kalapuya when he "perceived expressive potential therein."[61] As scholars like Dell Hymes and Charles Briggs have pointed out, ethnographers exert strong influence over informant performances, so that what we encounter in such texts are actually events "keyed" for outsiders, not necessarily stories as informants would tell them for people within the tribe.[62]

But Jacobs wanted to capture what he thought was American Indian life untainted by white contact and practice. He thus sought the oldest possible informants and asked them to talk about the past as far back as they could remember. He humorously referred to this practice as "rocking-chair linguistics," describing his work with Howard in his preface to the Clackamas texts thusly: "Few interruptions marred the hours spent in her home. Mr. Howard, the Howards' daughter, the latter's children, and occasional guests rarely intruded in the small quiet room where I sat writing comfortably on a Singer sewing machine, with Mrs. Howard in a rocking chair beside me."[63] He emphasized his search for the most "unacculturated" material, also revealing how he continued to steer the dictation sessions: "I tried to secure full reporting only of her songs and oral literature, that is, the portions of her heritage which she had retained in quantity, without acculturative distortions which analysis could display as complexly structured aspects of Clackamas life."[64]

Anthropologists and cultural critics today tend to find this kind of characterization of ethnographic work naive; they prefer to emphasize the ways ethnographers, approaching their work from particular historical and social positions, shape ethnographic texts, as well as the impossibility of preserving culture in any kind of static, authentic, original sense. And yet ironically, Jacobs also helped produce texts that dramatize these very shapings.

Jacobs worked by transcribing native languages phonetically, and he is remembered as a fast and clean transcriber.[65] However, he did not speak or understand these languages. His field notebooks from his work with Howard show that he spent a day or two collecting some vocabulary, but there his facility with the language more or less ended. To get his translations, then, Jacobs read the phonetic transcriptions back to Howard, word by word, asking her to translate the words into English. In the field notebooks this generates a palpable dialogue, so that the word *there*, for instance, will include a parenthetical note below it, like "it was near Oregon City, Mrs. Howard thinks," to indicate either that Jacobs asked her to elaborate further, or that she offered some additional information. Sometimes, too, it appears that Howard changed her mind about things on the re-reading; the left hand pages of the notebooks include short narratives or metanarrative comments she made while translating—sometimes in English, and sometimes in Clackamas, suggesting perhaps that Jacobs decided to elicit certain comments in the native language. Finally, Jacobs re-translated the literal translations of the field notebooks into relatively coherent English. Words in parentheses are his elaborations or additions, terms he believes will be helpful to the reader, although often the sheer number of parenthetically inserted phrases can be distracting. Howard was fluent, but she would have spoken a local variety of non-standard English. While Jacobs appears to be quite faithful to her word choice, then, he does make changes, as we saw in "A widow's mourning."[66] Even more than Sarah Winnemucca's writing, so crammed with the voices of her readers (real and anticipated), the Howard-Jacobs texts are intensely dialogic.

Jacobs wanted to give those texts as wide a distribution as possible; he wanted to create a large body of work for later study by a variety of methods and disciplines. He was thus adamant about including both languages on the printed page. This was anthropological convention; most of the BAE and other professional texts include both indigenous and English language versions. But Jacobs had to fight to get funding to do it, and as a result, the Howard narratives, collected in 1929–1930, didn't appear until 1958–1959, as two volumes of the *International Journal of Linguistics*.[67] Also, while many other ethnographic collections place the native and English versions on opposing pages, or even segregate the English and native language texts altogether, Jacobs split each page horizontally, putting the English translations at the top and the phonetic Clackamas transcriptions at the bottom, each sentence numbered for easier matching.

Reading this highly multivocal and conversational text is like hearing several voices talking at once. David Murray argues that this form makes the English look primary to the Clackamas by putting it spatially "above" the native language.[68] But the English is surely "primary" by virtue of its wider intelligibility; no one reads phonetic Clackamas as a "first" language. I would contend that the split-page form constantly reminds us of another, inaccessible voice. Jacobs could very easily have segregated the Clackamas and English versions altogether, so that a reader need never face the strange phonetic markings. But the presence of the Clackamas version at the bottom, with corresponding numbered sentences, continually intrudes on our reading of the English.

In so doing, the text returns us to resistance in the face of assimilation. For translation itself is a kind of assimilation; as Lawrence Venuti argues in his brilliant genealogical history, translation always practices some degree of "ethnocentric violence" on a text. To Venuti, the translator's assumed "invisibility . . . at once enacts and masks an insidious domestication of foreign texts, rewriting them in the transparent discourse that prevails in English and that selects precisely those foreign texts amenable to fluent translating."[69] One might argue that Jacobs's parenthetical

female or this male did not (become ill) just recently, he must have
become ill a long time ago. It is not a mere nothing. He is poisoned
(by a lethal spirit-power). That is what is doing it to him. 2. Possibly
the two of them (he and his wife) slept together, and they did something to one another (had sexual realtions). The following day he
went and drank a lot of water. It is lying all over his backbone
(inside his stomach), it (the water) has become yellow (inside him)."
Or he might say, "It became greenish, or it ıs black in there. 3.
Perhaps he will not become well. At the time that he voids the
water (or vomits), then he will be leaving us at that time (and he
will die), or she will be leaving us (and die)." They (shamans) used
to speak in such a manner.[466]

   4. Henry Wallace was his name. He became ill (at Grand
Ronde, Oregon), he lay there (sick) for a long long time. I went, I
went to see him. Then on the following day one old man (the shaman
whose name was Polk Scott) doctored him. I went that evening, I
went to see him. She (his wife whose name was i'ɫix̣ša) told me, "It
is good that you came. I shall tell you what the shaman diagnosed.
5. He said to him, You are not ill here for nothing. You were
sick, and then you had sexual intercourse (with your wife and so
you became even more ill). Right away I said to him (to Scott),
That is a big lie. You see this daughter of ours here, and now she
has become big. Since the time when we copulated (to conceive
her), we copulated (only at that time long ago and never since then).
That is what I said to him. I got angry at him."[467]

---

awači da'yax, a·'·nga ɫga i'yačgmam. nɛ'šqi qa'naga. idya'k'iɫawa.
dada'x tgi'yux̣t. 2. ɫu'xʷan nišx̣u'kšit, da'ngi nigišx̣ə'lux̣. ka'wux čɫu-
g̣u'mšt ɫa'bla iɫčə'qʷa. ka·'·nawi aya'kuč ɫakx̣a'ymat, gə'š·ɫki'x̣ax̣."
awači aɫgi'ma, "pčə'x ɫki'x̣ax̣, awači ɫə'l wakma'ɫayt. 3. ɫu'xʷan nɛ'š-
qi t'a'ya alix̣u'x̣a. qa'x̣bt ačɫxima'ya iɫčə'qʷa, aga kʷa'bt ačəlxima'ya,
awači agəlxima'ya." k'ʷaƛqi' nugʷagi'mx̣.
   4. wala's iya'x̣liw. iya'čgmam ni'x̣ux̣, i·'·yaƛqdix nix̣i'maxit. ganu'yx̣, ganyu'kšdamx̣. ka'wux aga gayugila'ytx̣ i'xt wiq'i'wqt. lawi'ska
ganu'yx̣, ganyu'kšdamx̣. gagnulxa'mx̣, "it'u'kdix imə'ti. ayax̣məlkʷɫi'-
čgʷa qa' idši'qɫataqɫq gʷidya'xilalit. 5. ičyu'lxam, ni'šqi qa'naga da'-
yax imi'čgmam. imi'čgmam, aga gamdə'x̣aštk. na'wi inyu'lxam, dada'x ida'gayƛ iƛ'mi'nxutiƛ'mi'nxut. mšgu'qmit axi'yax anda'xan, kʷa'bt
a·'ga iča'gayƛ. kʷa'bdix gandə'katx̣, gandə'x̣aštk. k'ʷaƛqi' inyu'lxam.
kala'lgʷli ičə'nux̣."

A sample of the Howard-Jacobs text. Reproduced from Jacobs, "Text 108:
Illness and Sexual Intercourse," from IJAL 25:2 (1959) pp. 514–15, courtesy
of University of Chicago Press.

interventions attempt precisely this; indeed, he says that "their function is to clarify in situations where a close translation would usually be obscure to persons of Western or other civilizations."[70] And yet his method also distinguishes his voice from Howard's, or at least gives the appearance of two distinct voices, a choice that has the effect of defamiliarizing the translation. *Clackamas Chinook Texts* thus moves toward the "supplementarity" that Eric Cheyfitz, another historian and critic of translation, has called for among languages—a "productive alienation" of constant movement among "a community of languages with mutual needs" rather than of repression of one language by another, or of one language within another.[71]

Jacobs's work is only part of the picture; there is also Howard to consider in the production of these texts. The contrast between her and her husband in their relationships to Jacobs is suggestive of his methods and their responses. Jacobs was frustrated with Eustace, from whom he was trying to get texts in Santiam. The problem was evidently that Eustace wasn't giving the right kind of "Indian" stories: in his field notes Jacobs complains that Eustace, in his "preposterously stupid overconscientiousness," refused to tell stories he couldn't remember perfectly and that he preferred to talk about events including white people—like jail breaks or sports.[72] Further, Eustace had an "adolescent, virtually schoolgirlish terror of sex," even though, to Jacobs's mind, "Indian life in the region reeks of sex." The field notebooks contain a long narrative of an evidently painful argument between Eustace and Jacobs. Some of that argument hinged on money, and in the course of the fight Eustace revealed that he hated the dictation sessions. Jacobs writes after the argument that it "showed to me that however desirous he was of earning $2 a day, he found it unconsciously desolatingly miserable labor."[73]

Indeed, dictating stories was first and foremost *work*, and it is hard to underestimate the pain and difficulties such work must have created for many American Indian people. Sarris recalls that his Pomo relatives called their own employment as informants "money-storytelling-time." It would not be surprising if money (rather than that old Indian tradition of sex with younger men) was Victoria Howard's primary motivation for working with Jacobs. He also records in his field notes that he felt very conscious of the employer-employee relationship and of Mrs. Howard's desire for the money.[74] Howard also apparently tried to smooth over conflicts between her husband and their employer, who scrawled in his notes that she "understood the problems of my work sympathetically and adequately, has tried to talk my point of view into [Eustace] also." Unlike her husband, Howard told Jacobs stories that include explicit sexual content (and, not incidentally, sexual violence) and accommodated him with stories of the Indian past. To his mind, she was "generally worldlier and abler and more respected, by comparison" to her husband.[75]

Eustace's dictations were so bad, as far as Jacobs was concerned, that the anthropologist never translated or printed them. But William Seaburg, returning to those texts, finds some jarring moments:

> It's not good to tell a story if you don't know all of it well, but Jacobs says never mind, tell what you do know. . . .
>
> I just want to get done with this story quickly. I'm getting tired of doing it like that. . . . Maybe I'll finish this story now. I just don't know it very well. That's why my storytelling is not very good. But maybe the white people won't mind. If it will be ok with them, it'll be that way with me too. Maybe there won't be anyone again who will know my language. There's nobody now living in my country. All the old timers are gone. Maybe no one will ever hear what I am telling [Jacobs]. Maybe no one will talk my language. Maybe somewhere someone will read what I am telling [Jacobs].[76]

It seems that Eustace felt financially pressured and emotionally bullied into working with Jacobs. The central events of his own life—working in the morgue at Salem, playing clarinet in the Grand Ronde band—failed to interest the anthropologist, who wanted him instead to dig in a past that was evidently painful to him, and that he did not feel qualified or willing to recount. This particular ethnographer-informant relation thus patterns itself on the pain and appropriation that are part of Grand Ronde history. It shows that Jacobs was sometimes more driven to acquire linguistic artifacts than he was concerned about those elements of storytelling that give it meaning for its practitioners. Jacobs's preconceptions, therefore, had costs personally for Eustace, collectively for the tribe, and further for literary history. In deciding in advance what were acceptable texts, Jacobs lost a chance to let Eustace be heard.

The sad passages quoted above suggest that Eustace had internalized the notion that his people really were disappearing all around him and that writing their narratives down might mark a kind of "posterity." They emerge both as a genuine expression of loneliness and loss and also as an address—whether heartfelt or ironic—to a white audience's preconceptions. At the same time, Eustace addresses an audience that is in a sense no audience, for his immediate listener cannot understand what he is saying, and he has little assurance that anybody who reads his published words will, either.

Eustace is talking about Jacobs, then, right under his nose and his phonetically recording pen; he is using his work time, not only to express what may have been genuine frustrations with his own lack of storytelling ability, but also to articulate his frustrations with the work itself, with his boredom ("I'm getting tired of doing it like that"), and with his sense that this work he feels compelled to do is somehow not right ("It's not good to tell a story if you don't know all of it well"). Sarris's relatives, not incidentally, called ethnographic dictations "giving-them-a-piece-work." That is, they gave anthropologists only random "pieces" of narratives or accounts, enough to make the researchers happy (and to make them fork over the pay) but not enough so that people had to feel they were really giving anything away. "Giving them a piece" is nothing short of "taking them for a ride."[77]

Both Howards, one suspects, had to put up with a good deal from Jacobs, but both also found ways to use him for their own ends. It is possible that both may have derived some personal satisfaction as well as monetary gain in being sought out as experts on their culture.[78] And, whether by intentional subversion or not, each told stories in a way that evades and staves off an unreliable interlocutor. Even though Victoria Howard appeared to Jacobs as a willing informant and performer, she, too, sometimes refused to give him what he wanted. Jacobs sensed this himself, as when he says, in a crucial footnote, that "I would have liked an autobiography and I tried to get one. But Mrs. Howard never seemed in a mood to describe her life in detail. Possibly I was too young for her to feel like revealing inward things, or perhaps I failed to handle the relationship in a manner which made clear what I wanted and how she could present the story of her life."[79]

Howard refuses to self-narrate, perhaps because self-narration is antithetical to her culture's thinking. As we saw in the critical history of Sarah Winnemucca, many scholars have argued that indigenous peoples do not practice autobiography, at least not as Euro-American literary culture construes it. One speaker in Brian Swann and Arnold Krupat's anthology, *I Tell You Now*, thus insists, "You should realize that focusing so intently on oneself like that and blithering on about your own life and thoughts is very bad form for Indians."[80]

But as we also saw in reading *Life Among the Piutes* as a cross-cultural text, it doesn't necessarily follow that Indians never self-narrate. A better model for reading Victoria Howard is suggested by Julie Cruikshank, who in her recent work with Yukon women elders found that their life stories blended personal recollection and cultural myths. The more she asked for personal or secular information, Cruikshank reports, the more persistently the women told traditional narratives. Cruikshank concludes that collective mythology *is* a form of self-expression: "These women talk about their lives using an oral tradition grounded in local idiom and a shared body of knowledge."[81]

In this model, women storytellers working with ethnographers create narration that can be read both as cultural expression and as resistance. It is cultural expression in the sense that it marks and is informed by aesthetics (and by a sense of "self") much different than those requested by Euro-American interlocutors. It is resistant not necessarily in a confrontational or oppositional sense, but in the sense that it redirects those requests and even gently instructs nontribal audiences in a more mutual kind of cross-cultural communication. While Jacobs thought, above, that he "failed" with Howard, his self-consciousness in this note also suggests that he was beginning to hear her, to be open to her different ways of expressing herself and her culture.

CRITICAL HISTORY: CONSTRUCTING A TRADITION

Beginning with Jacobs himself, a tradition of scholarship on Victoria Howard has been slowly emerging. Jacobs is both the producer and the most prolific interpreter of the Clackamas texts, publishing two content analyses of them, *The Content and Style of an Oral Literature* (1959) and *The People Are Coming Soon* (1960). These are grounded in two main methodologies, which have in turn informed most subsequent Howard scholarship. The first scrutinizes the narratives for an indigenous aesthetic or worldview, whether by using the texts as a window on indigenous culture, as Jacobs did, or by exploring divergences from and convergences with Euro-American literary forms. The second evaluates Howard's stories from feminist perspectives. For Jacobs, as we have seen, that meant interpreting the narratives as proof of tribal culture's denigration of women, rather than as actively participating in the construction of women's roles or even as interventions in those roles. Jacobs believed that "the literature ventilates the events and circumstances that cause anxiety and tension in the society, promoting its continuing emotional health."[82]

Decades later, Hymes and Ramsey refined this work.[83] As mentioned above, both see a "female standpoint" in the Howard collection, tending to attribute more agency to female characters and to Howard than does Jacobs. And both are interested in discovering the indigenous aesthetics underlying the stories.

Hymes, a linguist with facility in many American Indian languages, has retranslated and analyzed several of the narratives, breaking them down into verse patterns for interpretation. While other translators like Tedlock follow the speaker's pauses or breaths for such line breaks, Hymes tries to discern an underlying structure in the story. For example, he might use phrases like Howard's repeated "Now then" to mark the beginnings of poetic lines, or he might create stanzas around blocks of text that depict characters taking turns at talk, or he might organize the text into what he deems a common onset/ongoing/outcome plot. Hymes wants his approach to open avenues for discussing storytelling craft, and that is valuable.[84]

Hymes's translations lose that sense of dialogue among translator and speaker, Indian and English, that I have been applauding in the Jacobs texts. On the other hand, they are admittedly much more readable than Jacobs's, and it is for this reason perhaps that Hymes's translations of Howard's stories have begun appearing in anthologies, including William Bright's *A Coyote Reader* and Brian Swann's recent multitribal *Coming to Light*. Ramsey's *Coyote Was Going There* contains several Hymes-influenced translations of Oregon stories, including some of Howard's.

Clearly, Hymes has been crucial in bringing Howard's work to the fore, not only by precipitating the republication of her actual narratives, but also in spurring a critical discussion. Thanks to him, one story, "Seal and her younger brother lived there," which appears in the Ramsey and Swann volumes, has garnered national scholarly interest not only among linguists and anthropologists but also among scholars of literature.

The story features Seal, her daughter, her younger brother, and a woman who is the younger brother's sexual partner. The daughter tries to warn Seal that when the other woman goes outside at night to urinate, that woman sounds like a man. She also tells Seal that she feels something dripping on her face when the brother and the woman are lying together. Seal hushes the daughter, but the story ends with her discovering that the stranger has murdered her brother. The daughter says:

> "I told you something was dripping. You said to me, 'Oh don't say that. They are copulating. I told you there was something different about my uncle's wife. When she went outside she urinated exactly like a man. You said to me, 'Don't say that!'" She wept. Seal said, "Younger brother! My younger brother! They (the house posts in my younger brother's house) are valuable standing there. My younger brother!" She kept saying that. But the girl herself wept. She said, "I tried to tell you but in vain. My uncle's wife urinated not like a woman but just like a man. You said to me, Don't say that! Oh oh my uncle! Oh my uncle!" The girl wept.[85]

Jacobs saw this story as having a "nightmarish horror theme, murder of one's own kin by a sexually aberrant person." He said it promoted several moral lessons: "one should not marry a wife in such a manner; one should not speak disparagingly of in-laws and others' sexual intimacy; one should heed one's daughter."[86] Hymes argued, though, that the stranger is a trickster rather than a transvestite or homosexual, and he maintained that the story is chiefly about the conflict between Seal and the daughter, reading the latter as "the voice of a concern for personal loyalty as against social propriety; sensory experience as against verbal convention; personal feeling as against formal experience of grief."[87]

In 1977, Ramsey published an important article in *PMLA*, attempting to illuminate the narrative's aesthetics by way of comparisons to Shakespeare and Hemingway.[88] Two years later Karl Kroeber discussed the narrative in *boundary2*, trying to uncover its workings by contrasting rather than comparing it with Euro-American tradition; he concluded American Indian storytelling is more concrete and referential than Western tradition, with its fondness for explication and abstraction.[89] These later critics all read "Seal" as tragic, and all see the daughter as the heroine; where Jacobs thought her rude speech triggered the murder in the story, Hymes, Ramsey and Kroeber find Seal more to blame for suppressing the daughter's insight and warnings.

I am less interested in giving another reading of "Seal" here than I am in exploring what this critical history offers for future readings of Howard more generally. Returning to Jacobs's concern with an indigenous aesthetic and worldview, one can't help note this story's persistent unreadability, despite all of the exegetical energy expended on it. Howard, who had lived among white people as well as among American Indians and whose husband was fighting with Jacobs over what *kind* of stories to tell, had to have known that this narrative would puzzle and fascinate with its sexual violence and ambiguity. And yet she gives it a relatively laconic telling.

Most other stories in the collection include at least one or two illuminating footnotes, in which Jacobs either reports Howard's answer to some question he asked about the characters, or notes some explanatory detail that she offered, or describes some meta-narrative comment she made, such as a remark that a particular incident is funny. "Seal and her younger brother," however, contains only one note, which tells us only that Howard learned the story from her mother-in-law, and that it is probably a fragment of a longer tale. There is consequently so much we cannot know about this story—what Howard thought of it, how and why

Clackamas women told it to each other, and how and why one Grand Ronde woman told it to a white linguist. Jacobs and the other critics named above all give interesting and plausible readings, but those readings also underscore how a transcribed oral literature can stymie the textual work of a literary critic.

I do not want to disparage or rule out the possibility of textual reading, in which I am obviously invested. I am merely pointing out that readings of text originating in oral tradition continually encounter their own limits. Hymes, for instance, observes that at no moment in the story does anybody but Seal appear to hear the daughter speak about the urinating "wife."[90] This fact sustains his interpretation of the daughter as heroine and Seal as culpable, and he supports it with analogous stories, in which murders are not necessarily motivated. Yet in oral tradition, the daughter's culpability might have been assumed, and Clackamas listeners might have already understood that her rude speech triggered the murder, as Jacobs thought. We have little way of knowing. Similarly, Hymes, Ramsey, and Kroeber all assume that the story is tragic, but it is hard to be sure even of this. In other stories that turn on extreme violence, Howard sometimes remarks (via a footnote) that the perpetrator was "just being mean," and sometimes she even laughs. In "Seal," she tells us that the daughter wept, but without hearing and seeing Howard perform, and without some indication of her tone or some commentary from her, we are consigned to guesswork about even the mood of this story.

The readings of "Seal" tell us as much, or more, about the perspectives of the critics as they reveal about the story's meaning for Howard and Clackamas or Grand Ronde people. The psychoanalytic Jacobs, writing in the 1950s, sees the story as reflecting indigenous anxiety about women. Later critics are more inclined to read it as reflecting generational conflict and as valuing individual gumption in the face of stifling norms. I do not dismiss these readings as misapplications of Western paradigms, nor certainly do I pretend to move beyond them to the "correct" interpretation.

I cite them rather to illustrate that the reading of transcribed oral narrative is a deeply and inextricably cross-cultural event.

Once an oral story is written down, it becomes a transcultural reading encounter in which interpretations are to varying degrees both invited and frustrated. In this encounter, readers have several responsibilities. Faced with Howard's work, we as readers must try to reconstruct knowledge about Howard, her context, and the stories themselves to better understand them. In turn, we must also acknowledge the inevitable limits of such a process. All of the critics named here do both of these things. But a third responsibility is to repoliticize the stories—to acknowledge the historically inflected moment in which they were originally recorded and to scrutinize their power dynamics in an ongoing, often troubled cross-cultural reading context.[91] Hymes, for instance, ventures a provocative reading, but shyly, only in a footnote:

> I have not succeeded in phrasing in English the exact effect the myth conveys to me. One component of that effect is that I feel there may somehow be something implicitly expressive of the acculturation situation so thoroughly drawn between convention and experience—as if the mother accepts, or stands for the acceptance of, the strange newcomers, the whites . . . and as if the girl stands for a realization that the strange ways are not only different but dangerous and will destroy them (by destroying their men, who were the main casualty of the acculturation process). But all this is speculative.[92]

Hymes is duly cautious, but his speculation is actually highly illuminating, given that Howard told Jacobs this story at the tail end of the Era of Assimilation. His sense of Indian women's ingenuity as compared to men's vulnerability in the face of white usurpation matches the image of the frustrated and abused Eustace alongside his apparently more resourceful wife; it also matches many of the stories that Howard told about women who skillfully adapted to the changes ushered in by white people, while men at the reservation fell ill. Moreover, Hymes's is a politically appealing reading of the story as a form of cultural persistence. He could just as easily have read "Seal and her younger brother" as showing traditional values on the wane, with Seal standing not for acceptance of new ways but for misguided adherence to outdated ones. Ramsey, in fact, apparently imagining that he is following Hymes's "footnoted hint," does just this; he finds the story reflecting "the insufficiency of traditional social norms and the corresponding importance of keeping your eyes open and your tongue at the ready, as the little heroine tries to do."[93] This second reading is akin to Bernd Peyer's suggestion that Angel DeCora's story of the medicine man and the sick child describes a vanishing culture.

As I suggested in my discussion of that story, however, we can also read it as reflecting cultural persistence, as conveying the vitality of traditional practices without necessarily explaining them in much depth. Like DeCora's story or Winnemucca's elliptical accounts of Paiute practice, Howard's narratives gesture dramatically toward a whole world of values and behaviors that are markedly different from Euro-American ones and that, as much as readers try to get at them, remain in some ways veiled. These stories point strategically to what Sarris calls "the territory of orality"—a whole field of meaning beyond the printed page, to which the written version of the story purportedly gives us access, but which transcription and translation can never fully encompass.

Readers can and should learn as much as they can about that territory when they read transcribed oral narratives, but there is always a point at which they must proceed from certain assumptions about how stories convey meaning. Hymes's and Ramsey's suggestive readings of "Seal" as thematizing acculturation turn on a view of the characters as metaphors, as standing in for white or Indian culture. (Moreover, these readings turn on a view of Seal and her daughter as oppositional figures.) But it is hard to know whether Howard would have seen the story metaphorically or whether it ever could have circulated at Grand Ronde with this particular expressive potential, either consciously or unconsciously. We cannot know for sure which, if either, "acculturative" reading is truer to indigenous viewpoints—a reading, like Ramsey's, that calls out the story's expression of cultural loss or one, like Hymes's, that calls out the story's assertion of tribal knowledge and values.

In suggesting that Seal *can* represent a dangerous caving in to the colonizer's ways, however, Hymes at least re-places a highly elliptical story in the context in which Howard told it, a context in which white people were trying to translate, acquire, master, and incorporate American Indian ways. He allows that story to speak as an expression of tribal continuance. I am not saying that we can or should willfully read every transcribed oral narrative as another instance of resistance. For that would be another kind of appropriation. Readings that suggest that the story might express Indian resistance to assimilation also have to acknowledge that the story similarly resists its readers, with their efforts to assimilate it to their different knowledge and experience. Such readings, I would like to emphasize, come both from the text and from the reader. They come from Howard's evident lack of annotation for the story and from the way the story finally appears on the page, cryptically. But readings like Hymes's also utterly depend on readers who will be mobile, open to different possibilities, and willing to mark the end of their own interpretation.

CHAPTER FOUR

FEMALE AND INDIGENOUS RESISTANCE AND EXPRESSION IN HOWARD'S STORIES

In some sense the difficulties of reading the Howard-Jacobs texts, or any transcribed oral narratives, are not so different from the problems facing any literary critic: they have to do with what we think we are really doing when we interpret texts. Are we uncovering the writer or storyteller's intentions? Are we accounting for the narratives' cultural work, for their real effects on the people and cultures that have used them? Or are we doing something *productive*, not simply (or necessarily) in the judgmental sense of doing good, but in the sense of actually *producing* meaning and knowledge? Literary criticism, after all, reveals not just what texts *do* mean—for authors, readers, and listeners—but also what they *could* mean. As engaged and attentive readers themselves, literary critics want to alert fellow readers to possibilities in the works that have attracted their sustained attention, be those possibilities worrisome or potentially liberating. Literary critics, finally, hope to shape future readings by the light of those possibilities.

In my readings of Victoria Howard's work, then, I am trying to be as true as possible to her stories and her performance, but I am also making specific claims for specific ends. Looking at western Oregon Indian ethnography, at the history of Grand Ronde, at the record of Howard's life, and at the collaboration between her and

Melville Jacobs, I find some compelling reasons to read her work for both resistance and expression. Howard certainly faced dispossession in her relations with white people and with men. Yet in those same relations, she also found opportunities for self-authorization and collective empowerment. Reading her as expressing female and indigenous experience and as resisting assimilation and patriarchy can enrich and challenge literary history, and it can model forms of resistance and expression that might be useful at this seemingly evermore multicultural turn of a century.

We can imagine how Howard envisioned resistance and expression by observing what happens to female characters in her stories *as they speak* and how Howard renders or performs this speech. Such an approach is promoted by the ethnography of communication, a branch of linguistic anthropology that examines the situated use of language in social life. This approach need not be dependent on or limited to anthropological fieldwork, for practitioners have fruitfully looked to written documents, treating these as another kind of "informant," for indications of how and why people speak, under what conditions, and to what ends.[1] Howard's stories are ripe for such reading, for, like Jackson's and Winnemucca's, hers are loaded with speaking women: those who gossip, who challenge men and white people, who challenge and fight each other, and who in speaking *create* things—histories, communities, and even material things like husbands from fish sperm. Like Jackson and Winnemucca, too, Howard presents speaking women characters who sometimes refuse to speak, or who speak in unexpected ways.

Their speech often mirrors Howard's own performance, which emerges from and within an indigenous tradition. Hymes has drawn a distinction between storytellers who merely "report" or "repeat" their stories, perhaps out of reluctance to take on a more authoritative or dramatic role, and those who "perform" them, generally by assuming some kind of "responsibility to an audience." "Performance," he observes, doesn't really describe everything informants do: For example, members of a community may be able to recognize an event as culturally important but may not be able to perform it (e.g., the way a high-school A.P. English class might relate to something like *Hamlet*). Then again, they may be able to report that such an event occurred but be unwilling, for whatever complicated reasons, to take on the authority that comes with performing it.[2] Eustace Howard, insisting that his storytelling "was not very good," seems not to have relished performative authority—in particular, the authority constructed by a researcher asking a storyteller to perform "for the record."

Such disavowal of authority to perform may have some roots in traditional northwest Indian culture. Victoria Howard told Jacobs that one convention of elders' storytelling was their constant distancing of their own telling from past tellings—that they peppered their performances, as indeed she does herself, with meta-narrative statements that they weren't remembering things right, or that they weren't telling the story as well as those before them.[3] At the same time, Howard also did assume the authority to speak. Her stories and her storytelling performances dramatize both the assumption and the evasion of authority by indigenous women. In so doing, the texts provide another powerful working-out of the oscillation we have been seeing in women storytellers between self-disclosure and self-concealment, between transmitting information to another and redirecting that other's desires for certain kinds of information.

WRESTING BACK THE POWER TO SPEAK: THE GRIZZLIES AND MRS. WALLACE

Not everything in *Clackamas Chinook Texts* is as gratifyingly woman-centered as "She deceived herself with milt." I have already mentioned the grizzly ogresses—grotesque villainesses who do things like serving up their dead sisters' bodies for dinner. "Grizzly," a translation of the Clackamas *Ki'cimani*, appears in at least nine of

Howard's stories and in three of the ethnographic texts. The bear is explicitly sexed: besides having long hair and sharp claws, she paints her face with her own menstrual blood[4] and has breasts so huge she has to throw them over her shoulder when she runs to avoid tripping on them.[5] Grizzly Woman is pure evil; the psycho-analytic Jacobs called her a "murderous psychotic"—voracious, oversexed, vain, stupid, and destructive—"a caricature, or rather a horrible parody of what Clackamas perceived in many wives and maternal figures."[6] He posits that she "functioned as a scapegoat who permitted winter-long public ventilations of feelings toward purchased female commodities and maternal surrogates."[7]

A polygamous culture may have had ambivalent regard for wives and mothers, expressing that ambivalence in misogynistic narratives. More recently, however, feminist critics have been inclined to ask not just whether such narratives "release" animosity toward women, but also whether they construct and maintain such hostility. Reading across cultures, we cannot be sure how these narratives were received or used by Lower Columbian people. We can, however, tell something about Grand Ronde women's view of the grizzly stories (or at least, one Grand Ronde woman's view) by looking at Howard's performance of them. For that performance is both a kind of production, an active telling of the story, and a kind of reception, a transmission and possible reworking of a story she had long heard from others.

One of the richest examples of Howard's narrative production and reception is "Coon and Coyote went and stole," which she tells as a verbal battle of the sexes.[8] In this long, episodic story, Coon and Coyote live together, with Coon bringing home crawfish and Coyote bringing mice and grasshoppers for food. One day Coon happens upon an unoccupied house full of smoke-dried salmon, which he steals. Once back home, he pretends to Coyote that he is now producing food, magically, from his pillow. Coyote finally gets suspicious, however, and demands to be taken to the real source of the fish.

At the site of Coon's burglary, Coyote is discovered by the Grizzly ogresses who own the house. He stays with them for a time, during which various fights ensue. One of these is over some "water creatures," as the translation puts it, that the ogresses are keeping in their mountain home. Most interesting for our purposes, though, Coyote and the Grizzlies fight explicitly over the power to speak—to command the water creatures and to determine the outcome of events. Coyote finally wins, releasing the fish back into the river by proclaiming:

> "When should salmon ever remain in the mountains, or eels (or) various such things? Ah it should not be like that. Such things should be in the river. Whatever their (appropriate) month, then fish of various kinds will be there. . . . The Grizzly Women will not keep them in the mountains."[9]

As in other oral traditions, here Coyote is a trickster—both a creator, a force for the good, and a buffoon or ill-doer.[10] He is male, often explicitly embodied as such in Howard's tales; in one story he snakes his long penis downriver to rape two girls.[11] "Coon and Coyote" therefore pits a male hero much revered in the oral tradition against specifically female villains.

The story turns, moreover, on the male figure's performative utterance, his command that makes something happen: "Whatever their (appropriate) month, then fish of various kinds will be there." In Chinookan and in other oral traditions, it is common for Coyote or some other figure, often male, to bring something into being by pronouncing. "Coon and Coyote" thus has two clear messages, both drawing on the gender of the story's characters. The first message is etiological: Coyote paved the way for the people; he made the world the way it is. The second is didactic: hoarding food in a society so dependent on seasonally available sources is evil and will be punished. In both cases, as Hymes reads it, the story conquers the Grizzlies "to the discomfort of the women, but to the general good."[12]

We have exactly one shred of evidence that indigenous listeners found the story more supple than this. Jacobs tells us that Clackamas people "identified humorously" with Coon,[13] who delightfully pretends to conjure salmon out of his bedding thus: "(uttering fake magic words), 'Right where I am lying here, I raise this pillow. That is where I pull out smokedried strips of salmon.'"[14] At this point in her narration, Jacobs tells us, Howard remarked, "When some person yawned, then that person would say, 'Oh I wish I were eating something.' The person would name it."[15] This raises the possibility that Grand Ronde listeners and storytellers didn't necessarily "identify"—if that is even the correct word—with only one character, but possibly with several, simultaneously or in succession. If Coon, ostensibly a villain here, can be quoted and performed not only by the storyteller but also by a range of people in daily life, then perhaps other figures, including the terrible ogresses, might likewise be available for a range of identifications and uses. Howard's account of people "playing Coon" also suggests how deeply embedded such stories were in everyday speech, that they were not only lessons or entertainment but also a way of making sense of the world, and of communicating.

It would be too much, I think, to extrapolate directly from such a local observation to any broad claims about a communitist ethos here. However, Howard's metanarrative remark helps us observe that this mode of storytelling, which encourages narrator and listeners to move among many different characters, is very different from one that privileges a single hero to the exclusion of other figures and vantage points. We might thus be able to read against the story's ending, and against its seemingly overarching conflict between male savior and female evildoers.

Indeed, in telling the story, Howard speaks not just as Coyote, who saves the day with his pronouncement over the fish, but also extensively as the Grizzlies, as they try to prevent that pronouncement. Direct discourse, according to Zenk, "is a ubiquitous feature of narrative structure for all of the local indigenous languages . . .

characterizing not only myths but prosaic reportage and personal anecdote as well."[16] Thus, when Coyote commands the water creatures out of the house,

> [The Grizzly Women] said (to their water creatures), "Coyote merely said that!" Woops (rising then falling tone), they (the water creatures) halted. (But) Coyote called out loudly, "Let us go into our river!" (five times in a high monotone). Then they (the water creatures) went on again. They (the women) called out (five times), they (the water creatures) stopped. Coyote called out (five times), then they (the water creatures) went on again.[17]

When the ogresses call out that Coyote "merely said that," they temporarily assume the power to undo his words; a more colloquial translation might read, "Coyote was just kidding," suggesting that his words don't count or are deceptive. Howard's telling thus generates a kind of play with the resolution of the story. Hereafter, the transcription suggests that she may have abbreviated her performance for dictation, turning to reportage ("they called out,"), but the initial quoted speech ("Coyote merely said that!") highlights the effect of struggle.

That struggle is rendered dramatic by another feature that Zenk specifies as a deeply embedded part of Chinookan discourse—onomatopoeia. "Woops" (and, elsewhere in the story, a long "w—ow") is an attempt to translate a particle that may have been part of ordinary language, although the parenthetical "rising then falling tone" also suggests that Howard may have added some dramatic effect tonally.[18] Both of these features make something of the Grizzlies' resistance to Coyote, dwelling on it for a bit before he wins. More broadly, the techniques suggest that Howard was a skilled and energetic performer, although the transcription also shows how she must have been shaping this performance for the dictation. But that, of course, is precisely the point: *Clackamas*

Chinook Texts represents a particular set of narrative encounters between a Grand Ronde woman and a professional linguist; it is not "authentic" Indian storytelling, which is in any event a highly varied and variable practice. For example, Coyote calls to the fish five times and the Grizzlies challenge Coyote five times. In Lower Columbia traditions, five is a ritual number, and events often occur in fives. Since "five times" comes in parentheses (and in the field notebooks, in brackets), it appears that, at this point, Howard simply indicated that the call would be thus repeated, rather than actually reciting each event five times for Jacobs.[19]

Those parenthetical notes are descriptive not just of Howard's particular performance for Jacobs, but of many other tellings of this story, which would of course have preceded and succeeded his recording. It is a movement toward the territory of orality, as if to say "when we *really* perform it, we do it like this." A performance that actively repeated "Coyote merely said that!" five times could have many functions. It could allow storyteller and audience to linger on, even revel in, the temporary trouncing of the powerful male Coyote. Repetition in oral storytelling can fuel audiences' investment and participation in the performance. It can be a way of building tension or identification, of helping listeners mark the progress of the tale, of providing a hook that audiences can even recite along with the storyteller. Then again, it could bore some listeners, or allow them to think about other things while still remaining partially engaged in the recital of something familiar.

The transcription of this story raises many possibilities, without giving definitive answers. It is thus that Howard (and Jacobs) uses the transcription process both to preserve something of an indigenous tradition and to point to the limits of that preservation process in really capturing such a tradition; it is thus, too, that she can use translation both for indigenous expression and for resistance.

"Coon and Coyote" dramatizes speech acts that bring about change; it illustrates the difference between fake speech and genuine speech, good speech and malicious. But it also puts high-spirited and humorous pressure on some of the story's resolution. Even without actually repeating these speech events five times in this long narrative, Howard does seem to have provided quite a bit of elaboration and repetition, as the following passage illustrates. In the delightful final scene, the Grizzly Women literally clobber Coyote, one after the other, with the rootdiggers he has made,[20] while he tries to protect himself with wooden bowls:

> They (the Grizzly Women) went toward him, they hit him (with their rootdiggers), she broke the wooden bowl that he had on his head. He took out another, he put it (the bowl) on (his head), and then they hit and hit him. Another bowl (on his head) broke in two. They would halloo (five times), they (the water creatures) would halt. (But) Coyote hallooed even louder (five times). Then far away and off (the water creatures rushed). Now they (the water creatures) had gone (never to return upon calls of Grizzly Women). They (the women) hit him, another one (bowl) broke in two. Coyote thought, "Now only one more (bowl). Maybe they will kill me." They hit and hit him, the (next to the last) bowl broke in two. He put on another, now that was the last one. Then they had become tired out, (but) they hit and hit him. (Now) they turned and looked, they turned and saw, now all of them (the water creatures) were getting into the (main) river.[21]

Coyote wins, but not until the Grizzlies and their storyteller have put up a fight. By keeping so many voices in play, the Howard-Jacobs transcriptions, created in the conversation and work of at least two people, allow us to examine the dialectics between storyteller and received narrative. In the end, it is impossible to say exactly what happened in this or any other transcribed oral performance, but the multilayered translation offers several possibilities, all of which point in a compelling direction, from a feminist perspective: whether in actual performance for Jacobs, or in the potential performance that the translation signals, Howard's version of the story milks the struggle between Coyote and the Grizzlies, and it prolongs the contest over the power to speak and create.

Indeed, many of the myths that Howard told Jacobs paint speech as a turf war between men and women. In some, female speech is doomed. One story, for example, kills off a young cannibal girl who extensively mocks her half-brother.[22] But even when mouthy female characters die in Howard's stories, her performance of these narratives elongates their fatal speech acts, often with a repeated song. In another story, for instance, a rich young girl evades a headman who wants to marry her by disguising her dog as herself. Though he finally kills her for her deception (in a most "gendered" way, by sending snakes to impregnate her), she celebrates her resistance by singing "I fooled him with my dog" five times.[23] Another vociferous female figure, Greyback Louse, drowns four successive Grizzly men by luring them into her canoe, playing off their vanity by suggesting they'll get women if they come with her. The fifth Grizzly finally kills her, but not before she has sung over each dead male.[24] In these latter two tales, as in "Coon and Coyote," female figures are eliminated for their unruly behavior and speech. That Howard chose such stories at all, told them to Jacobs, *and* told them in ways that milks their songs for performative gusto pries at the stories' punitive endings and suggests that this Indian woman informant was not completely co-opted by the ethnographic encounter.

Comparisons to the works of other storytellers will also be instructive, further illuminating the story's gender dynamics as well as the interplay between Howard and Jacobs. Other storytellers in the region around the same time told versions of this "impounded water and release" story,[25] all of which involve a male figure conquering females who have been hoarding a food source and most of which culminate with that male figure's performative utterance. Louis Simpson tells a much shorter version of the story in *Wishram Texts*, translated by Edward Sapir (who, like Jacobs, could not speak the native language and in fact needed an interpreter to communicate with Simpson).[26] This version describes only Coyote's rescue of the fish. Coyote hears about two women who are keeping fish in a pond. Instead of accidentally stumbling upon the women, he disguises himself as a child to trick them into taking him in, expressly so that he can free the fish. He makes five rootdiggers, which he uses, not for any subsequent clobbering, but to break open the earth so that the fish have an outlet to the Columbia River. No struggle with the women transpires. After releasing the fish, Coyote pronounces the two women Swallows, with much performative fanfare: "Whenever a fish will be caught, you two will come. Your name has become Swallows. . . . Thus will the people say: 'From these two did Coyote take away their fish preserved in a pond; now they have come.'"[27]

Stylistically, much is different here: not only are the Simpson-Sapir texts much shorter than the Howard-Jacobs texts, but they also contain much less glossing and they begin and end much more formulaically. For example, one finishes with: "This is the story of Coyote. Thuswise did men of old in ancient days relate the tale. Today there are no longer such men of old."[28] The version not only favors Coyote more pointedly but also suggests a different kind of relationship between teller and anthropologist. Sapir may have demanded short, formulaic units; or Simpson may have sensed that this was what the anthropologist wanted, thinking that a greater number of stories would seem more "productive" to his transcriber (therefore proving more lucrative to himself); or Simpson may have found the sessions boring and chosen to generate such short texts.[29] It is, as always, impossible to be sure. But by contrast, the Howard-Jacobs texts do more to underline their own difference from indigenous storytelling practice by offering more diverse kinds of information about it.

Even in versions collected from other raconteurs by Jacobs himself, we can see key differences from the Howard texts. John B. Hudson (Santiam Kalapuya) and William Hartless (Mary's River) also pit Coyote against female figures. And both, like Simpson, conclude with Coyote's performative utterance as victory. In Hartless's version, Coyote is battling, not grizzlies, but female frogs. Here his utterance is quite long and pronounced; Coyote escapes the frogs, who are hitting him, then proclaims:

> You are not to be keeping the water! Everyone will drink (free), they will not purchase it. You must not be keeping the water. You will be bull frogs, you will live on the river bank. That is where your place (home) is to be. But you must never keep the water (back). You are to live on the river bank.[30]

From this small sampling, it appears that a roughly identifiable version of the impoundment and release story was in circulation, or was at least called forth by employed raconteurs, at a particular moment and in a particular region. It appears, too, that this version depends on specifically gendered heroes and villains and generally concludes with a performative utterance from Coyote that confirms his status as benevolent transformer. Howard's version thus differs sharply from that of the male raconteurs, because it uses Coyote's utterance rather to *initiate* the struggle with the ogresses, not to finish it. And when she does finish the conflict, she in fact does so rather elliptically, saying of the Grizzlies:

> Then they had become tired out, (but) they hit and hit him. (Now) they turned and looked, they turned and saw, now all of them (the water creatures) were getting into the (main) river. So there they lay down (exhausted), while he himself then went along, I do not know where to. Now story story.[31]

No dramatic punishment of the ogresses, no final grand pronouncements from Coyote. We might say that Howard uses this story differently than do Hudson, Hartless, and Simpson—not so much to show how Coyote brought things about, perhaps, as to play with that masculine authority a bit.

I am not claiming that Victoria Howard, a lone feminist voice in the indigenous Northwest in 1929, independently revised an inherently sexist narrative. Many factors comprise and shape her telling, including her working relationship with Jacobs—one that seems to have lent itself to longer, more dynamic performances than did some other informant-ethnographer relationships—and the community from which she learned this story. As we'll see, Howard always defines that community as female. We can and should consider Howard's possible individual intentions and innovations within those of her community, and in dialogue with them.

We also need, as I've been insisting, to consider those innovations in dialogue with Jacobs. While I've painted him as a relatively nonintrusive translator, one who helps to create productive dialogues and multiple meanings, there are nevertheless times when he cannot seem to resist the rather intrusive parenthetical gloss and closure. Shortly *before* the concluding paragraph we have just seen, for instance, he glosses one line as follows: "Now they (the water creatures) had gone (never to return upon calls of Grizzly Women)."[32] Whether Jacobs arrived at this highly dramatic obliteration of all future Grizzly Ogress speech with Howard's help, or embellished it on his own, we can't know, but the gloss has a hyperfinality to it that seems countermanded by all of the juicy reveling in the Grizzlies' behavior that has preceded this moment and by the anticlimactic departure of Coyote that follows ("he himself then went along, I do not know where to"). Even the phrase "I do not know" (a recurrent locution in *Clackamas Chinook Texts*) chafes against firm narrative resolution. Hymes indicates that it is in fact a mistranslation, that the Clackamas original contains neither a negative nor a personal pronoun, and that what appears as "I do not know" is really more like "to be thinking"—a "definite indefinite" that contrasts with the story's apparent finality.[33] "I do not know" thus helps open the way back to that "territory of orality," even as the transcription process seems to move toward stasis. It generates conflicts and dissents, possibly intracultural and possibly intercultural, between the impulse to "fix"—to fix words, voices, and narrative outcomes—and the impulse to leave things open and continuous.

I have been making much of the tiny possibilities lurking in admittedly problematic transcribed oral texts in order to construct an account of a struggle between ethnographer and informant and their possible respective agendas. In some of the ethnographic texts, though, that struggle between voices and the uses to which Howard is able to put that struggle is much more blatant. "Illness and sexual intercourse," for example, is structured as two paragraphs of quoted speech and, as such, pits female against male talk and indigenous experience against ethnographic demand. First, Howard speaks as a prototypical male shaman: "When a man or woman became ill, they went somewhere to fetch a shaman. When he doctored he might say, 'Yes. This female or this male did not (become ill) just recently, he must have become ill a long time ago. . . . Possibly the two of them (he and his wife) slept together, and they did something to one another (had sexual relations).'"[34] In the second paragraph, she tells a specific story of one particular shaman, Polk Scott, and a sick man named Henry Wallace. Scott had attributed Wallace's sickness to sex with Mrs. Wallace. In turn, Mrs. Wallace gave the shaman an earful, and Howard quotes her at some length in this second half of the text.

"Illness and sexual intercourse" is not just about Mrs. Wallace's challenge to Polk Scott. It is also about female challenges to male power more broadly and—less directly but still compellingly— about lived Indian experience as a challenge to anthropological fixing and fixation. Quite ethnographically, the first half of the two-paragraph text, with its prototypical shamanistic diagnosis, concludes: "They (the shamans) used to speak in such a manner." Many of the ethnographic texts use this phrase, "They used to," often beginning with it, suggesting, perhaps, an answer to a question (e.g.,

"How did shamans diagnose illness" or even "What did shamans say about sex?").[35] Concluding with this phrase seems to bracket the shaman's words, to place them firmly in the remote past, in an exotic place where superstitious people account for sickness in mysterious ways.

And yet Howard moves on, as though this generalized account is not quite the story she wanted to tell. In the story that follows, the story of Mrs. Wallace and her husband, Howard figures importantly as a witness: "I went that evening, I went to see him." Just as she (and Jacobs, of course) built the first part of "Illness and sexual intercourse" around the generalized shaman's words, she builds this second paragraph around Mrs. Wallace's retort:

> Right away I said to him (to Scott), That is a big lie. You see this daughter of ours here, and now she has become big. Since the time when we copulated (to conceive her), we copulated (only at that time long ago and never since then). That is what I said to him. I got angry at him.[36]

The text ends here, very different from the first paragraph. In contrast to "They used to speak in such a manner," Mrs. Wallace is still talking when this story ends. Unlike the Grizzly women, Greyback Louse, or other female figures who speak out of turn in Howard's telling, Mrs. Wallace gets the last word. "Illness and sexual intercourse" ends powerfully with her anger, her hostility toward a belief, exchanged between men, that would denigrate female sexuality. Moreover, it ends with Mrs. Wallace speaking of that anger—privately, to a man, the shaman, and then publicly, to another woman, Howard. Finally, that anger is spoken of publicly once again, as Indian woman recounts it for white male anthropologist.

The crucial point, then, is not just that Mrs. Wallace articulated this anger herself; we have no way of knowing whether she actually confronted Scott this way, since people often aggrandize their own behavior in the retelling, and for that matter we have no way of knowing how much she actually said to Howard. Nor can we know for sure what really happened as Howard told this story for Jacobs—whether she began by giving him the kind of ethnographic account he seemed to want, then broke into her own kind of storytelling, or not. The crucial point, instead, is that Howard structures her account specifically as an exchange between women (herself and Mrs. Wallace) and that she launches the challenge to Scott's masculine authority as a woman's monologue. In so doing, she underscores the gendered and spoken nature of the exchange.

Jacobs thought that "Illness and sexual intercourse" showed "Mrs. Howard's mixed feelings about shamans," adding, "I think that acculturated people, like Mrs. Howard, were often much more severe than pre-contact Indians in their observations about the integrity of shamans."[37] As we have seen, though, a number of people at Grand Ronde in the 1930s circulated stories about shamans in a powerful form of cultural persistence. Polk Scott himself, the reader will remember, was the subject of such stories, even among other women, as when Mrs. Simmons told Berreman that she was able to outlive the much-loathed Agent Kershaw thanks to Scott's healing work. And taken together, the stories in *Clackamas Chinook Texts* do not really reflect much "post-contact" or "civilized" antipathy toward shamans, though they do express a healthy ambivalence about people in power. What seems important about the ambivalence toward the shaman Polk Scott in "Illness and sexual intercourse," rather, is that it expresses an Indian woman's displeasure with a cultural belief, not necessarily as a belief, but as it gets deployed at her expense. This is a communitist story, one that—unlike Helen Hunt Jackson's vision, perhaps—does not construct feminine resistance and power in opposition to a monolithic notion of male power or of tradition, but that rather insists that tradition be supple enough to accommodate changing needs and thus to endure.

SELF-NARRATION

"Illness and sexual intercourse" is one of six stories Howard tells about shamans, accounts of traditional healers singing over the sick, laying their hands on painful body parts, and removing disease-powers.[38] These stories would seem to confirm the cultural persistence of shamanism at Grand Ronde at this time, as Zenk has suggested, as well as the persistence of storytelling. Howard's shaman stories are a verbal continuation of a culture that is by no means dead; they assert that indigenous culture continues, despite and perhaps even because of cultural change, and despite or because of challenges to shamanistic authority like Mrs. Wallace's. Howard may have told these stories at Jacobs's prompting, as he asked for stories of the past; we can't be sure. But her doing so would not preclude the possibility of their also acting as genuine expressions of indigenous and female experience. Howard's narratives are never simply acquiescence to the ethnographer's questions, nor merely resistance to those demands, but complex ways of expressing what Valaskakis calls "the affective or experiential quality of 'being Indian.'"[39]

For example, while the short narrative "A shaman doctored me for my eyes" is hardly what Jacobs would call very "inward," it still expresses Howard's experience, as a woman and a Grand Ronde Indian, as an individual and as a member of overlapping communities:

> I became nearly blind. My mother-in-law told me, "Do not wash your face with warm water. Pour cold water on yourself (on your eyes)." It became worse during the day, I could not see about me. It was nighttime before I could see. So then I thought, "I shall go to my mother." I got to her house. On the following day she said to me, "I shall go. I shall go fetch your father's aunt (a shaman named *se'msxn*). She will come to see (and doctor) you." She went. In a short time she returned, she said to me, "She will come." We waited for her.[40]

The shaman comes and doctors Howard, feeling Howard's head. Then she tells Howard, "Well well! . . . After a still longer period, you might then have become blind. Do not again wash your face with cold water. Warm water is the thing with which to wash your face. Possibly your mother-in-law just thought that she would make you blind!"[41]

Told to a white person at an historical moment when shamanism was supposed to have disappeared, this story effectively rehearses the power of traditional healing. It can thus function as a powerful statement of Native cultural continuance at the latter end of the Era of Assimilation. At the same time, it is a vivid picture of connections among Grand Ronde women. Like the myths that Howard tells, this narrative is loaded with direct discourse, confirming the speculation that everyday Chinookan speech proceeded this way. And the effect of that direct discourse in this story, about women and told by a woman, is to underscore the centrality, the work, of female speech. Through speech, these women both sustain tradition and, if we are to believe Howard's account of her mother-in-law, also subvert or ruin it; by talking, they help each other and maintain familial bonds even as they foil those bonds. This story reads like a wry anti-mother-in-law joke, even with a little humor in its punch line.

This is curious, since Howard cites her mother-in-law, with evident respect, as a major source for her narratives and, as we will see below, tells stories of that woman's experience. Howard's "feelings," such as they are, thus stay somewhat out of reach, as they often do in American Indian literatures and in transcriptions of the oral. Yet this text also offers rich suggestions of her experience, constructing it specifically as Indian, female, and relational: women's collective sustaining of a tradition along with tensions between two women who appear to have lived very much in each other's presence. The story is, in a sense, as much about these women's affective connections as it is about shamanism.

Though Jacobs felt frustrated in his attempts to "get" Howard's "life story," then, it appears that she did tell him things about herself, though not in the linear, psychological ways that he might have recognized as "true" autobiography. Howard's self-narration is not only a matter either of her unilateral and spontaneous self-expression, or of Jacobs's benign interest in her life, or of his arguably imperialist desire for a story about the last Clackamas Indian. Her story emerges instead out of a complicated combination of these and other factors, out of traditional practice, individual self-expression, and the cross-cultural situation of the translation itself.

Howard's mother-in-law resurfaces much more sympathetically in "*Wa'susgani* and Watcheeno," a long contact narrative that would appear to be the "real stuff" of ethnoautobiography.[42] It tells of Wa'susgani's marriage to the tribe's nominal chief, Old Wacheno, of the arrival of whites in northwest Oregon and their trade with the Indians, of the increase in winter spirit-power dances after whiskey was introduced into the indigenous community, of the disease that periodically ravaged Oregon Indians, of the eventual removal of the Clackamas and other tribes to the Grand Ronde Reservation, and of Howard's Clackamas grandmother's criticisms of Wacheno. Much of this story therefore takes place before Howard herself was born. It begins, "My mother-in-law would think of something, and then she would talk about it. Once in a while when she arose in the morning, she made the fire, and then she would be talking." Similarly, she concludes a brief initial narrative about Wa'susgani's shaman father by saying, "That is what she (my mother-in-law) said."[43]

Again, Howard's narration thematizes women's speech, making it absolutely central to female and indigenous life and experience. It underlines the habitual and daily nature of Wa'susgani's verbal recollections, shared with Howard herself as part of household life. This narrative also ends with women speaking, as Howard shifts from Wa'susgani's story to her grandmother:

My grandmother had another one (another narrative about olden days). She used to say, 'Something occurs to me.' Now

ki'lipasada (a Clackamas woman who married a Molale) would
be chatting with her. She (the latter woman) would laugh and
laugh, she would say, 'Where did we ever see Watcheeno do
anything (although he is now an acting chief)?'" "Yes, possibly
he did do something (befitting a chief) long long long ago,"
said my grandmother. Then the other old woman said (cyni-
cally), "It is only where he sees some woman who has many
possessions, then that is just the person he wants. He will be
going to purchase her (in marriage)."[44]

Howard continues reconstructing her grandmother and the neighbor's talk for what amounts to almost two pages of text, noting
repeatedly how the two women would "laugh and laugh." This
picture valuably fills out the history of indigenous Oregon women,
whose status is complicated by polygamy and the purchase of
wives, but who, as implied by Howard's narration, also found
forms of power in such a life. Howard's lengthy recital of the gossip between her grandmother and the neighbor similarly emphasizes talk as the means by which women in Howard's world fashion
emotional bonds, keep their histories alive, and contest masculine
authority.

For much of the text, Howard even drops the tag "she said" in
quoting her mother-in-law. This Chinookan feature creates a narrative that speaks not only *for* Wa'susgani but also *as* her. By thus
switching from reporting what happened in the past to performing
it as though in the present, Howard gives an immediacy to her
mother-in-law's story. These shifts also amount to what Richard
Bauman calls "traditionalization," to be specifically distinguished
from the static notion of "tradition." Bauman spoke with a male
Icelandic narrator who, in telling a story, invoked previous sources
for his tale. Bauman finds this kind of storytelling to be "directly
and explicitly engaged in an act of symbolic construction, drawing
the links of continuity by which he may tie his story to past discourses as part of his own recounting of it."[45]

Howard, likewise, actively creates links to the past; further, she actively constructs that past as female. Never does she explicitly name a male source for her tales; rather, she focuses heavily on her mother-in-law and grandmother. Probably, this is because Jacobs asked for Clackamas tales, and her mother-in-law and grandmother were Howard's nearest Clackamas relatives. But her citing them also compels us to look at her work in a more agent-centered light in which Howard doesn't simply cite those two women because they happened to be her only sources (we don't know whether they were or they weren't). Instead, she actively creates a female tradition and a female speaking position while telling.

As the above examples suggest, the female tradition that Howard builds shows women using speech as a form of resistance against patriarchy. It also shows American Indians using speech as resistance to whites and to assimilation. In some cases, this spoken resistance takes the form of very direct survival strategies. Wa'susgani talks at considerable length of the diseases brought by white settlers—tuberculosis, ague, and measles. Under these conditions, talk among Indians is quite literally a form of survival. When the whites bring a sick Indian to the hospital, an orderly who is either Indian or part Indian tells the patient not to take the whites' medicine:

"Be on your guard!" He (the orderly) gave him a handker-chief. He said to him, "He (the doctor) will give you medicine. Do not swallow it. Spit it out. Here is a handkerchief. Wipe (inside) your mouth. He will try to give you water. Do not drink it." "Yes," he replied to him. And soon afterward the shaman (the white doctor) came, he brought him medicine. He told him, "Drink the medicine now!" He gave it to him, he held his handkerchief, he poured it into his mouth, he hurried and wiped it (out from inside his mouth), he spit out the medicine. He said to him, "Here is water. Drink it!" He replied to him, "No." Where the medicine ran out (from his lips), his mouth (lips) was all burned. . . . He said to them,

"Had not that other person (the orderly) seen me I should now be long since dead. The shaman (the white doctor) is giving bad medicine to people (to Indian patients), they are dying (because of that)." The shaman (the white doctor) fled that very night I do not know where to. He was gone. They never saw him again anywhere.[46]

This lengthy narration suggests a very vivid memory and the power of keeping such memory alive through narration. But more than merely recounting, it also uses nested narration to dramatize the importance of talk among Indians. The story concludes, "So she used to say. 'The myth (white) people just fixed up the disease for us. They wanted this country of ours.'"[47] These words seem to confirm Zenk's thesis about the emergence of an "Indian" identity in opposition to a white one at Grand Ronde in the early twentieth century and to show how narrative aided in the construction and maintenance of that identity. In other cases, the coming of whites has even more deleterious effects, especially on the men. The story describes them abusing whiskey that the whites gave to them.

The women, meanwhile, are more successful in Wa'susgani's account:

They gave her a skirt. She put it on, she showed it (to other Indians), they saw her, they laughed at her. They said to her, "Let us see you walk about." She walked around, they laughed at her skirt. They also had a name for apron. They said that it was made the same way too, just like a skirt (it was held up by a waist string and was wide).

We baked potatoes in the ashes (for the first time), and they popped (in the fire). We said, Oh dear these potatoes are a different kind of thing. We laughed at them (at such a food). That is what they did. Some people would not eat these potatoes, but there were others who ate them forthwith.

> We did not know how they made this wheat bread. One Boston (that is, an American) woman showed me how they made wheat bread. I showed it to them (to other Indians) the very first time that I made it. We laughed at my wheat bread. I learned all sorts of things from that Boston (American) woman there. Her name was Barclay, (and she was) a good Boston woman.[48]

Elsewhere, Wa'susgani reports, "They gave us new pans, and these we used for looking (for use as mirrors). We laughed and laughed when we looked at ourselves."[49] As in the grandmother's and neighbor's gossip about Old Wacheno, it is the *laughter* of women that is so striking here; it presents them not as unwitting dupes who are too primitive to understand what a pan really is, but as savvy cultural collators. "Acculturation," as presented here, doesn't merely act upon or happen to Indian women. Rather, they make active choices among cultural practices. Earlier, Wa'susgani proudly says, "I saw how they cut calico, I (myself then) cut it that way. And I sewed (and) I made quilts. I do it like that today. I sew all day long (today yet),"[50] in evident contradistinction to the men who drank whiskey, or the people who were afraid to eat new foods and became sick.

This is not a history that proceeds by either a simple "progress" or "loss of culture" model; it is one in which women adapt, suvive, and continue their culture through humor and narration. Finally, while Howard's stories may reflect something of an oppositional Grand Ronde Indian identity, these passages are also notable for their illustration of cross-cultural alliances, specifically alliances among women. As in Jackson's and Winnemucca's stories, it is talk among women, white and Indian, that provides the vehicle by which these women survive, fashion their identities, resist masculine and white authority. We might observe that this talk is less romanticized than it is in *Ramona*'s pantomiming graveyard scene, and less anxious than *Life Among the Piutes* about showing that Indians are more egalitarian than the U.S. government when it comes to women's status. That is not very surprising, given when Howard told her stories, and to whom. Still, Wa'susgani's account of friendship with the "Boston woman" marks another voluntary affiliation that is itself a form of resistance to assimilation, at least to assimilation conceived as a model of simple cultural loss.

Reading Howard ethnoautobiographically, we can situate her in a long line of American Indian women who have made their personal and tribal histories public, from Sarah Winnemucca to Wilma Mankiller. Howard's self-narrations do not proceed from a model centered only on her "self," nor are they particularly linear or psychological. Rather, they blend accounts of historical and personal experience with mythic narrative, and they incorporate the stories of many women's lives. At the same time, this communitism does not preclude more individualistic forms of self-narration that should have been more familiar to the disappointed Melville Jacobs. One of Howard's most dramatic ethnographic texts, "They said the cat is crying," is primarily about Howard, and like the story about her leaving her cousin behind without a horse, it seems to reflect her lingering worry that her behavior helped bring about someone else's suffering or death.

The story begins like a typical ethnographic datum: "They said that when a cat urinated in a bed, or when he defecated (inside a house), they said that it was a bad omen." But then, as in "Illness and sexual intercourse," Howard proceeds to a specific memory: her mother-in-law once called her to see that the cat had wet Howard's bed. Howard says

> I took her cane, I beat him, he dropped off (the bed), he rolled over, there I killed the cat. My mother-in-law said to me, "If you had not killed it, it would be a good deal longer before someone died. However, you did kill it, and so you have speeded it up (and someone will die soon now)."[51]

A footnote to this last line reads, "Mrs. Howard added that one after another of her children died, after this episode of the cat. . . . She inclined to believe that the episode accounted for her family mortality."[52] Why this information is relegated to a footnote is hard to say, especially given Jacobs's self-professed desire for auto-biographical information. In this story Howard insistently figures herself as an agent, beating and killing the cat, and her style dwells rather boldly on those active verbs. This retelling suggests a preoc-cupation with the relations between her individual actions and the mortality of those she loves. The text suggests that we should look for self-expression among the many ends for which Howard used her work with Jacobs.

"SHE DECEIVED HERSELF WITH MILT": ALLUSIONS TO CLACKAMAS NARRATIVE PRACTICE

Future Howard scholarship might continue reconstructing the connections among her ethnographic texts, metanarrative remarks, and myths—connections that shed some light on how she used narrative within the dictation sessions with Jacobs, and on how Clackamas or Grand Ronde women used it outside such situations. Returning to "She deceived herself with milt," for instance, such a project would place the exuberant woman-centered myth along-side a snippet that Howard told in the course of translation:

> One house (at Grand Ronde Reservation was) close to the road. When some (white) person would pass by, she (my mother-in-law) would look at (that white person), and she would laugh. She would say, "Dear oh dear it is a light one! Possibly it is Milt!" And then she would sing. This is what she would say (in the words of the song),
> "Milt! She changed him into a man!"[53]

Reading the myths in concert with such purportedly extranarrative comments and accounts, we can garner more information about how and why women at Grand Ronde told stories. Howard cites both her mother-in-law and her grandmother as sources for the milt story. And she appears to have enjoyed telling it herself. In *The People Are Coming Soon*, Jacobs writes that she "laughed heartily" over the light-skinned Milt.[54] In a footnote to the actual story, he also mentions that at the precise point where the widow observes her new husband's light skin, "Mrs. Howard bubbled with mirth and added the comment, 'He must have been a half-breed.'"[55] In telling Jacobs the milt story, then, Howard also seems to be telling him something about how Indian women used storytelling—against and within patriarchy and racism and as a form of cultural continuance.

Curiously, other Pacific Northwest collections do not contain any direct analogs for this tale.[56] Stories of "inadvertent wishing" abound, as do narratives in which women (or men) marry mythic or semi-human figures. In one recurrent tale, for instance, young girls wish that stars would become husbands; that they get their wish becomes a cautionary element.[57] Of course, the ethnographic collections cannot come anywhere near encompassing indigenous storytelling practice, and so we have no way of knowing whether any version of the milt story was ever widely told or not. It is worth noting, however, that while some of Howard's other stories (like "Coon and Coyote") appear fairly closely replicated in other collections, her mostly male peers did not recount "She deceived herself with milt."

After all, the story does suggest considerable humor at men's expense, with its choice of milt as the "seed" that becomes the husband: the widow fashions a husband from the mere gland of the fish, useless unless filled with seminal fluid, and apparently just as easy for the widow to discard as to desire or take. This widow is independent and enterprising; she has enough fish to sell during the winter when others get hungry and acquires "many valuables" besides. She thus stands out both in her status within her community and in her position of power in her new marriage.

Further, the narrative hinges on a performative utterance that is unusual in that it is a woman's: "Oh that you become a person." It is not as definitive perhaps as Coyote's declaration that Grizzlies will never hoard water creatures, but it is readable as a mark of feminine power. And we have a song, "She deceived herself with milt," which the widow sings five times in response to the second woman's verbal harassment. Our familiar theme of female power garnered through speaking has resurfaced once again.

The widow gains additional power by defining herself against the second wife, the one who most dramatically "deceives herself with milt." In Jacobs's view, "[t]he title appropriately refers to the second woman who enters the plot, because she, not the first woman, is deceived. In most other instances it is an actor who appears initially in the plot who is referred to in the title."[58] This doesn't preclude the possibility of reading the widow's song as self-referential, a kind of third-person exorcism of her own folly. And yet the "milt" title does point humorously to that second wife. At the story's end, she beats a hasty retreat from the widow, who in turn chases her while singing and throwing the milt (again in his lowercase form).

These interpretations, of course, rely on close reading of the phrase "she deceived herself." But Hymes claims that the translation should really be "The Honorable Milt! I supposed him for myself!"[59] Based on this retranslation, Ramsey re-reads the song as referring to its singer, with a kind of double meaning for "suppose" that includes "I conjured him up for myself" and a more rueful "I thought he was mine."[60] And yet according to Jacobs's field notebooks, Howard's own translation (or at least, the translation she worked out in conversation with him) was "Milt! She changed him for a man!"[61] This version, we might observe, gives the woman much more agency than does Hymes's "correct" reworking or, for that matter, any of Ramsey's multiple possibilities. It generates some ambiguity with the third person pronoun (which is possibly what led Jacobs to his version), but its use of "changed" focuses entirely on the act of transformation, without any elevation of "him" as desirable or "honorable."

Like "Coon and Coyote," this narrative indicates that the song would be sung five times: "the fifth time (when she had sung the song five times) she extended her spirit-power regalia (toward the couple)."[62] Based on this line, it seems reasonable to conclude that Howard abbreviated the story for the dictation situation, that she turned to "reporting" rather than "performing." However, it would not be quite safe to posit that the "correct" version of the story includes five actual repetitions of the song; in none of these readings do I wish to suggest that there is some original "real" version of the tale. Howard could abbreviate the story just as easily for a female Grand Ronde audience; indeed, as her mother-in-law's brief citation of the story suggests, people may have been so familiar with the story that it didn't need a full performance every time to have meaning.

Storytelling always emerges in and is shaped by a specific context, and the result must be evaluated in terms of that context—whether it be an "authentic" indigenous context or an "inauthentic" recording context. Having said that, however, the provocative thing about the Howard-Jacobs transcriptions is that they *write in* the possibility of five repetitions. In so doing, they point to a whole field of oral use and performance that exceeds the print version before us. Whether or not Howard or Jacobs intended such moments as resistance, that is precisely one of the translation's effects: it resists any expectation of a transparent window onto authentic Indian practice by delineating the limits of the translation itself.

Thus, although it does not definitively or completely reveal anything, the translation suggests a world of female storytelling use and performance in which women, through speech, story, and song, create male sexual partners and dismiss them; distinguish themselves from other, less powerful women who would be hoodwinked by those false polygamous males; and create ties with still other women.

Those effects cross into the way the story alludes to its own racial valences. The brevity, coupled with evident enjoyment, of Howard's performance of this tale points us back to our light-skinned husband, to Howard's chuckling about him and her allusion to her mother's joke about whites as milt. Jacobs concludes that the story "exemplifies one kind of humor which Clackamas resorted to in order to ventilate their anger toward Caucasians."[63] Somewhat surprisingly, he also asserts, "Every Indian informant I have worked with in Oregon and Washington . . . assured me that lighter skins had been preferred in pre-Caucasian times."[64] Possibly this reflects another use of myth, in that the stories' didacticism resided not just in showing how the world was made or in modeling proper behavior but also in showing *improper* behavior, for Howard often remarks that the characters of myth "were very foolish." Yet another possibility is astutely suggested by Ramsey, following Hymes: "Probably there is a sense of satisfaction in being able to name the situation of the presence of a white as one encompassed by Indian tradition stretching back before whites came. Certainly there is satisfaction in being able to entertain the proposition, through quotation of myth, that whites are shameful and that a widow could both conjure them up for sexual satisfaction and dismiss them."[65]

Of all of the ways that Howard's stories generate resistance, however, one of the most striking is the way they resist critical efforts to seal them up, patronizingly, as minor expressions of frustration with the long, painful, and ongoing business of colonization and racism. Such readings are ethically motivated in that they seek to understand how stories intervene in this history, but they are dangerous when they purport to have resolved the story's meaning and use. Howard's non-repetition of the song in this telling (given that she does repeat songs in other, less charged, stories), together with her laughter, the cryptic comment "he must have been a half-breed," and her later reference to her mother-in-law's use of the story to mock passing whites—all these elements point to uses of this story such as those that Jacobs, Hymes, and Ramsey have described. And yet they also point to a field of usage much larger than that suggested by the print version. These elements use the literate medium, the moment of transcription and translation, to *transmit* an anti-white use of the story at the same time that they partially conceal the use of the story. They point, once again, to that broader "territory of orality," a territory that can never be more than glimpsed in a printed transcription of oral tales and to which the reader of this printed transcription cannot have access. Howard's texts do less, I think, to encourage conclusions like "this must have been how Indians vented their anger" than they do to illustrate that, quite without the aid of ethnographic textualization, Clackamas people textualized their own culture in highly dynamic and complicated ways.

Ethnographic collections, as the Howard-Jacobs texts remind us, are not simply the record of what elderly speakers of Native languages could remember of their people's oral traditions. Recalling Hymes's observation that "the persistence of the tradition disclosed in performances" is all about people's continuing ethical uses of narrative, we might qualify that insight now by adding that the Howard-Jacobs texts also underscore "the persistence of tradition *not* disclosed in performances." Howard has a penchant for stories that will strike outsiders as highly "Other," for avoiding extensive cross-cultural explanation, for leaving things unintelligible, and for indicating where oral practice exceeds the written representation of that practice. We can explain such moments by way of Jacobs's desire for the "unacculturated," but we can also see them as a kind of American Indian assertion of cultural difference and viability, a refusal of the assimilation that is part of translation. We can also see these moments as further instances of Weaver's notion of communitism, in that they reveal an activist commitment to indigenous community in their self-preserving rehearsal of practices and narratives that have long enabled Indian peoples to survive.

Collections like *Clackamas Chinook Texts* have been, nevertheless, highly controversial. I have praised Jacobs for his faithfulness to Howard's words, but it is really impossible to reconstruct exactly how faithful he was. And while I have praised the collection's ability to call attention to its own limitations, critics of these ethnographic collections find them pernicious precisely because they purport to reveal or contain sacred traditions. Leslie Marmon Silko is perhaps the most blunt:

> [S]ince white ethnologists like Boas and Swanton first intruded into Native American communities to "collect" prayers, songs and stories, a number of implicit racist assumptions about Native American culture and literature have flourished. The first is the assumption that the white man, through some innate cultural or racial superiority, has the ability to perceive and master the essential beliefs, values and emotions of persons from Native American communities. . . . The second . . . is that the prayers, chants, and stories weaseled out by the early white ethnographers, which are now collected in ethnological journals, are public property.[66]

Those piles of ethnological journals, many now languishing on dusty library shelves, create definite dilemmas. Some include private and unethically published materials, and most pretend to capture or reveal a tradition that they come nowhere near representing ethically or with anything like accuracy. At the same time, such texts are a fact of American Indian literary production in the late nineteenth and early twentieth centuries. Countless Indian people, many of them women, sat down with ethnographers, with varying motivations, to record what some felt was a passing culture. While many people may have felt coerced into participating, others could also convert that experience of translation and trans-cription into creative expression and resistance.

What is remarkable about Victoria Howard's texts is not what Jacobs "weaseled" out of her, but what he didn't. She alludes to sacred practices without describing them in depth; she evades some of his demands for specific kinds of material. In so doing, she helps illuminate the very cultural blindness that Silko attacks—the notion of whites' "ability to perceive and master the essential beliefs, values and emotions of persons from Native American commun-ities." If we avoid the temptation to approach transcribed oral narratives as "real" tradition, as the unmediated record of some authentic indigenous voice, they emerge instead as the product of a conversation, an often asymmetrical conversation, between two people and two cultures. They have much to reveal about that asymmetrical encounter, and in turn about the encounters of reading and speaking; they also have something to say about American Indians' resources for cultural expression and about the ability to protect that cultural expression from usurpation.

There is at least one more way that Howard's strategically unreadable narratives resist assimilation, and that is the way they resist the assimilative work of the literary critic trying to incor-porate them into the American literary canon. Literature antholo-gies now almost uniformly stake out indigenous literatures as the "original" literatures of the United States; take, for example, the odd concentration of Indian oral narrative at the very beginning of The Heath Anthology, which suggests that oral narrative was only told before Europeans descended on the continent and that only Indians told oral stories. Hymes, too, is eager to claim Indian liter-ature as "the first literature of North America."[67]

But canon revision, to which this book obviously hopes to con-tribute, should never be just additive. The value in "rediscovering" forgotten authors, texts, and genres lies, indeed, not just in expanding the canons we already have or in subsuming Indian literatures into some pre-existing ideal, but in changing our ways of reading, in shaking up the way we think about the category of "Literature," and in giving us new models for understanding how texts do their cultural work. Reading texts like Victoria Howard's alongside those of authors who were more conventionally *writing*, we can get a view of works like *Ramona* and *Life Among the Piutes* as literal dialogues. Like Howard's sessions with Jacobs, these texts are cross-cultural, communicative encounters. They do not simply transmit Indian culture and an Indian aesthetic to non-Indians; nor are they wholly compromised reflections of little more than the colonizer's desires. They are instead intense, constant negotiations with readers, and in reading these negotiations, we can learn to read ourselves a little bit better.

THE POLITICS AND PERILS OF REPRESENTING TRIBAL DISCOURSE

One of the threads in this reading of Helen Hunt Jackson, Sarah Winnemucca, and Victoria Howard has been a series of questions about reading itself—how to read such women, why to read them, and what is at stake in reading them for specific political ends. The literary profession has long been divided over such questions, witnessing an apparent conflict between readings that are "true to the text," that purport to discover a work's seemingly innate patterns and rationales, and readings that are political, that advance particular interpretations of literature for particular ends. As many writers have observed, this is largely a false opposition. Critics who imagine or present themselves as above or beyond politics, like T. S. Eliot in his insistence that high art is essentially fragmentary and anti-emotional, can actually be highly political insofar as they help shape a canon that excludes other kinds of writers and works. Meanwhile, politically motivated critics, like the feminists who have championed and resuscitated the nineteenth-century sentimental novel, have helped to give us a richer picture of literary history itself and indeed of what and how literature does its work. Their readings have helped us appreciate not only the enormous political import of books like *Uncle Tom's Cabin* but also their aesthetics—the governing patterns that make these works worthy of study as literature.

Scrupulous critics therefore try to keep the two goals in sight, trying to read both accurately and ethically. In that spirit, this book tries to provide a more precise picture of literary history by locating a resistance to assimilation that has not been hitherto heard or acknowledged. Writers and storytellers at the turn of the century imagined and rendered a whole host of social issues—women's suffrage, immigration, industrialization, reconstruction, and economic dispossession. Unfortunately, their imaginings of Indian cultural persistence in the face of assimilation campaigns have been omitted from literary history, an omission this book seeks to redress.

My argument has been that resistance to assimilation may have taken different literary forms, like ethnography and oral narrative, as well as different rhetorical forms, like cagey silence or an indigenous aesthetic, which are not ultimately invested in cultural self-representation. This phenomenon is not peculiar to the Era of Assimilation, though it has operated as an historically situated response. Contemporary writer Sherman Alexie, for example, has said, "We all know our religion is not meant for the page, not meant for mass consumption."[1] If American Indian authors seek alternative modes of representation, readers will need new methods to call out tribalism as resistance. Like so much else in the world, literature is usually full of conflict and contradiction, and so a reading that locates indigenous resistance to assimilation will sometimes actively foreground apparently muted traces of that resistance against a text's or storyteller's evident concessions to Euro-American values.

Such strategic foregrounding can have its own dangers. Some scholars have taken issue with reading for resistance on the grounds that it, too, can be a kind of appropriation. As Betty Louise Bell has warned, "[I]f we are truly to decolonize the representation of indigenous peoples and not simply locate them in positions of reaction to Western history, then we must allow ourselves to discover their actual and original contributions to the telling of history."[2] To claim that every moment where Winnemucca and Howard "fail" to deliver a story as Euro-Americans might expect amounts to "resistance" is to fall into the trap of always putting Americans Indians in relation to white people—a subordinate relation. In such a reading, Indians resist because they can do little else, not because they have their own complex modes of storytelling and ways of seeing. We cannot afford to ignore these ways of telling and seeing, even if we cannot decipher them precisely; indeed, my argument has been that many times they are not intelligible to non-tribal readers or to readers at an historical distance.

At the same time, saying that Victoria Howard didn't give Melville Jacobs the autobiography he was looking for simply because "Indians don't talk about themselves" is to risk occluding the historical and political circumstances under which she told her stories. Reading for resistance and reading Native aesthetics in concert with that resistance are a necessary part of approaching these women accurately and ethically. Such approaches acknowledge the *social* conditions of narrative production. Winnemucca and Howard did not create their texts in a pristine cultural arena, devoid of their audiences' influence, any more than any other author (among canonical authors, Twain springs to mind) could work independently of cultural and economic forces. Reading for resistance thus acknowledges the long histories of oppression and dispossession to which American Indian narratives are responses, and amidst which they are forms of cultural expression and survival.

I began from the premise that American literary history contains little or no record of resistance to Indian assimilation—resistance in the sense of what Warrior calls nationalist, treaty-based forms of opposition; conservative assertions and delineations of tribal ways of life against Euro-American ones; and open rejections of the Era of Assimilation in general and allotment in particular.[3] These kinds of resistance may not, and indeed, need not have existed textually. Indigenous people had other ways of resisting, from armed conflict to the private maintenance of sacred practice, that were just as powerful as written representations, if not more so.

To find written resistance, we need to expand both the kinds of texts we read and our ways of reading. Further, we may discover more resistance to Indian assimilation as more literary historians continue bringing forgotten works to light. One example is the ambitious project undertaken by Daniel Littlefield and James Parins in their bibliographic record of tribal newspapers. American Indian people writing for Indian audiences undoubtedly would have said different kinds of things about assimilation, told different kinds of stories.

Such recovery work has continued as I've worked on this book, and recent reprintings of early Native works also confirm the picture I'm drawing of resistance to assimilation. One especially important republication occurred in 1998, when the University of Nebraska, as part of its Native American authors series, reprinted what was until then an obscure archival text, Muscogee (Creek) S. Alice Callahan's *Wynema* (1891). This short novel draws on many conventions that will be familiar to readers of Jackson and Winnemucca. Its first chapters read almost like an ethnography, with chapters on Indian food, dancing, mourning rituals, and healing practices. Meanwhile, Callahan initiates several simultaneous plots: a developing friendship between white schoolteacher Genevieve Weir and her Indian student, Wynema; and parallel marriage plots for these two women (Genevieve marries the white missionary, Gerard Keithly, while Wynema is successfully wooed by Genevieve's brother, Robin). The last third of the novel, an apparent digression into the U.S. conflict with the Sioux over the Ghost Dance, stages several discussions among Genevieve, Gerard, Wynema, and other characters about U.S. Indian policy.

Wynema includes a chapter titled, dramatically enough for our purposes, "Shall We Allot?" In this, Genevieve avers that the policy "seems to me a plan by which the 'boomers' who were left out of Oklahoma are to be landed. For years the U.S. Senators and citizens have been trying to devise ways and means by which to divide the Indians' country."[4] As we have seen, very few people anywhere were willing or able to expose allotment's underlying goal of divesting American Indian peoples of still more land. Yet Genevieve articulates this radical argument to Wynema, who in turn makes an argument that could have come from an Indian Progressive like Zitkala-Sa or a white reformer like Carl Schurz:

> I don't see how dividing our lands can materially damage us. . . . We should have our own homes, and contrary to ruining our fortunes I think it would mend them. . . . There are so many idle, shiftless Indians who do nothing but hunt and fish; then there are others who are industrious and enterprising; so long as our land remains as a whole, in common, these lazy Indians will never make a move toward cultivating it. . . . while, if the land were allotted, do you not think that these idle Indians, knowing the land to be their own, would have pride enough to cultivate their land and build up their homes? (pp. 50–51)

Genevieve rapidly persuades Wynema to see the error of this position. Setting the white woman up as the naive Indian's corrective is admittedly paternalistic, but it is also potentially radical, a strategy for rendering the message more audible to non-Native readers, perhaps, and moreover a drastic revision of the role of the white schoolteacher, who was historically one of assimilation's most avid agents. Genevieve does not exactly say that allotment would be a bad thing in itself, conceding that it would "do very well for the civilized tribes"; still, she argues:

> Laws are made for people and not people for laws. The South Sea Islander could not be governed by the laws of England, nor can the North American Indian become a fit subject of the United States. Do you not see, my friend, that if your land were divided, your territory would then become a state—a subject of the United States Government. Do you think the

western tribes sufficiently tutored in the school of civilization
to become citizens of the United States, subject to its laws and
punishments? (p. 52)

In the social-evolutionist 1890s, this looks surprisingly close to
an argument for cultural relativism or pluralism. Indians are not
yet "sufficiently tutored," not yet "fit" subjects, but this fitness is
not necessarily so much a question of their "readiness" or worth as
it is of their cultural *difference*, as suggested by the comparison to
South Sea Islanders and English imperialist law. Citizenship is not
presented here as a necessarily desirable end, for it would make
the Indian "a subject" of the American government, "subject to" its
laws and punishments. Indeed, Genevieve acknowledges Indian
sovereignty when she warns against statehood's capacity to abridge
that sovereignty.

Callahan craftily turns pro-allotment rhetoric on its head,
painting Indians as "like" white people, not to show that they can
become "as good as" whites, but to suggest that they have equal
rights to self-determination and equally legitimate cultures. For
example, the novel deploys the ideal of Indian educability sub-
versively: Wynema reads Shakespeare, Dickens, and Tennyson;
Genevieve talks of teaching the Indians ancient (Western) languages and higher mathematics; some of the older Indians write
political letters. To so many white reformers, such images would
have underscored the idea that Indians could become civilized;
they would have proved that Indians could one day become fit
citizens of the United States. But as Callahan's book proceeds and
its Indian characters seem to become more educated and civilized,
they also begin to use their newfound skills for other, more subversive ends. They write letters to protest U.S. government action,
they ponder the possibilities and limitations of cross-cultural
alliances, and they eloquently assert their own resistance, as does
Chief Wildfire, repeating a message revealed to him by the bodies
of slain Indians:

[T]hey told me we had suffered long enough at the hands of the white man; they cried out for revenge; they told me to fight the pale-faces until they or I lie bleaching in the sun, as those dead bodies were; but they told me to *never*, NEVER listen to a tale of peace, even if told by a friend. Peace! Let those talk of peace who live in quiet homes, who are surrounded by friends and loved-ones, happiness and affection; but peace is not the watchword of the oppressed. (p. 82)

This speech, which renders speechless the benign white negotiator visiting Wildfire, shows the same concerns we have seen in Jackson, Winnemucca, and Howard over what kinds of resistance are available to Indian peoples when white settlers have closed off all options.

In addition to her stark and open disagreements with allotment and assimilation, Callahan shares with Jackson, Winnemucca, and Howard cagey silences and indigenous aesthetics. Like *Ramona*, *Life Among the Piutes*, and many of Victoria Howard's stories, *Wynema* thematizes communication and translatability. Translating Indian culture into white terms seems to be a necessary rhetorical strategy for securing some kind of cross-cultural sympathy and respect for Indians. The missionary Keithly, therefore, explains medicine men in terms of Western healing and discusses Indian women in terms of Victorian modesty. This translating is also a kind of assimilation, one that renders indigenous practices intelligible in terms *only* acceptable or non-threatening to white culture, and *Wynema* seems both drawn to and nervous about that translation process. For example, its first chapters use ethnographic convention only to question it, to dwell on what cannot be told. Genevieve complains that she "could find no one to explain so that I could understand" (p. 17); she is presented with a soup with "an unspellable name" (p. 11); a medicine man's actual words "could not be told by any of the Indians" (p. 13); and things like distances "could not be exactly told for an Indian never measures distance"

(p. 15). When Genevieve inquires about a mourning practice, Wynema replies, "The death-chant? How can I tell you, Mihia? It begins by telling the good deeds of the dead person; of his virtues; what a good hunter he was; how brave he always was; and ends by carrying him over the mountain side to the happy hunting-ground, there to live forever, among dogs and horses, with bows and arrows and game of all kinds in abundance" (p. 24). Like Wild-fire's speech, which marks an impasse in his colloquy with the white mediator, Wynema's account turns on a question about the impossibility of transparent communication. Callahan incorporates Indian self-representation of indigenous practices into her novel, but she does so in ways that turn on misgivings about the possibility of explaining and that don't explicate those practices in the expected or desired ways.

Like other women of the period, then, Callahan oscillates between rendering Indian practice intelligible and keeping it veiled, between showing that Indians are "just like us" and wanting to insist that they are not like us. She balances mediation with resistance. These women who write and tell stories about Indians during the Era of Assimilation, we have seen, attempt to make legible the otherwise strange: painting American Indian agrarian land use in highly Anglocentric terms of property, as does *Ramona*, or describing tribal councils and consensus as being like the U.S. Congress, as does *Life Among the Piutes*. But they are even more compelling when they announce the impossibility of such mediation—when they announce the presence of cultural materials they will *not* translate or reveal, as Winnemucca and Howard do when they merely allude to further oral or sacred traditions. To indicate that a tribal practice exists without fulfilling the vociferous demand of Euro-American audiences for annotation is a powerful gesture, for it not only radically asserts that these practices are viable and con-tinuing but it also ironically keeps the door open to cross-cultural communication. Jackson, Winnemucca, and Howard may be skep-tical of their interlocutors, may wish to keep them at arm's length, but they do, extraordinarily, keep talking, and in ways that try to instruct readers and reconstruct communities. They thus show an impulse to use distinctly communicative media for communicative purposes—to express one's culture and one's "self" or community—at the same time as they disrupt common notions of "communication," "self," "culture," and "expression."

When Callahan refuses mediation she, like her contemporaries, does so less to widen the rift between Indian and non-Indian than to explore the conditions that have created that rift and to explore how it might be more honestly reckoned with. Thus, she builds her novel around interracial alliances, especially among women. The friendship between Genevieve and Wynema is not without its imbalances, reminiscent of those in Ramona's talks with Aunt Ri and Carmena, in Winnemucca's work with Mary Mann and her appeal to white suffragists, and in Howard's stories of her mother-in-law learning from the "Boston woman." But this friendship is a voluntary feminist affiliation across cultures that begins to move toward mutual cultural recognition and toward the breakdown of many hierarchies—racial, sexual, and national. Like the relationships between women described by Jackson, Winnemucca, and Howard, that between Wynema and Genevieve begins to explore the politics and conditions that have made cross-cultural communication so vexed.

Callahan points expressly to the subversive potential of this alliance, and to the changes it induces in Genevieve, when she has the schoolteacher's scurrilous fiancé declare, "I do not want my wife to stock her mind with sentiments that, if held by all, would be injurious to the commonwealth" (p. 55). Women who wrote and told stories about Indians during the Era of Assimilation and who did so in a way that insisted on an examination of the power structures that enabled and disabled certain forms of speech at the expense of others were precisely this—injurious to the commonwealth that was trying to enclose, absorb, and ultimately disavow the indigenous nations within its borders.

NOTES

PREFACE

1.   I am using the term *American Indian*—as well as the whole range of vexed terms such as *Indian, non-Indian, Paiute, Clackamas Chinook,* and *tribal*—advisedly and guardedly. I am also using them interchangeably and flexibly, in an attempt to honor a variety of preferences. For these terms are always contested; far from representing "real" essences, they work to represent people in certain ways for certain purposes. Among many people, the preferred usage is the tribal name rather than more totalizing designations, for instance, and so I try to use terms such as *Paiute* wherever possible. At the same time, I acknowledge that even these can be problematic. In the Pacific Northwest, where intermarriage has crossed so many linguistic and geographic boundaries, many indigenous peoples and anthropologists prefer to use broader terms like *Lower Columbia*. I try to use *Clackamas*, then, when referring to the language or when following Melville Jacobs's lead, and *Chinookan* or *Lower Columbian* when referring to indigenous peoples of coastal Oregon. At still other times a larger term

such as *American Indian* is in fact desirable, as when I am talking about the kinds of things that diverse indigenous peoples do share—most notably, material dispossession and histories as the targets of assimilationist and racist policies and practices that have treated them as though they were all the same. As James Clifford says of the term *culture*, then, I must say for now that *American Indian*, along with other similar terms, is a "compromised idea I cannot yet do without" (*The Predicament of Culture*, 10).

As for the word *tribe*, I use it following Vine Deloria's observation that the modern sense of the word in fact came from the 1934 Indian Reorganization Act, which prompted remnants of larger historical tribal groups on reservations to collectively self-govern as "tribes" (*Custer Died for Your Sins*, 16).

2. *Paiutes* is currently the most widely used spelling.

3. Forbes, "Intellectual Self-Determination and Sovereignty," 20.

INTRODUCTION

1. Hoxie, *A Final Promise*, 4 ff. Standing Bear went on a lecture tour in the East to drum up support for his landmark civil-rights case, which he was trying to bring to court. He did finally win *Standing Bear v. Crook*, in which Nebraska District Court Judge Elmer Dundy decided that an Indian was a person, with the right to sue for a writ of *habeas corpus* in court. For a contemporary account, see Tibbles, *The Ponca Chiefs*.

2. Helen Hunt Jackson, *A Century of Dishonor*, 346. Hoxie discusses the Ute case in *A Final Promise*, 5–6; for a more detailed account, see Brown, *Bury My Heart*, 367–89.

3. O'Brien, *American Indian Tribal Governments*, 78. Some American Indians therefore already had citizenship when the Indian Citizenship Act was passed in 1924. That act, according to Walter Benn Michaels, helped mark the failure of the assimilation effort; it kept Indians from *becoming* citizens by claiming they already *were*. It thus ironically normalized and marginalized Indians further while appearing to include them in the national polity. See Michaels, *Our America*, 30–32. For more on the Dawes Act, see D. S. Otis, *The Dawes Act and the Allotment of Indian Lands*; Loring Benson Priest, *Uncle Sam's Stepchildren*; and Wilcomb Washburn's excellent and concise book, *The Assault on Indian Tribalism*.

4. For a useful anthology of reformers' writings on allotment and assimilation, see Prucha, *Americanizing the American Indians*.

5. Trachtenberg, *The Incorporation of America*. Other useful overviews of the period include John Higham's *Strangers in the Land* and Jay Martin's *Harvests of Change*.

6. Earlier in the nineteenth century, Americans had tended to believe that Indians were fundamentally and ineradicably different from Europeans, that primitive peoples would never transcend their "lower stage." Hence, they could be isolated on reservations. As demand for land increased, however, this theory changed, and Americans began to call for patterns of settlement that were more integrated, at least superficially, so that Indians could "learn" from their white neighbors. The defining feature of "civilization," not surprisingly, turned out to be the acquisition and ownership of private property. In Morgan's teleology, "savages" owned nothing and foraged or hunted; "barbarians" had "progressed" to agriculture, owning common farms; and "civilized" people acquired land individually, "improving" it using complex machinery and domestic animals. See Hoxie, *A Final Promise*, 17–24. For more on Morgan and Powell, see Hinsley, *Savages and Scientists*; and Harris, *Rise of Anthropological Theory*, esp. chaps. 6–11.

7. Cited in Hoxie, *A Final Promise*, 24. Helen Hunt Jackson resided in Colorado while Teller was senator and had a friendly correspondence with him, sharing information on such matters as broken Ute treaties. This correspondence is reprinted in Mathes, ed., *Indian Reform Letters*.

8. Alternately praised by liberal historians like Brian Dippie and vilified by reactionaries like Dinesh D'Souza, Boas was a cultural relativist; his famous thesis was that the human mind was the same everywhere (as opposed to progressing in stages) and that differences among people were to be accounted for by culture and material circumstance. Boas is commonly described as reacting against the evolutionism of Morgan and Powell, and as bringing with him a strong antiracist, democratic impulse to counter evolutionary determinism. See, for example, Harris, *Rise of Anthropological Theory*, chap. 10.

9. Dippie, *The Vanishing American*, 274–79. For more on the Bursum Bill, see Lawrence C. Kelly, *The Assault on Assimilation*, 201–11, 296.

10. Quoted in Dippie, *The Vanishing American*, 316. For more on the IRA, see O'Brien, *American Indian Tribal Governments*, 82–83.

11. In *Native American Tribalism*, McNickle says the act "made explicit in statutory law for the first time the principle, which the courts had followed since Justice Marshall's rulings in the 1830s, recognizing the residual right of Indians to govern themselves. In this respect the 1934 act

was an integral segment of the humanistic tradition started by Spain, advanced by England, and incorporated into the early laws and court decisions of the American republic" (94). See also Warrior, *Tribal Secrets*, 20. In Vine Deloria's more mixed assessment: "[O]verall the IRA was a comprehensive piece of legislation which went far beyond previous efforts to develop tribal initiative and responsibility, but one provision was unfortunate. Once having voted down the acceptance of the provisions in the act, a reservation was forbidden from considering it again." See *Custer Died for Your Sins*, 48. Brian Dippie also notes many protests against the act: Prominent American Indian leaders like Arthur Parker and members of the Five Civilized Tribes adamantly opposed the IRA on the grounds that it was separatist; a group including Elaine Goodale, a white poet and activist who married the Sioux physician Charles Eastman, accused Collier of wanting to keep Indians entrenched; and in 1978, the activist magazine *Akwesasne Notes* condemned the act as part of a long history of governmental attempts to "terminate" American Indians. See *The Vanishing American*, 319–20. Additionally, some people interviewed at the Grand Ronde reservation in Oregon, where Victoria Howard lived, expressed dissatisfaction with the IRA, even though Grand Ronde had voted to accept it (Berreman, GRNR II, p. 94).

12.   For a fascinating account of how artistic representations, including some literary representations, of American Indians changed during the period, see Hoxie, *A Final Promise*, 85–103. Reading World Fair exhibits, for example, Hoxie finds that reform-minded displays (showing live Indians in schoolrooms, among other spectacles) elicited sympathy and an optimism that American Indians' fate was a national responsibility; by the second decade of the twentieth century, however, static, romanticized Indians à la James Fenimore Cooper had come back into vogue, suggesting that the idea of extinction had again supplanted that of assimilation in the popular imagination.

13.   Dippie, *The Vanishing American*, 312.

14.   Zitkala-Sa, "Why I Am a Pagan," 803.

15.   Warrior, *Tribal Secrets*, 11.

16.   Francis LaFlesche, "An Indian Allotment," 2688.

17.   DeCora, "The Sick Child." Originally in *Harper's Monthly* (February 1899), 446–48. Reprinted in Peyer, ed., *The Singing Spirit*. For Peyer's interpretation, see xiii.

18.   Suzette LaFlesche, "Nedawi." Originally in *St. Nicholas* (January 1881), 225–30. Reprinted in Peyer, *The Singing Spirit*, 3–13.

19. Ibid., 9.

20. Ibid., 5.

21. Ibid., 3.

22. Ibid., 4.

23. Ruppert, *Mediation*, 3. Another well-known book on this topic is Margaret Connell Szasz, ed., *Between Indian and White Worlds*. I will discuss mediation and critics' use of the idea in more depth in my chapter on Sarah Winnemucca.

24. Ruppert, *Mediation*, 4.

25. Ibid., 16.

26. Weaver, *That the People Might Live*, 35.

27. LaFlesche, "Nedawi," 12.

28. Ibid., 13.

29. See, for example, the essays in *Writing Culture*, ed. James Clifford and George E. Marcus.

30. DeCora, "The Sick Child," 45.

31. Some of the best known examples in women's literature are Nina Baym's *Woman's Fiction*; Hazel Carby's *Reconstructing Womanhood*, on African-American women writers; and Elizabeth Ammons's *Conflicting Stories*, which strives for the most multicultural approach.

32. Weaver, *That the People Might Live*, 43.

33. LaFlesche, "Nedawi," 6.

34. See, for example, Bhabha, *The Location of Culture*. A helpful introduction to postcolonial theory is Ashcroft, Griffiths, and Tiffin, eds., *The Empire Writes Back*.

35. Clifford, *The Predicament of Culture*, 12.

36. Ibid., 10.

37. The best-known articulation of strategic essentialism is Diana Fuss's *Essentially Speaking*. For a cogent critique of Fuss, see hooks, *Teaching to Transgress*, 77–92.

38. Batker, "'Overcoming All Obstacles,'" 190.

39. Hedges, "The Development of Women's Narrative," 34. In her *American Women Writers and the Work of History*, Nina Baym observes that "[we] may find in time that representations of female selves as privatized and domesticated beings are actually minority strands in American women's literature, owing their prominence to present-day occupations" (4).

40. Ammons, *Conflicting Stories*, 138.

41. Warrior, *Tribal Secrets*, 44.

42.   Silko, "An Old-Time Indian Attack Conducted in Two Parts"; Tedlock, "On The Translation of Style in Oral Narrative," chap. 1 in *The Spoken Word*, 31–61; and Sarris, *Keeping Slug Woman Alive*, esp. 35–84.

43.   See Gates, *The Signifying Monkey*; Hine, "Rape and the Inner Lives"; Miller, "Emphasis Added." Another interesting example is Seeiwong Oh's concept of "strategic defamiliarization," as described in "Cross-Cultural Reading versus Textual Accessibility."

44.   Kaplan, "The Erotics of Talk," 118.

45.   Sarris, *Keeping Slug Woman Alive*, 23.

46.   Lynch and Warner, eds., *Cultural Institutions*, 4.

47.   Ibid.

48.   Razack, *Looking White People in the Eye*, 10.

CHAPTER 1

1.   From a letter to Thomas Wentworth Higginson, dated January 17, 1880; widely cited. This letter and others cited in this chapter are now available in Mathes, *Indian Reform Letters*. See p. 84.

2.   Also widely cited; letter to an unknown recipient, dated January 22, 1885. In Mathes, *Indian Reform Letters*, 341. In a letter to Thomas Bailey Aldrich, dated December 1, 1884, Jackson also used medicinal language, saying she wanted readers to "swallow a big dose" of information on the Indian issue without knowing it. *Indian Reform Letters*, 337.

3.   Biographer Ruth Odell provides a thorough discussion of Jackson's pseudonyms, which included not only "H. H." but also "Marah," "Saxe Holm," and even "Rip Van Winkle." For a more recent and nuanced discussion of Jackson's shifting and very strategic uses of pseudonyms, see Susan Coultrap-McQuin's chapter on Jackson in her book *Doing Literary Business*, 138–66. Denial of authorship was not only a feminine mode of self-concealment but also a literary game and marketing strategy; for the most part, readers knew that Jackson was behind the pseudonyms. For more on this subject, see Catharine Hale Phillips's dissertation on Jackson. For discussion of a short-lived rumor that Emily Dickinson collaborated with Jackson on the "Saxe Holm" stories, see Richard Sewall, *Life of Emily Dickinson*, 223.

4.   Seltzer, *Bodies and Machines*, 3.

5.   Ibid., 81.

6.   Helen Hunt Jackson, *Ramona*, 216. Hereafter, all references to this novel will be cited parenthetically in the text.

7.   Jackson and friends frequently and self-consciously described her writing of *Ramona* in terms reminiscent of Stowe's "possession" while writing *Uncle Tom's Cabin*; Jackson was reportedly driven to write her novel extremely fast—up to three thousand words a morning—with spates of nervous prostration in between. See Mathes, *Helen Hunt Jackson*, 79.

8.   Readers who know Jackson well might be surprised at my ready search for feminist valences in her work. Earlier in her career she had publicly pitted herself against agitators for women's rights, with diatribes like the following: "There is an evil fashion of speech which says it is a narrowing and narrow life that a woman leads who cares only for her husband and children; that a higher, more imperative thing is that she herself be developed to her utmost." Quoted in Banning, *Helen Hunt Jackson*, 99–100. At times Jackson can sound like a nineteenth-century Phyllis Schlafly, but she was also a canny self-marketer and relied heavily on positioning herself as an embattled female voice. Moreover, I operate from the premise that Jackson's texts may have feminist resonances whether she intended them or not.

9.   See Custer, "Comulos." Comulos was a ranch that Jackson visited before writing the novel and on which she reportedly based the home of Señora Moreno. See also George Wharton James's *Through Ramona's Country*, one of the most famous Ramona-tourism books, published in 1909. For more detailed discussion of the circulation of Jackson's novel in popular culture, see Antoinette May's *Annotated Ramona* and Michele Moylan, "Reading the Indians."

10.   The films, all titled *Ramona*, include a silent directed by D. W. Griffith and starring Mary Pickford (1910); a version that inspired a hit song, starring Dolores Del Rio and Warner Baxter (1928); and another starring Loretta Young and Don Ameche (1936). The Ramona pageant plays every spring in Hemet, California; for information write The Ramona Pageant, 27400 Ramona Bowl Road, Hemet, CA 92544-8108.

11.   Nevins, "Helen Hunt Jackson," 284; Dorris, introduction to *Ramona*, xvii.

12.   Tompkins, *Sensational Designs*, xi.

13.   In chapter 3, the novel fills in Ramona's complicated history, which the Señora manages to keep secret from her until Alessandro gets involved in the household. Ramona was born to an unnamed Indian woman and a Scots seaman, Angus Phail—an apparent lapse of judgment on the latter's behalf ("he realized to the full how wickedly he had thrown away his life" [27]). Wanting the baby to be brought up properly, Phail takes Ramona to his former lover, the beautiful noblewoman Ramona

Gonzaga, dismissing the child's mother as unimportant ("She has other children, of her own blood. This is mine" [27]). When Ramona Gonzaga dies, the care of the child reverts to her sister, the Señora Moreno; but Ramona, who is naturally (i.e., by nature and predictably) noble, gets a legacy of riches. As Phail's comments illustrate, the book deploys a fascinating and complex range of attitudes toward miscegenation: It clearly demonizes characters who repudiate interracial unions, like the man Ramona Gonzaga haplessly marries, who calls the baby an "Indian brat" (29) and—at times—the Señora, who dislikes "crosses." At the same time, its erasure of Ramona's Indian mother can only be called horrific.

14.   Roy Harvey Pearce, in his *Savagism and Civilization*, was one of the first to argue that nineteenth-century literature established noble/evil savage dichotomies as a way of justifying genocide; by killing off their savages, many plays and poems relegated Indians to prehistory. Pearce's thesis has been variously taken up by scholars including Robert Berkhofer, Richard Drinnon, Richard Slotkin, Paula Gunn Allen, and William Scheick. Scheick argues that novelistic uses of mixed-blood characters showed Indians moving toward extinction (*The Half-Blood*, 1).

15.   See Shipek, "History of Southern California Mission Indians," 613. In *Indians, Franciscans, and Spanish Colonization*, Robert Jackson and Edward Castillo describe the early southern California economy as based on hunting, fishing, collecting wild plants; skillful resource management through techniques like grassland burning; and stratification of roles through gender and social status. Lowell Bean calls the Cahuillas, who appear in this novel, "proto-agricultural." Alessandro is said to be Luiseño; to this tribe, according to Bean and Shipek, "the concept of private property was important and violation of trespass on these areas was seriously punished," ("Luiseno," 551). Throughout their histories with Mexican and Anglo-American colonizers, Mission Indians maintained traditional settlement patterns and economies that combined agriculture and hunting, while incorporating Catholic and other non-Indian customs.

16.   On the popular fascination with southern California, see Starr, *Inventing the Dream*; and McWilliams, "Southern California."

17.   In one of the novel's characteristic contradictions, however, Aunt Ri remarks that he and Ramona are "dark's any nigger" (286).

18.   Andrew Jackson, "Second Annual Message to Congress," December 6, 1830, quoted in Takaki, *Iron Cages*, 101.

19.   Quoted in Prucha, ed., *Americanizing the American Indians*, 115.

20.   Quoted in Hoxie, *A Final Promise*, 34.

21. See Bannan, "'True Womanhood.'"

22. Quoted in Prucha, *Americanizing the American Indians*, 46.

23. Ibid., 34.

24. Priest, *Uncle Sam's Stepchildren*, 189.

25. Quoted in Prucha, *Americanizing the American Indians*, 85.

26. In a December 23, 1879, letter to the *New York Tribune*, Jackson attacked Carl Schurz for suggesting that non-Indians should be permitted to harvest hay and other products from Ute lands that the Utes weren't "using." In Mathes, *Indian Reform Letters*, 57.

27. Even the minority report of the House Committee on Indian Affairs in 1880, objecting to allotment, stated: "This communistic idea has grown into their very being and is an integral part of the Indian character. From our point of view this is all wrong; but it is folly to think of uprooting it . . . through the agency of a mere act of Congress." Quoted in Otis, *Dawes Act*, 54.

28. The Schurz-Jackson correspondence was reprinted in Jackson, *A Century of Dishonor*. This letter, dated January 17, 1880, appears on pp. 361–62.

29. Washburn gives a helpful list of actual alternatives to allotment and reasons these were not pursued; *Assault on Indian Tribalism*, 3–4.

30. Harsha, *Ploughed Under*, 4.

31. Ibid., 5.

32. Washburn, *Assault on Indian Tribalism*, 10.

33. Priest, *Uncle Sam's Stepchildren*, 207.

34. See Wald's fascinating discussion of *Cherokee Nation v. State of Georgia* in her *Constituting Americans*, 20–47.

35. Hoxie, *A Final Promise*, 75. For a fuller chronology of the case, see Bodayla, "Can an Indian Vote?"

36. Quoted in Mathes, *Helen Hunt Jackson*, 93.

37. Washburn, *Assault on Indian Tribalism*, 13. Washburn's characterization of Fletcher's early reaction suggests that her thinking about allotment was vexed: she may have been concerned not only that 160 acres wouldn't have been enough for some people in some areas but also that it might have been too much for others.

38. Mark, *Stranger*, 73.

39. Dated December 11, 1879. In Mathes, *Indian Reform Letters*, 35–36.

40. Odell, *Helen Hunt Jackson*, 162; Rolle, introduction to *A Century of Dishonor*, xi.

41. Washburn, *Assault on Indian Tribalism*, 7.

42. Quoted in Mardock, *The Reformers*, 213.

43. Ibid., 186.

44. January 22, 1880. Reprinted in Helen Hunt Jackson, *A Century of Dishonor*, 363–64; Mathes, *Indian Reform Letters*, 86–87.

45. *New York Times*, February 21, 1880. Reprinted in Helen Hunt Jackson, *A Century of Dishonor*, 368.

46. Reprinted in *A Century of Dishonor*, 466–67.

47. Ibid., 467.

48. Ibid.

49. Quoted in Prucha, *Americanizing the American Indians*, 80.

50. The National Indian Defense Association is often cited as one of the few groups supporting the idea that Indians should decide their own fates. And yet George Manypenny, one of its staunchest proponents and a former Commissioner of Indian Affairs who had vigorously defended reservations against white encroachment, could also implore his readers to "let [the Indian] have a fixed and settled home" (with the important addendum that "the Indian women must cease to do the outdoor work") and write, "As the habit of roaming must cease, and all Indians have their fixed homes, the young of both sexes will always be within reach, and then an inviting and interesting field will be open, not only for the work of the agent, but for the Christian missionary." Manypenny, *Our Indian Wards*, xxiv–xxvii.

51. Brodhead, *Cultures of Letters*, 137.

52. Starr, *Inventing the Dream*, 61.

53. For an excellent discussion of colonization and resistance at the missions, see Jackson and Castillo, *Indians, Franciscans, and Spanish Colonization*. Some writers, including Alfredo Mirandé and Evangelina Enríquez in *La Chicana*, attempt to argue that Spanish colonization wasn't "as bad" as American colonization. While the imperialism of the U.S. take-over of parts of Mexico in 1848 shouldn't be overlooked, nor the painful history this produced for chicano/as, mission life under the Franciscans and Jesuits can hardly be said to have been idyllic for the Indians.

54. Helen Hunt Jackson, *Glimpses of Three Coasts*, 54.

55. Ibid., 66–67.

56. Dorris, introduction to *Ramona*, xvi.

57. Dobie, "Helen Hunt Jackson," 95.

58. Thus Chopin's novel doesn't indict Edna for not being an artist like Mlle. Reisz or a good mother like Adele Ratignolle, but comments, though cryptically, on the limitations of a world in which a wife and

mother cannot express sexual longing and autonomy. Similarly, Lily Bart's cryptic death is just as much an attack on the economy that makes her an object of consumption as it is of her behavior as a consumer.

59.   For a fascinating discussion of how madness was construed as connected to psychological interiority in highly gendered and classed ways, see Tom Lutz's *American Nervousness*. For a literary work to grant a non-white person the ability to become mad was, from this point of view, a radical move.

60.   In *The Winning of the West*, Roosevelt laments that "the purely sentimental historians take no account of the difficulties under which we labored nor of the countless wrongs and provocations we endured, while grossly magnifying the already lamentably large number of injuries for which we really deserve to be held responsible" (81). Of *A Century of Dishonor* specifically, he says, "the purpose of the book is excellent, but the spirit in which it is written cannot be called even technically honest. . . . It is not too much to say that the book is thoroughly untrustworthy from cover to cover, and that not a single statement it contains should be accepted without independent proof"; hence, perhaps, this book became "much quoted by a large class of amiable but maudlin fanatics" (81–82).

61.   Hoxie, *A Final Promise*, 14.

62.   See Bhabha, *Nation and Narration*, 291; Anderson, *Imagined Communities*.

63.   Quoted in Prucha, *Americanizing the American Indians*, 101.

64.   Although we needn't doubt Jackson's sincerity about her cause, we can note that the "Indian" issue also gave her career a welcome boost. While she had generally enjoyed cordial and profitable relations with most of her editors, she was in the late 1870s estranged from Josiah Holland, then at *Scribner's*. He had rejected *Mercy Philbrick's Choice* (the prestigious *Century*'s Richard Watson Gilder likewise worried that it might "offend"). Thomas Niles's No Name series finally picked up the novel and, like her other Saxe Holm stories, it proved highly lucrative. Still, Holland's rejection agitated Jackson, and the novels never got the critical praise her poetry did—critical praise Jackson understandably longed for—and Saxe Holm was a name she distanced herself from until her death. By 1879, as Ruth Odell puts it, Saxe Holm was "worked out," and Jackson was "halfheartedly" continuing her travel sketches (151). Indian reform was just the tonic she needed.

65.   Helen Hunt Jackson, *Glimpses of Three Coasts*, 95.

66.   As Nina Baym puts it, following the philosopher Jürgen Haber-mas's conception of the public sphere, "if print formulates and consoli-dates public opinion, and women are printed, then they are part of the public sphere." Baym, *American Women Writers*, 6.

67.   For further discussion of women's reform movements in general and the WNIA in particular, see Pascoe, *Relations of Rescue*. Pascoe examines the ways that women used Victorian ideals of piety and purity not just to effect benevolence but also to oppose a male-dominated society; she is careful, however, to qualify their work as having "moral influence, not social power" (xvii).

68.   Not in equal numbers, of course; Helen Bannan offers some anecdotal evidence of American Indian field matrons ("'True Woman-hood,'" 9–10).

69.   Bannan, "'True Womanhood,'" 7–9.

70.   Ibid., 4.

71.   Ibid., 3.

72.   "Not Enough Sacrifice," *Southern Workman* (February 1885), 19.

73.   Hoxie, *A Final Promise*, 25.

74.   In Mathes, *Indian Reform Letters*, 55. To William Hayes Ward, dated December 20, 1879.

75.   Quoted in Mathes, *Helen Hunt Jackson*, 78.

76.   Ibid., 132.

77.   Ibid., 130ff.

78.   Mark, *Stranger*, 107.

79.   Ibid., 267.

80.   Ibid., 269.

81.   Letter to William Hayes Ward, editor of the New York *Inde-pendent*, dated January 1, 1884. In Mathes, *Indian Reform Letters*, 307.

82.   Tompkins, *Sensational Designs*, 145.

83.   Dorris, introduction to *Ramona*, xvii.

84.   It is important to qualify a reading of the Señora as "masking," however, with a firm recognition of the stereotype itself; disruptive though her strategy may be, the Señora is hooked to a familiar ster-eotype: black-clad, controlling, manipulative, and, even in her time of life, highly sexualized in her jealous overprotectiveness of her son. As Alfredo Mirandé and Evangelina Enríquez note in *La Chicana*, this character turns on gendered tropes of "Spanish temperament" (151–52). The Señora is finally destructive—and exotic—because of that Spanish pride.

85.   In his well-known study of late-nineteenth-century American writers who worked with dialect, Richard Bridgman suggests that in scenes like this, quotations and italics bracket "vulgar" voices from the more "distinguished" types surrounding them, relegating the dialect voice to a comic or grotesque role. And yet Jackson here clearly reverses that hierarchy. Aunt Ri's voice is hardly the "vulgar" party in the exchange with the Agent; it's the right voice for the situation. See Bridgman, *Colloquial Style*, 22.

86.   Helen Hunt Jackson, *Bits of Talk*, 194.

87.   Odell, *Helen Hunt Jackson*, 171.

88.   Tourgée, "Study in Civilization," 250. See also the anonymous review in the *Atlantic* of January 1885.

89.   To *Harper's* editor Charles Dudley Warner, December 25, 1884. In Mathes, *Indian Reform Letters*, 338.

90.   See Antoinette May's *Annotated Ramona* for a brief account of Sam Temple, the "real" murderer of "Alessandro," who promoted himself as such at World Fairs and other commercial events (203).

91.   At times, it is true, the implied author cannot resist stepping in, as when this voice remarks of the embittered Señora: "No wonder she believed the Americans thieves, and spoke of them always as hounds. The people of the United States have never in the least realized that the taking possession of California was not only a conquering of Mexico, but a conquering of California as well; that the real bitterness of the surrender was not so much to the empire which gave up the country, as to the country itself which was given up. Provinces passed back and forth in that way, helpless in the hands of great powers, have all the ignominy and humiliation of defeat, with none of the dignities or compensations of the transaction" (12–13).

92.   In this critics are influenced by Mikhail Bakhtin, who famously argues in *The Dialogic Imagination* that the novel is characteristically multivocal, embracing many different languages. It has become common in much literary criticism to yoke multivocality with political liberation, sometimes uncritically.

93.   Helen Hunt Jackson, *Glimpses of Three Coasts*, 44.

94.   It is important to note, though, that the novel's crisscrossing of voices renders Juan Canito's voice just as suspect and complicated as the Señora's. In these opening scenes, he histrionically bemoans the loss of the Señora's husband as head of the estate, and the book is generally sympathetic to a vision of the ranch under a benign Spanish patriarchal hand;

however, it also renders Juan Canito foolish and weak, as he tries hopelessly to shore up a sense of his own masculinity against the Señora's undeniable power. He is further mocked for his failure to share in the Señora's relatively elevated view of Indians, calling them "idle mooning louts" (p. 4). The novel frequently plays different kinds of racism off each other in this manner; here, the Spanish shepherd's failure to embrace Indian workers and their conversion directly calls up allotment-era discourse that insisted on the Indians' potential as civilizable material. In the end, Juan Canito grudgingly agrees that "it is a good thing for those poor Indian devils to get a bit of religion now and then; and it's like old times to see the chapel full of them kneeling" (p. 5). Compared to Juan Canito, the Señora is enlightened, and yet she will also serve as a foil for more racially progressive characters later in the novel.

CHAPTER 2

1.   In Helen Hunt Jackson, *A Century of Dishonor*, 396. This letter was originally printed in *Harper's*, May 1870.

2.   In 1849 the Bureau of Indian Affairs had been taken from the War Department and transferred to the Department of the Interior. The end of the Civil War, however, ushered in an increasingly fervent debate over whether the "persuasion" of Protestant reformers or the force of the military was the best means of "taking care" of the Indians—that is, of bringing them onto the reservation. The Grant Administration Peace Policy of 1869 was an effort to compromise between these two factions by giving appointments in the Indian agency to religious personnel and giving the army control over Indians who refused to stay on reservations—hence, Winnemucca's often sarcastic references to "that praying agent" and to the conflicts that arise as the Indians shuttle back and forth from military to agency "protection."

3.   Washburn, *Assault on Indian Tribalism*, 3.

4.   Sale, "Reconceptualizing America," 31–32.

5.   Winnemucca, *Life Among the Piutes*, 221. Subsequent citations from this work will appear parenthetically in the text.

6.   For a wonderful reading of Winnemucca's images, see Scherer, "Public Faces."

7.   In this, Indian women may actually have had an edge among women speakers, who failed to command large audiences until the time

of Ida B. Wells and Emma Goldman. See Kelley, *Private Woman, Public Stage*. In addition to Winnemucca and Suzette LaFlesche, Americans in the 1880s were familiar with Toby Riddle, or "Wi-ne-ma," veteran of the Modoc War and cousin to the famous Captain Jack. She toured the country in 1875 with Albert Meacham, a former peace commissioner. See Meacham, *Wi-ne-ma*.

8. Ronda, ed., *Letters*, 414. On Peabody and Mann, see also Tharp, *The Peabody Sisters*.

9. The attacks turned on Winnemucca's alleged untruthfulness and promiscuity. One sanctimonious writer describes paying her to have sex with him; another letter includes a news clipping from *The Bedrock Democrat* of Baker City, Oregon, which in turn cites a Nevada newspaper's account of "the Piute Princess, Sallie Winnemucca" who "has recently been making the atmosphere of Elko county decidedly torrid" (United States Office of Indian Affairs, "The Case of Sarah Winnemucca"). These letters, with their nested accusations, aimed to end Winnemucca's career as an interpreter at Malheur, where she had been a vocal critic of Agent William Rinehart, who replaced Parrish and provoked hostilities with the Paiutes with his corrupt management.

10. Ruoff, "American Indian Autobiographers," 262.

11. Ronda, *Letters*, 414, italics in original.

12. Canfield, 212–15.

13. Bruce Ronda, personal communication, June 2000.

14. Walker, *Indian Nation*, 142.

15. Lape, "'I Would Rather,'" 275.

16. Sale, "Reconceptualizing America," 30.

17. Ibid., 33.

18. Lukens, "Her 'Wrongs and Claims,'" 96.

19. Anderson, *American Indian Literature*, 125.

20. Ibid., 129.

21. Walker, *Indian Nation*, 141.

22. Quoted in Prucha, *Americanizing the American Indians*, 18–19.

23. Canfield, *Sarah Winnemucca*, 40.

24. Ibid., 36.

25. See, for example, Hinsley, *Savages and Scientists*; Rydell, *All the World's a Fair*.

26. Canfield, *Sarah Winnemucca*, 37, 39.

27. Ibid., 41.

28. Watson, *Silver Theatre*, 323.

29.   Canfield, *Sarah Winnemucca*, 41.

30.   Quoted in Canfield, *Sarah Winnemucca*, 41.

31.   This wasn't a singular discourse; a fear of "degradation" and "inauthenticity" frequently surfaces among non-native "sympathizers" when Indians franchise themselves. In a fascinating article on the I.laponki. (Seminole), for instance, Patsy West describes the resourcefulness of indigenous families who wanted to avoid becoming wards of the government— such things as alligator wrestling and sewn patchwork clothing gave them the means to continue to live semi-autonomously and govern themselves. But as West says, such activities "appeared 'degrading' to some, who did not see the Seminoles as clever, adaptable people engaged in a novel economy. The government only saw these Florida Indians shunning aid and not conforming to the current administration's plans to make them 'white.'" See West, "I.laponki.," 28.

32.   Canfield, *Sarah Winnemucca*, 43.

33.   This could be said of many—even most—autobiographies, however. Scholars of the genre have observed that autobiography is a relatively late arrival, literarily; some have argued that women autobiographers and autobiographers of color generate works that are less psychological, individualistic, and linear than do canonical writers of the self like Benjamin Franklin and Henry Adams. For examples of such scholarship, see the essays in *Life/Lines: Theorizing Women's Autobiography*, edited by Bella Brodzki and Celeste Schenck. On autobiography more generally, see Lejeune, *On Autobiography*.

34.   Georgi-Findlay, "Native American Women's Writing," 238. Historically, American Indian women represented a romantic adventuresomeness that appealed to self-proclaimed enlightened whites of both sexes. On white women activists' fascination with and use of images of egalitarian Indian cultures, see Landsman, "The 'Other' as Political Symbol." The status of women within Indian tribes has long been a subject of debate, both among Natives and non-Natives. Some American Indian critics, most notably Paula Gunn Allen, have maintained that indigenous cultures are gynocentric. Allen has been criticized for being overly essentialist, yet her argument was a potent antidote to the stereotypes, quite beneficial to the United States as a nation, that Indian societies are misogynistic—in Thomas Jefferson's words, that they "submit their women to uncommon drudgery," as though white women have never known dull and grueling work. Catherine Fowler and Sven Liljeblad write that traditional Paiute social organization was based on a division of labor, with men hunting

and women gathering seeds and roots. While group leaders tended to be men, shamans could be men or women ("Northern Paiute," 439–41). Martha Knack and Omer Stewart confirm this view, adding that despite the division of labor, cooperation between the sexes was strong (*As Long as the River Shall Run*, 23). It is likely that Paiute culture, like most others, had some practices that were oppressive to women and some that were not, and that these varied over time and place and were taken up and resisted by individual Paiute women in different ways. Thus, while we can worry over the "real" sources of the feminist moments in *Life Among the Piutes*—be they an essentially woman-centered Paiute culture, an essentially misogynistic Paiute culture, or Victorian women's projected desires—perhaps it is more useful to think of these moments as traces of the dialogue between women and cultures, and to consider what uses they may serve.

35. According to Katherine Gehm's biography, *Sarah Winnemucca*, thousands signed this petition (182).

36. However, even a passage like this could be ironically appropriated to shore up Euro-American identity; see Werner Sollors's excellent discussion of the cult of the cursing Indian in *Beyond Ethnicity* (119–25). Sollors notes that American audiences "liked even the 'anti-white' curse scenes in [nineteenth-century] Indian plays—as if they had been blessings!"

37. Nudelman, "Harriet Jacobs," 957.

38. Ibid., 947.

39. Quoted in Canfield, *Sarah Winnemucca*, 203.

40. See, for example, Sands, "Indian Women's Personal Narrative," 275; and Brumble, *American Indian Autobiography*, 62.

41. Stewart, "Sarah Winnemucca," 32. Albeit outside the scope of this project, those references to blacks are indeed fascinating. See, for instance, Winnemucca's description of the Indians' surprise on finding out what an apparition of some burning creatures really was: "Ha! ha! oh, what a laughable thing that was! It was two negroes wearing red shirts!" (8); and, quite different in tone, her account of Captain Truckee's refusal to ride with a white man who was whipping some blacks (23–24).

42. Tharp, *The Peabody Sisters*, 327.

43. Ruoff, "American Indian Autobiographers," 192.

44. Brumble, *American Indian Autobiography*, 67. Paiute contestation over Winnemucca's power and work has continued through the twentieth century. For example, *Karnee*, a 1936 WPA book narrated by Annie Lowry (1867–1943) and compiled by Lalla Scott (presented more or less as an as-

told-to narrative), tries to wrest control over Paiute history back from the Winnemuccas. It mocks Captain Truckee and Old Winnemucca and tries to install in their place a "Cap John" who, like Truckee, allegedly traveled with Fremont and who carried around a letter from that man. At certain points, Lowry directly contests Winnemucca's authority over Paiute history, saying, "You see, the historians got their information from the followers of Winnemucca or Natchez, and not from the followers of Cap John" (16). She also suggests that she herself was the first Paiute to go to school, an honor usually reserved for Sarah Winnemucca. In the summer of 1999, meanwhile, a display on Sarah Winnemucca at the Pyramid Lake Reservation visitors' center noted that she was a controversial figure, thought by some Paiutes to have done harm to her people.

45.   Lott, *Love and Theft*, 39.

46.   Knack and Stewart, *As Long as the River Shall Run*, 111.

47.   Cooper, *The Pioneers*, 13–14.

48.   Quoted in Meeker, *The Ute Massacre*, 21.

49.   Ibid.

50.   For a compelling contrast, see Standing Bear's account of the Ponca reservation before the forced removal; it is given over mainly to listing his possessions—"civilized" possessions like farming implements and cutlery—that were taken away from him (Tibbles, *The Ponca Chiefs*, 12–13). This underscores the dangers of romanticizing Indians as essentially communal or selfless or not interested in "property."

51.   Knack and Stewart, *As Long as the River Shall Run*, 110.

52.   Ibid., 109.

53.   Oytes, not incidentally, is also the "blackest" of the tribe (113). I would like to thank Jocelyn Barrett, a student at the University of Maine in Farmington in 1999, for writing a wonderfully incisive paper on Oytes that helped me see better how Winnemucca might be deploying him.

54.   Fowler, "Sarah Winnemucca," 40.

55.   A letter in the Office of Indian Affairs file on Winnemucca from the agent at Yakima refers to "that unfortunate letter" that Winnemucca brought him from Schurz—a letter he'd told her he couldn't honor (U.S. Office of Indian Affairs, "The Case of Sarah Winnemucca").

56.   Fowler, "Sarah Winnemucca," 39.

57.   James Clifford, "On Ethnographic Allegory" in *Writing Culture*, ed. Clifford and Marcus, 115.

58.   Hinsley, *Savages and Scientists*, 8.

59.   Fabian, *Time and the Other*, 112, 80, 81, 87.

60. Winnemucca, "The Pah-Utes," 108. Subsequent references will appear parenthetically in the text.

61. In *Writing Culture*, Clifford and Marcus valuably point out that the ethnographic present isn't really a present, as it removes its object from the dynamic temporality of reader and writer. In this sense, Winnemucca may be seen disrupting the ethnographic present in her insistence on the historical contingency of culture and cultural contact. Moreover, her article doesn't fully follow the ethnographic present, often shifting abruptly into past tense or imperfect forms ("they would signal")—but this is possibly a matter of editing, as in, "Our men used to hunt, and after that, our women go into the valleys to gather different kinds of seeds" (108). We can't even be sure that the ethnographic present in this text was genuinely Winnemucca's choice or how much it was the product of an editor.

62. General Fremont, for example, talked about how "fat" the Paiutes were, assuming from this that "they live an easy and happy life." Quoted in Knack and Stewart, *As Long as the River Shall Run*, 40.

63. Landsman, "The 'Other' as Political Symbol," 247.

64. In Bruce Ronda, ed., *Letters of Elizabeth Palmer Peabody*, 423 (italics in original).

65. As for fur traders, Sylvia Van Kirk and others have argued that these early travelers made much less effort to convert American Indians to their ways of life than later, agrarian settlers did. See Van Kirk, *Many Tender Ties*. Mann's invocation of fur traders thus suggests that late-nineteenth-century reformers may have invoked those earlier settlers as an additional way of constructing themselves as "civilized."

66. Weaver, *That the People Might Live*, 49.

67. Sollors, *Beyond Ethnicity*, 44.

68. Ibid., 49.

69. On the definition of the Paiutes, see Knack and Stewart, *As Long as the River Shall Run*, 14–16. Maggie Sale has also observed that "Winne-mucca Hopkins's work and writing helped to constitute the formerly kin-related but loosely-tied bands into the tribe of Northern Paiutes" ("Recon-ceptualizing America", 32).

70. Knack and Stewart, *As Long as the River Shall Run*, 42.

71. James Clifford, "On Ethnographic Allegory," in *Writing Culture*, ed. Clifford and Marcus, 117–18.

72. Foreman, *Indian Women Chiefs*, 51.

73. Bhabha, *The Location of Culture*, 107. In his landmark essay, "Signs Taken for Wonders," Bhabha describes the re-rehearsed narrative in

English colonial discourse, giving the example of Hindu people reading the Bible with excitement (not unlike Helen Hunt Jackson's spectacles of converted Indians, or the widely circulated images of the Winnemuccas singing the anthem). This narrative, Bhabha contends, marks "the disturbance of [the English book's] authoritative representations by the uncanny forces of race, sexuality, violence, cultural and even climatic differences which emerge in the colonial discourse as the mixed and split texts of hybridity." In this scenario, we see an "effect of uncertainty that afflicts the discourse of power, an uncertainty that estranges the familiar symbol of English 'national' authority and emerges from its colonial appropriation as a sign of its difference" (113).

As Winnemucca describes them, the canny Paiute uses of the Star-Spangled Banner may persist in some of the songs known as "flag songs"—for example, those recorded by Judy Trejo (*Circle Dance Songs of the Paiute and Shoshone*, Canyon Records). One is translated as "What a wondrous sight the American flag is!"

74. Richey, "Sagebrush Princess," 30.

75. Gehm, *Sarah Winnemucca*, 29.

76. Howard, "Famous Indian Chiefs," 815.

77. Lott, *Love and Theft*, 24.

78. Michele Moylan outlines a similar dynamic in her brilliant reception history of *Ramona*, "Reading the Indians."

CHAPTER 3

1. Melville Jacobs, *Clackamas Chinook Texts* (hereafter abbreviated as CCT), Part II, Text 39. I present story titles as Jacobs does, with only the first word capitalized.

2. In what Stith Thompson dubs "transformation through wish" tales, a character casually makes a wish and then gets it, often to unhappy ends (Thompson, *Motif-Index*, D521).

3. Dennis Tedlock, an anthropologist and translator who has worked with the Zuni, is perhaps the most famous proponent of such translations. His are typically in verse form, with line and stanza breaks indicating storytellers' pauses. He also uses boldface and small type to indicate changes in volume, and will sometimes add parenthetical notes describing gestures or intonation. For Tedlock's discussion of his rationale, see his chapter, "On the Translation of Style" in his book *The Spoken Word*.

For a handy glimpse at varying translation styles, see Brian Swann's excellent anthology *Coming to Light*, which seeks to represent not only different peoples and kinds of stories, but also different transcription methods.

4. Pratt, *Imperial Eyes*, 7.

5. CCT II, Text 96.

6. Meville Jacobs Collection (hereafter abbreviated as MJC), Notebook 3, p. 82.

7. See Spivak, "Can the Subaltern Speak?" In a useful parallel to "A widow's mourning," Spivak's landmark essay interprets British colonial interventions into the Indian practice of *suttee*, or widow burning, as a history of "white men saving brown women from brown men"; in this scenario, Spivak concludes that there is no place from which the subaltern, or dispossessed woman, can speak. The question of whether she can, indeed, is deliberately unanswerable, meant to provoke critics who want to investigate subaltern politics into questioning the politics of speaking for others, a politics in which critics, speaking for the subaltern and appropriating her voice, wind up re-rehearsing the very imperialist history they purport to critique.

8. See Seaburg, "Collecting Culture," esp. 26–27.

9. For a more detailed but still concise account of languages and peoples in the region, see Hymes's "Ethnological Note" in *"In Vain I Tried,"* 15–23.

10. At least one Oregon newspaper, however, had already given the honor on May 8, 1915, to "Soosap," or Joseph Andrews, in an obituary proclaiming this old "character" to be the "last of the once haughty Clackamas tribe" (Oregon Historical Society scrapbook 55, p. 132. The Oregon Historical Society keeps a wealth of scrapbooks, amply indexed, of newspaper clippings on topics of local interest, but unfortunately the collectors neglected to provide full bibliographic information for many of the entries.)

11. "Victoria Howard," *Portland Oregonian*, September 28, 1930.

12. In many cases, such labels are simply dramatic, slightly sloppy exaggerations of the truth, as when the otherwise careful critic Craig Thompson writes, "The Clackamas Chinook Indians, a tribe whose last member died over 50 years ago . . ." (See his "Gender Representation," 19).

13. CCT I, p. 1.

14. Seaburg, "Collecting Culture," 49.

15.   As we will see, however, Jacobs's goals were even broader; he insists that he "neither initiated nor conducted Clackamas studies in order to serve linguistics principally." CCT I, p. 1.

16.   Hymes, "Anthologies and Narrators," 80.

17.   For a more detailed discussion of culture areas, see Seaburg, "Collecting Culture," esp. 87–90. A methodology of culture elements was initially developed by Alfred Kroeber in the 1930s. As Seaburg argues, Kroeber had made up his mind in advance of collecting his data that the Yuroks of northern California represented the "richest" culture in the area, while he devalued western Oregon cultures. Kroeber thus based his argument about "impoverished" or "primitive" western Oregon cultures on a lack of rich data for them—data he hadn't really bothered to collect, since he wasn't interested in those Indians. The method is thus somewhat dated and troubled, although it makes it possible to compare, say, oral tales across cultures in the region, if we are cautious about such comparisons.

18.   Most of the early sources describing the region are hopelessly stereotypical. Of the English-language travel accounts like Lewis and Clark's journals, narrative treatments like Washington Irving's *Astoria* and Edward Curtis's (in)famous ethnographic descriptions, most can only turn out some variation on Curtis's line that Chinook "tribal life was one of indolent, licentious ease, dignity, and filth" (*The North American Indian*, 87). For an extensive bibliography of such materials, see Silverstein, "Chinookans," and Murdock and O'Leary's *Ethnographic Bibliography*. For a readable and concise introduction and overview to west Oregon Indian culture and history, see Beckham, *Indians of Western Oregon*.

19.   See CCT I, Text 16, "Black Bear and Grizzly Woman and their sons."

20.   CCT II, Text 90.

21.   CCT II, Text 94, lines 5–6.

22.   Laurence Thompson's highly praised obituary also makes a good mini-biography of Jacobs. He married Elizabeth Derr, a former student of psychiatry who did her own anthropological work with Jacobs's encouragement, and whose intellectual interests informed his. When reading Jacobs's musings on the status of Indian women, it is usefully tempering to remember this balanced and mutually self-sustaining relationship. Jacobs was also a member of the Communist Party, an involvement for which he was publicly persecuted at the University of Washington during the Red Scare. During the 1960s, he was a dedicated public speaker against racial intolerance. Like his mentor Franz Boas, Jacobs might sometimes

appear racist to us today, but his egalitarian political commitments still deserve our attention as well.

23. Melville Jacobs, *Content and Style*, 159, 171.

24. In *The Sacred Hoop*, Paula Gunn Allen discusses American readings of American Indian cultures as misogynist and the political ends those readings served. See especially "When Women Throw Down Bundles," 30–42.

25. For one of the few direct treatments of Oregon Indian women's roles, see Leslie Scott, "Indian Women as Food Providers."

26. GRNR II, p. 121.

27. Berry, *Trask*, 14.

28. Babcock, "'No Womens Are Storytellers,'" 382 n. 33.

29. Silverstein, "Chinookans," 543.

30. Beckham, *Indians of Western Oregon*, 90.

31. Zucker, *Oregon Indians*, 54.

32. Ruby and Brown, *The Chinook Indians*, 9.

33. Ibid., 64. One wonders what really generated these stereotypes— the behavior, which of course was not solely the women's, or the observers and historians reading the behavior. For a more sympathetic view of inter-racial relations in the Northwest, see Sylvia van Kirk's *Many Tender Ties*, which sees indigenous women who were involved with fur traders not merely as objects of exchange, but as subjects who gained power through such relations.

34. Ibid., 127.

35. Sarris, *Keeping Slug Woman Alive*, 93.

36. See Zenk, "Chinook Jargon," esp. 96 and 104–5. Zenk provides several useful tables and maps of tribal makeup and distribution on the reservation. He breaks the groups down into three main elements: Willamette Valley groups (including Kalapuyan-speaking groups, Molale, and Clackamas); Umpqua Valley groups (including Athabascan-speaking Umpquas), and Rogue River and Cow Creek Valley groups (including Takelma-speaking groups and Shastans).

37. See www.grandronde.org.

38. Some, though, including Howard, may have "pretended" to convert. The Catholic Church records edited and published by Munnick and Beckham certainly show bizarre inconsistencies in the numbers and names of children that Indians baptized, as I'll discuss in Howard's case below.

39. When I attended the Grand Ronde powwow in the summer of 1995, some of the elders I talked to (who would have been children in the

1930s) remarked that, in contrast to today's cultural revival, they themselves had to grow up with "no culture."

40.   GRNR II, p. 48.

41.   CCT II, Text 131, lines 54–55. Words and phrases in parentheses are Jacobs's interpolations.

42.   Agent J. B. McLane is usually credited with ending such practices. Older Indians interviewed by Berreman remembered him fondly, however; Andrew Smith recalls "that McLane tried to get them to stop dances and Indian doctoring, but says he did it nicely, and the Indians liked him very much, the best agent they ever had" (GRNR II, p. 38). It is possible that shamanism at Grand Ronde was kept alive, but underground, or, if it was indeed on the wane by the 1920s and 1930s, that its energies were channeled elsewhere, as into personal narratives about traditional healing.

43.   GRNR II, p. 82.

44.   Ibid., 81–82.

45.   Ibid., 102.

46.   Hymes, "In Vain I Tried," 133.

47.   There have been some important recent attempts to reconstruct informants' lives: in his dissertation, "Collecting Culture," William Seaburg has reconstructed the life story of Coquille Thompson, an Upper Coquille Athabaskan informant who worked with several anthropologists, including Jacobs's wife Elizabeth; and Lionel Youst's *She's Tricky Like Coyote* is a book-length biography of Annie Miner Peterson, a Miluk Coos woman who also worked with Melville Jacobs. More recently, oral storytellers like the Okanagan Harry Robinson have been getting credit as authors for their collection of narratives [*Write It on My Heart* (1989)]. And Jacobs had the company of anthropologists like Ruth Bunzel, who at least noted the names of some of her Zuni informants.

48.   Valaskakis, "The Chippewa," 268.

49.   CCT II, Text 130, lines 6–9.

50.   According to Berreman, John Wacheno (Howard's brother-in-law) was the only person at Grand Ronde in 1934 with the flattened head. This status mark suggested the prestige the Wacheno family enjoyed at one time on the reservation (GRNR II, p. 106).

51.   MJC, Box 92, file "Acculturation and Childhood."

52.   Ibid., file "Childhood." Jacobs adds, "I infer that her mother-in-law, and possibly all Clackamas mothers-in-law, were controlling of their daughters-in-law."

53. Munnick and Beckham, eds., *Catholic Church Records*, 123. According to Henry Zenk (personal communication, August 1999), the editors of these volumes made an error in transcribing her maiden name, which was actually "Wishikin"—a doubly interesting Americanizing of the surname, coupled with the gallicizing of her first name.

54. As some Grand Ronde elders told me, it was "almost like people then had two sets of children"—one that lived and one that didn't.

55. MJC, Box 92, file "Marriage."

56. In MJC, Box 94, file "Women."

57. GRNR II, p. 106.

58. In some areas, as at Zuni, men remain the traditional storytellers, so that the large number of female informants who worked with researchers like Ruth Benedict represent a complex departure from tribal tradition. In western Oregon, however, both men and women appear to have told traditional stories, with both boys and girls listening.

As some of Jacobs's notes describe it, storytelling was traditionally a winter evening activity; people would invite to supper an elderly neighbor, who would tell stories into the night, sometimes continuing the following night (MJC, Box 94, Folder 16).

59. Jacobs thought that Howard enjoyed telling the stories. He also thought that his Northwest informants were motivated to preserve oral tradition in writing, though he said he "never had any certain cues to the feelings which many of the last-informed survivors have had concerning their role as sole providers of permanent records of their people's almost vanished cultural heritage" (MJC, Box 94, Folder 16).

60. Elizabeth Derr Jacobs, *Nehalem Tillamook Tales*, xix.

61. Melville Jacobs, *Kalapuya Texts*, 5.

62. See Hymes, "Models of Interaction"; and Briggs, *Learning How to Ask*.

63. CCT I, p. 2. Laurence Thompson also quotes Jacobs describing how to convert domestic space to professional ends: "[T]he thing to do, is to get yourself comfortably seated reasonably close and where you can see the informant's mouth—usually you can hope to use the flat closed top of the old Singer sewing machine you'll surely find—it's just right for such purposes—and keep writing what you hear" (p. 642).

64. CCT I, p. 2.

65. I am grateful to William Seaburg and Henry Zenk (personal communications, August 1995) for helping me flesh out this account.

66. For example, in MJC notebook 67, Howard's field English translation reads "oh she said oh maybe it is something flooey." In the published version in *Texts in Chinook Jargon* (1936), however, the translation reads "'Oh,' she said, 'oh, maybe there is something queer'" (Text 2:3(2)). Thanks to Henry Zenk (personal conversation, August 1999) for providing this example. Zenk adds (in another personal communication, August 1999) that "Probably, none of our English translations from Chinookan are fine-grained enough to give us a really good handle on the stylistic nuances of the originals." He notes that even the interlinear English translations in Jacobs's field notebooks tend to vary widely in style; such variety might, however, reinforce the idea of a dialogue between Jacobs and Howard, since such stylistic changes could have been motivated by him, by her, or by the two of them together.

67. Partly this was because, as Seaburg has demonstrated, public funding was diverted elsewhere around the time of World War II. And partly it was because, as Jacobs felt in his own lifetime, professional interest in transcribed oral narratives was on the wane. Sol Tax had suggested printing the Clackamas collection on microcard to save money, an option Jacobs decried in his letters. Indiana University Press, under Thomas Sebeok, finally agreed to print the entire collection if the University of Washington, where Jacobs was on the faculty, would pay half the costs. Initially, though, the University of Washington paid only a quarter of the cost, so the collection is split into two volumes. Jacobs insisted that "the merit of the texts does not reside largely in their service to linguistics. We have never shown how texts contain riches for the varied purposes of ethnographic, literary, and psychological analysis" (MJC, Box 120, Letter to A. L. Kroeber, May 11, 1955).

68. Murray, *Forked Tongues*, 110.

69. Venuti, *The Translator's Invisibility*, 16–17.

70. CCT I, p. 7. Too, Jacobs may have shared the feelings of Elizabeth Jacobs, who once remarked that she "fixed" informants' grammar so that their texts wouldn't be devalued by readers (Seaburg, "Collecting Culture," 59).

71. Cheyfitz, *The Poetics of Imperialism*, 135.

72. Unless otherwise indicated, all of Jacobs's remarks about Eustace come from MJC Notebook 57.

73. Note what immediately follows, however: "A pitifully stupid, humorless, introverted, cowardly, beaten, infinitely lazy, childish man, trying for ghastly and weakly willed efforts to recall fragments of memory

weighted with an early happier aura." The field notebooks reveal Jacobs as a complicated man—often sympathetic and liberal-minded, but prone to arrogant impatience when he didn't get what he wanted. He also relentlessly psychoanalyzes his informants (Eustace has "a mother fixation, of course"), reflecting not only his historical moment but also a real conflict over control in his relations with his informants.

74. MJC Box 94, Folder 16.

75. MJC Notebook 57, p. 32.

76. Quoted in Seaburg, "Collecting Culture," 55, and translated therein by Howard Berman. Eustace may not have been as unreliable as Jacobs complained. In his introduction to *Kalapuya Texts*, which he took from Santiam informant John Hudson, Jacobs calls Eustace "unfortunately a most inarticulate person," adding that Hudson was never able to translate the other man's dictations (8). But Seaburg reports that Hudson did in fact translate about 60 percent of Howard's almost one thousand notebook pages of dictation ("Collecting Culture," 54).

77. Sarris, *Keeping Slug Woman Alive*, 105. One is reminded, too, of the account by Zora Neale Hurston (also a Boasian) in the beginning of her own anthropological work, *Mules and Men*:

> Folk-lore is not as easy to collect as it sounds. The best source is where there are the least outside influences and these people, being usually under-privileged, are the shyest. They are the most reluctant at times to reveal that which the soul lives by. And the Negro, in spite of his open-faced laughter, his seeming acquiescence, is particularly evasive. You see we are a polite people and we do not say to our questioner "Get out of here!" We smile and tell him or her something that satisfies the white person because, knowing so little about us, he doesn't know what he is missing. The Indian resists curiosity by a stony silence. The Negro offers a feather-bed resistance. That is, we let the probe enter, but it never comes out. It gets smothered under a lot of laughter and pleasantries (18).

Hurston's remarks underscore the real power struggle over ownership of knowledge in ethnographic encounters, though in light of Sarris's comments and of Eustace's metanarrative rambles, her wooden-Indian stereotype takes on a double irony.

78. I have already discussed Howard's possibly complicated position within her community, and the difficulties of understanding that position by studying the printed information. Jacobs felt that Eustace was not

respected at Grand Ronde, but we really have only his word on that. During the summer of 1985, the Grand Ronde tribal center included a photograph of Eustace in its historical display; today, at least, he is fondly remembered, hardly the social anathema that Jacobs's angry notes to himself would have one believe.

79. CCT II, p. 656 n. 506.

80. Swann and Krupat, eds., *I Tell You Now*, ix.

81. Cruikshank, *Life Lived*, 2.

82. Quoted in Laurence Thompson, "Melville Jacobs," 644.

83. There were only a few other readings of Howard between the work of Jacobs and that of Hymes and Ramsey. See, for example, Alexander Scharbach's 1962 "Aspects of Existentialism in Tribal Chinook Myths."

84. Hymes has been taken to task by some readers, including Sarris, who faults him for assuming that some essential "true structure" underlies oral narrative (*Keeping Slug Woman Alive*, 22).

85. CCT II, Text 37, lines 7–9.

86. Jacobs, *The People Are Coming Soon*, 242.

87. Hymes, *"In Vain I Tried,"* 296.

88. Ramsey, "Two Oregon Indian Narratives."

89. Kroeber, "Deconstructionist Criticism."

90. Hymes, *"In Vain I Tried,"* 284.

91. Craig Womack has been one of the few scholars of American Indian literature to observe that oral tradition is always already political and that ethnographic collections might yet prove to be valuable literary and political resources. See chapter 2 of *Red on Red*, "Reading the Oral Tradition for Nationalist Themes" (51–67), for his powerful discussion of how an obsession with "authentic" "Indian" tradition has worked to obliterate or occlude oral tradition's work in Native sovereignty: "[O]perating under the assumption that the oral tradition is a static body of narratives located inside areas of translation problems, performance problems, and textual representation problems, among other 'Indian problems,' scholars have glossed over their political meanings" (66).

92. Ibid., 297.

93. Ramsey, "Two Oregon Indian Narratives," 17.

CHAPTER 4

1. This is Richard Bauman's approach, for example, in *Let Your Words Be Few*, his study of seventeenth-century Quaker speech. Also,

Hymes is a prominent practitioner of the ethnography of speaking. For a good overview of the field, see Bauman and Sherzer, eds., *Explorations in the Ethnography of Communication*.

2. Hymes, "*In Vain I Tried*," 83–85.

3. MJC, Box 94, Folder "Introductory Notes."

4. CCT II, Text 16.

5. This is a common motif in diverse oral traditions; see Stith Thompson, *Motif-Index*, F531.1.5.1, F232.2, F460.1.2., G.123.

6. Melville Jacobs, *Content and Style*, 159.

7. Ibid.

8. CCT I, Text 3.

9. Ibid., line 42.

10. For more on trickster, see Babcock, "A Tolerated Margin."

11. CCT I, Text 9. In some other oral traditions, as in the Zuni, the trickster's gender may vary. Coyote may be male in one version of a tale and female in another; or his gender traits might range more widely, as in the case of a Coyote who maternally feeds his children; or his gender might seem almost incidental to the narrative, never mentioned other than pronominally. Among the Pacific Northwest tales I have examined, including Howard's, however, this gendering seems much more stable and explicit. Howard's Coyote stories (which Jacobs has grouped as Texts 1–9) would warrant a study in themselves, especially since Jacobs notes of the last (and longest) text that Howard did not seem to enjoy telling Coyote stories very much. She sometimes figures Coyote as a nonentity who does nothing, or an evil-doer who gets quickly killed off. Jacobs thought that in Howard's hands Coyote grows, following "a sequence from a trickster who is impelled by youthful drives, to a conscience-controlled announcer and transformer" (*Content and Style*, 137–38).

12. Hymes, "Anthologies and Narrators," 75.

13. CCT I, Text 3, n. 10.

14. CCT I, Text 3, line 6.

15. CCT I, Text 3, n. 10.

16. Henry Zenk, personal communication, August 1999.

17. CCT I, Text 3, lines 45–46.

18. Zenk says that Howard could have dictated such particles without much dramatic inflection at all, "as appropriately descriptive Chinookan, and/or as a stylistic verisimilitude of 'real' performance." Personal communication, August 1999.

19. Unfortunately, the field notebooks are not much more certain on this point. Under the English translations, Jacobs has written "[rep. 5x,

high monotone], probably following something Howard told him, or ever so possibly abbreviating a performance she really enacted. In general, though, Jacobs does not seem to have truncated Howard's telling for his own recording convenience.

20.   Rootdiggers are just what they sound like—long, pointed tools for digging out roots, in this case a local bulb called camas.

21.   CCT I, Text 3, lines 47–49.

22.   CCT I, Text 4.

23.   CCT II, Text 27.

24.   CCT II, Text 36.

25.   "Impounded water" is a motif found in the Thompson *Motif-Index* (A1111). Of course, I am not suggesting that any particular version is authentic or that Howard only revises some alleged original.

26.   Sapir, *Wishram Texts*, Text 1, pp. 29–33. Simpson's narratives, in fact, almost exactly replicate the episodes in Howard's Text 9—hers are just strung together into longer sections.

27.   Ibid., p. 33.

28.   Ibid., p. 49. As this language undoubtedly suggests, Sapir's translations reflect the egregious anthropological "editing" we have seen critiqued by Tedlock and others. The wording not only sounds like a phony rendition, like the way a white person thinks an Indian is supposed to talk, but it also, like John Neihardt's famous last lines for *Black Elk Speaks*, reinforces the stereotype of the vanishing race. Zenk observes, though, that Wishram has six tenses, including one referring to distant time past, and so this might have motivated Sapir's translation (personal communication, August 1999).

29.   We could say a similar thing about Howard, of course—that she may have felt that Jacobs wanted long stories and so strung together many episodes to keep the four dollars per day coming. I don't mean to mystify or romanticize her long tellings by suggesting that they must mean that she loved storytelling, and loved doing it for Jacobs. By the same token, it might be that Simpson actually gave short dictations to Sapir *against* the anthropologist's wishes.

30.   Melville Jacobs, *Kalapuya Texts*, p. 237, lines 7–8.

31.   CCT I, Text 3, lines 49–51. "Now story story" is like a formulaic narrative conclusion. It doesn't appear in every text in *Clackamas Chinook Texts*. Jacobs thought that Howard concluded with it when she had particularly enjoyed a story, but Hymes finds no apparent correlation between the appearance of the tag and a satisfactorily resolved narrative;

indeed, in my reading, "Coon and Coyote" has plenty in its final paragraph that seems unresolved. See Hymes, *"In Vain I Tried,"* 326.

32.   CCT, Text 3, line 48.

33.   Hymes, *"In Vain I Tried,"* 303–304.

34.   CCT II, Text 108, lines 1–2.

35.   In the field notebooks, indeed, many of the ethnographic texts appear on the left-hand pages, which Jacobs used for corrections or addenda while he was transcribing or translating the mythic texts on the right-hand pages. This setup indicates that, during retranslation, Howard sometimes remembered something she wanted to add and that, while they were both translating words into English, Jacobs sometimes asked her for further explanation.

36.   CCT II, Text 108, line 5.

37.   Ibid., n. 467.

38.   CCT II, Texts 105–10 and 114. As Jacobs describes it briefly in *The Content and Style of an Oral Literature*, "Occasionally an older person who had encountered a spirit-power granting one or another kind of doctoring ability became a curing shaman and received fees from the sick or their relatives. . . . Some shamans accepted fees to 'poison' people; others only cured the sick or controlled the weather" (p. 10).

39.   Valaskakis, "'Dance Me Inside,'" 40.

40.   CCT II, Text 105, lines 1–2.

41.   Ibid., line 5.

42.   CCT II, Text 131.

43.   Ibid., lines 1–3.

44.   Ibid., lines 84–85.

45.   Bauman, "Contextualization," 136.

46.   CCT II, Text 131, lines 56–60.

47.   Ibid., line 61.

48.   Ibid., lines 17–19.

49.   Ibid., line 14.

50.   Ibid., line 11.

51.   CCT II, Text 122, line 3.

52.   Ibid., n. 498.

53.   CCT II, Text 136.

54.   Jacobs, *The People Are Coming Soon*, 244.

55.   CCT II, p. 632 n. 297.

56.   My search was by no means exhaustive, but it included the collections of oral narratives by Melville Jacobs, Elizabeth Derr Jacobs, Jarold

Ramsey, Edward Sapir, Leo Frachtenberg, Franz Boas, Ella Clark, and Vi Hilbert. Ramsey suggests some analogs both in his reprinting of the tale in *Coyote Was Going There* and in "Genderic and Racial Appropriation," but none of these involves a female figure who wishes and then undoes her wish.

57. See, for example, Elizabeth Derr Jacobs, *Nehalem Tillamook Tales*, Text 28.

58. Melville Jacobs, "Titles in an Oral Literature," 161.

59. Hymes, "A Theory of Irony," 324–25.

60. Ramsey, "Genderic and Racial Appropriation," 274.

61. MJC Notebook 67.

62. Jacobs recorded this song on wax cylinder, a cassette copy of which can still be heard in the Melville Jacobs archives. The sound quality is unfortunately very muffled, however.

63. CCT II, p. 661 n. 542.

64. Jacobs, *The People Are Coming Soon*, 345.

65. Ramsey, "Genderic and Racial Appropriation," 273.

66. Silko, "An Old-Time Indian Attack," 211–12.

67. Hymes, "*In Vain I Tried*," 5. See Robert Dale Parker ("Text, Lines, and Audiotape") for a full critique of Hymes's "rhetoric of discovery."

EPILOGUE

1. Gibson, "Artists of Change," 57.

2. Bell, Comments in "Forum," 411.

3. Warrior, *Tribal Secrets*, 11.

4. Callahan, *Wynema*. Subsequent citations will appear parenthetically in the text. For a more developed reading of the novel, see my forthcoming "The Politics and Perils of Representing Tribal Discourse: S. Alice Callahan's *Wynema*." For a very different reading of *Wynema* as a failure to adequately represent Creek tribalism, see chapter 4 of Craig Womack's *Red on Red*, entitled "Alice Callahan's *Wynema*." LaVonne Brown Ruoff's introduction to *Wynema* provides an excellent short biography of Callahan and a discussion of the novel in its context.

BIBLIOGRAPHY

MANUSCRIPTS AND ARCHIVES

Berreman, J. V. "Duplicates of Grand Ronde Notes and Report, 1934." 3 parts: "Part I: Background and History of the Grand Ronde Tribes." "Part II: Field Notes, Grand Ronde." "Part III: Cultural Adjustment of the Grand Ronde Indian Tribes." Unpublished manuscripts in the possession of Gerald Berreman, University of California, Berkeley.

Melville Jacobs Collection. Manuscripts and Archives. University of Washington, Seattle.

Oregon Historical Society. Scrapbook 55. Portland, Oregon.

United States Office of Indian Affairs. "The Case of Sarah Winnemucca." Special File no. 268. M 574. National Archives.

United States Census of Indians Belonging to Grand Ronde, 1885–1913.

BOOKS AND ARTICLES

"Not Enough of a Sacrifice." *Southern Workman* (February 1885): 19.

Review of *Ramona*, by Helen Hunt Jackson. *Atlantic Monthly*, January 1885, 127–30.

"Victoria Howard." *Portland Oregonian*, September 28, 1930, section 2, p. 3.

Allen, Paula Gunn. *The Sacred Hoop: Recovering the Feminine in American Indian Traditions*. Boston: Beacon, 1986.

Ammons, Elizabeth. *Conflicting Stories: American Women Writers at the Turn into the Twentieth Century*. New York: Oxford University Press, 1991.

Anderson, Benedict. *Imagined Communities*. London: Verso, 1991.

Anderson, Eric Gary. *American Indian Literature and the Southwest: Contexts and Dispositions*. Austin: University of Texas Press, 1999.

Ashcroft, Bill, Gareth Griffiths, and Helen Tiffin, eds. *The Empire Writes Back: Theory and Practice in Post-colonial Literatures*. New York: Routledge, 1989.

Babcock, Barbara A. "At Home, No Womens Are Storytellers: Potteries, Stories, and Politics in Cochiti Pueblo." *Journal of the Southwest* 30 (Autumn 1988): 356–89.

———. "'A Tolerated Margin of Mess': The Trickster and His Tales Reconsidered." *Journal of the Folklore Institute* 11 (1975): 147–86.

Bakhtin, Mikhail M. *The Dialogic Imagination*. Edited by Michael Holquist. Austin: University of Texas Press, 1981.

Bannan, Helen. "'True Womanhood' on the Reservation: Field Matrons in the United States Indian Service." Tucson, Ariz.: Southwest Institute for Research on Women, 1984.

Banning, Evelyn I. *Helen Hunt Jackson*. New York: Vanguard, 1973.

Batker, Carol. "'Overcoming All Obstacles': The Assimilation Debate in Native American Women's Journalism of the Dawes Era." In *Early Native American Writings: New Critical Essays*, edited by Helen Jaskoski. New York: Cambridge University Press, 1996.

Bauman, Richard. "Contextualization, Tradition, and the Dialogue of Genres: Icelandic Legends of the Kraftaskald." In *Rethinking Context: Language as an Interactive Phenomenon*, edited by Alessandro Duranti and Charles Goodwin, 136–54. New York: Cambridge University Press, 1992.

———. *Let Your Words Be Few: Symbolism of Speaking and Silence among 17th-century Quakers*. Prospect Heights, Ill.: Waveland, 1983.

Bauman, Richard, and Joel Sherzer, eds. *Explorations in the Ethnography of Speaking*. New York: Cambridge University Press, 1991.

Baym, Nina. *American Women Writers and the Work of History, 1790–1860*. New Brunswick, N.J.: Rutgers University Press, 1995.

———. *Woman's Fiction: A Guide to Novels by and about Women in America 1820–1870*. Ithaca, N.Y.: Cornell University Press, 1978.

Bean, Lowell John. "Cahuilla." In *California*, edited by Robert Heizer, 575–87. Vol. 8 of *Handbook of North American Indians*, edited by William C. Sturtevant. Washington, D.C.: Smithsonian, 1978.

Bean, Lowell John, and Florence Shipek. "Luiseño." In *California*, edited by Robert Heizer, 550–63. Vol. 8 of *Handbook of North American Indians*, edited by William C. Sturtevant. Washington, D.C.: Smithsonian, 1978.

Beckham, Stephen Dow. *The Indians of Western Oregon: This Land Was Theirs*. Coos Bay, Oreg.: Arago Books, 1977.

Bell, Betty Louise. Comments in "Forum". *PMLA* (May 1995): 411.

Berkhofer, Robert F., Jr. *The White Man's Indian: Images of the American Indian from Columbus to the Present*. New York: Vintage, 1978.

Berry, Don. *Trask*. New York: Viking, 1960.

Bhabha, Homi. *The Location of Culture*. New York: Routledge, 1994.

——. *Nation and Narration*. New York: Routledge, 1990.

Boas, Franz. *Chinook Texts*. U.S. Bureau of American Ethnology, Bulletin No. 20. Washington, D.C.: Government Printing Office, 1894.

Bodayla, Stephen. "Can an Indian Vote? *Elk v. Wilkins*, a Setback for Indian Citizenship." *Nebraska History* 67 (Winter 1986): 372–80.

Bridgman, Richard. *The Colloquial Style in America*. New York: Oxford University Press, 1966.

Briggs, Charles L. *Learning How to Ask: A Sociolinguistic Appraisal of the Role of the Interview in Social Science Research*. New York: Cambridge University Press, 1986.

Bright, William. *A Coyote Reader*. Berkeley and Los Angeles: University of California Press, 1993.

Brodhead, Richard H. *Cultures of Letters: Scenes of Reading and Writing in 19th-Century America*. Chicago: Chicago University Press, 1993.

Brodzki, Bella, and Celeste M. Schenck, eds. *Life/Lines: Theorizing Women's Autobiography*. Ithaca: Cornell University Press, 1988.

Brown, Dee. *Bury My Heart at Wounded Knee*. New York: Henry Holt, 1970.

Brumble, H. David. *American Indian Autobiography*. Berkeley and Los Angeles: University of California Press, 1988.

Callahan, S. Alice. *Wynema: A Child of the Forest*. 1891. Reprint, Lincoln: University of Nebraska Press, 1998.

Canfield, Gae Whitney. *Sarah Winnemucca of the Northern Paiutes*. Norman: University of Oklahoma Press, 1983.

Carby, Hazel V. *Reconstructing Womanhood: The Emergence of the Afro-American Woman Novelist*. New York: Oxford University Press, 1987.

Cheyfitz, Eric. *The Poetics of Imperialism: Translation and Colonization from The Tempest to Tarzan*. New York: Oxford University Press, 1991.

Clark, Ella E. *Indian Legends of the Pacific Northwest*. Berkeley and Los Angeles: University of California Press, 1953.

Clifford, James. *The Predicament of Culture: Twentieth-Century Ethnography, Literature, and Art*. Cambridge: Harvard University Press, 1988.

Clifford, James, and George E. Marcus, eds. *Writing Culture: The Poetics and Politics of Ethnography.* Berkeley and Los Angeles: University of California Press, 1986.

Cooper, James Fenimore. *The Pioneers.* New York: Signet, 1964.

Coultrap-McQuinn, Susan. *Doing Literary Business: American Women Writers in the Nineteenth Century.* Chapel Hill: University of North Carolina Press, 1990.

Cruikshank, Julie. *Life Lived Like a Story: Life Stories of Three Yukon Native Elders.* Lincoln: University of Nebraska Press, 1990.

Curtis, Edward S. *The North American Indian.* Vol. 8. 1870. Reprint, New York: Johnson Reprint, 1911.

Custer, Elizabeth B. "Comulos, the Home of Ramona, as Seen by the Widow of General Custer." *Boston Evening Transcript,* May 14 1887, 6.

DeCora, Angel. "The Sick Child." 1899. Reprinted in *The Singing Spirit: Early Short Stories by North American Indians,* edited by Bernd C. Peyer, 45–47. Tucson: University of Arizona Press, 1989.

Deloria, Vine, Jr. *Custer Died for Your Sins.* Norman: University of Oklahoma Press, 1988.

Dippie, Brian W. *The Vanishing American: White Attitudes and U.S. Indian Policy.* Middletown, Conn.: Wesleyan University Press, 1982.

Dobie, Frank. "Helen Hunt Jackson and Ramona." *Southwest Review* (Spring 1959): 93–98.

Dorris, Michael. Introduction to *Ramona.* New York: Signet, 1988.

Drinnon, Richard. *Facing West: The Metaphysics of Indian-Hating and Empire-Building.* Minneapolis: University of Minnesota Press, 1980.

Eastman, Charles Alexander. *From the Deep Woods to Civilization.* 1916. Reprint, Lincoln, Nebr.: Bison Books, 1977.

———. *Indian Boyhood.* 1902. Reprint, New York: Dover, 1971.

Fabian, Johannes. *Time and the Other: How Anthropology Makes Its Object.* New York: Columbia University Press, 1983.

Forbes, Jack D. "Intellectual Self-Determination and Sovereignty: Implications for Native Studies and for Native Intellectuals." *Wicazo Sa Review* 13, no. 1 (Spring 1998): 11–24.

Foreman, Carolyn Thomas. *Indian Women Chiefs.* Washington, D.C.: Zenger, 1976.

Fowler, Catherine S. "Sarah Winnemucca." In *American Indian Intellectuals,* edited by Margot Liberty, 33–42. St. Paul. Minn.: West Publishing, 1978.

Fowler, Catherine S., and Sven Liljeblad. "Northern Paiute." In *Great Basin,* edited by Warren D'Azevedo, 435–65. Vol. 10 of *Handbook of North*

American Indians, edited by William C. Sturtevant. Washington, D.C.: Smithsonian, 1983.

Frachtenberg, Leo J. *Coos Texts*. Columbia University Contributions to Anthropology, vol. 1. New York: Columbia University Press; Leyden: E. J. Brill, 1913.

Fuss, Diana. *Essentially Speaking: Feminism, Nature and Difference*. New York: Routledge, 1989.

Gates, Henry Louis. *The Signifying Monkey: A Theory of African-American Literary Criticism*. New York: Oxford University Press, 1989.

Gehm, Katherine. *Sarah Winnemucca: Most Extraordinary Woman of the Paiute Nation*. Phoenix, Ariz.: O'Sullivan Woodside, 1975.

Georgi-Findlay, Brigitte. "The Frontiers of Native American Women's Writing: Sarah Winnemucca's Life Among the Piutes." In *New Voices in Native American Literary Criticism*, edited by Arnold Krupat, 222–52. Washington, D.C.: Smithsonian, 1993.

Gibson, Dan, et al. "Artists of Change: Breaking through the Millennium." *Native Peoples* 13 (June-July 2000): 50–57.

Harris, Marvin. *The Rise of Anthropological Theory*. New York: Thomas Crowell, 1968.

Harsha, William Justin. *Ploughed Under: The Story of an Indian Chief, Told by Himself*. New York: Fords, Howard & Hulbert, 1881.

Hedges, Elaine. "The Development of Women's Narrative." In *The Heath Anthology of American Literature*, edited by Paul Lauter, et al., 34–35. Lexington, Ky.: D.C. Heath, 1990.

Higham, John. *Strangers in the Land: Patterns of American Nativism, 1860–1925*. New York: Atheneum, 1963.

Hilbert, Vi. *Haboo: Native American Stories from Puget Sound*. Seattle: University of Washington Press, 1985.

Hine, Darlene Clark. "Rape and the Inner Lives of Black Women in the Middle West: Preliminary Thoughts on the Culture of Dissemblance." In *Unequal Sisters: A Multi-Cultural Reader in U.S. Women's History*, edited by Vicki Ruiz and Ellen Carol DuBois, 342–48. New York: Routledge, 1990.

Hinsley, Curtis M. *Savages and Scientists: The Smithsonian Institution and the Development of American Anthropology, 1846–1910*. Washington, D.C.: Smithsonian, 1981.

hooks, bell. *Teaching to Transgress: Education as the Practice of Freedom*. New York: Routledge, 1994.

Howard, O. O. "Famous Indian Chiefs." *St. Nicholas Magazine* 32, no. 2 (May-October 1908): 815–22.

Hoxie, Frederick E. *A Final Promise: The Campaign to Assimilate the Indians,*
1880–1920. Lincoln: University of Nebraska Press, 1984.

Hurston, Zora Neale. *Mules and Men.* New York: Negro Universities Press,
1969.

Hymes, Dell H. "A Theory of Irony and a Chinookan Pattern of Verbal
Exchange." In *The Pragmatic Perspective: Papers from the 1985 Inter-*
national Pragmatics Conference, edited by Jef Verschueren and Marcella
Bertuccelli-Papi, 293–337. Philadelphia: John Benjamins, 1987.

———. "Anthologies and Narrators." In *Recovering the Word: Essays on*
Native American Literature, edited by Brian Swann and Arnold Krupat.
Berkeley and Los Angeles: University of California Press, 1987.

———. *"In Vain I Tried to Tell You": Essays in Native American Ethnopoetics.*
Philadelphia: University of Pennsylvania Press, 1981.

———. "Models of the Interaction of Language and Social Life." In
Directions in Sociolinguistics: The Ethnography of Communication, edited
by John Gumperz and Dell H. Hymes, 35–71. New York: Holt, Rinehart
& Winston, 1972.

Jackson, Helen Hunt. *A Century of Dishonor.* 1881. Reprint, Norman:
University of Oklahoma Press, 1995.

———. *Glimpses of Three Coasts.* Boston: Roberts Brothers, 1886.

———. *Bits of Talk about Home Matters.* Boston: Roberts Brothers, 1873.

———. "The Indian Problem: Questions for the American People." *New*
York Tribune, December 15, 1879.

———. *Mercy Philbrick's Choice.* Boston: Roberts Brothers, 1876.

———. *Ramona.* 1884. Reprint, New York: Signet, 1988.

Jackson, Robert H., and Edward Castillo. *Indians, Franciscans, and Spanish*
Colonization: The Impact of the Mission System on California Indians.
Albuquerque: University of New Mexico Press, 1995.

Jacobs, Elizabeth Derr. *Nehalem Tillamook Tales.* Corvallis: Oregon State
University Press, 1990.

Jacobs, Melville. *Clackamas Chinook Texts, Part I.* Indiana University
Research Center in Anthropology, Folklore, and Linguistics, Publication 8, vol. 24, no. 2. Bloomington: Indiana University Press, 1958.

———. *Clackamas Chinook Texts, Part II.* Indiana University Research
Center in Anthropology, Folklore, and Linguistics, Publication 11, vol.
25, no. 2. Bloomington: Indiana University Press, 1959.

———. *The Content and Style of an Oral Literature.* Chicago: Chicago
University Press, 1959.

———. *Kalapuya Texts.* Publications in Anthropology, vol. 11. Seattle:
University of Washington Press, 1945.

————. *The People Are Coming Soon: Analyses of Clackamas Chinook Myths and Tales*. Seattle: University of Washington Press, 1960.

————. "The Romantic Role of Older Women in a Culture of the Pacific Northwest Coast." *Kroeber Anthropological Society Publications* 18 (Spring 1958): 79–85.

————. *Texts in Chinook Jargon*. Publications in Anthropology, vol. 7. Seattle: University of Washington Press, 1936.

————. "Titles in an Oral Literature." *Journal of American Folklore* 70 (1957): 157–72.

James, George Wharton. *Through Ramona's Country*. Boston: Little Brown, 1909.

Kaplan, Carla. "The Erotics of Talk: 'That Oldest Human Longing.'" *American Literature* (March 1995): 117–43.

Kelley, Mary. *Private Woman, Public Stage: Literary Domesticity in Nineteenth-Century America*. New York: Oxford University Press, 1984.

Kelly, Lawrence C. *The Assault on Assimilation: John Collier and the Origins of Indian Policy Reform*. Albuquerque: University of New Mexico Press, 1983.

Knack, Martha C., and Omer C. Stewart. *As Long as the River Shall Run: An Ethnohistory of the Pyramid Lake Indian Reservation*. Berkeley and Los Angeles: University of California Press, 1984.

Kroeber, Karl. "Deconstructionist Criticism and American Indian Literature." *boundary2* vol. 7 (1979): 73–89.

Krupat, Arnold. *For Those Who Come After: A Study of Native American Autobiography*. Berkeley and Los Angeles: University of California Press, 1985.

LaFlesche, Francis. "An Indian Allotment." *The Independent*, November 8, 1900, 2686–688.

LaFlesche, Suzette. "Nedawi." 1881. Reprinted in *The Singing Spirit: Early Short Stories by North American Indians*, edited by Bernd C. Peyer, 3–13. Tucson: University of Arizona Press, 1989.

Landsman, Gail H. "The 'Other' as Political Symbol: Images of Indians in the Woman Suffrage Movement." *Ethnohistory* (Summer 1992): 247–84.

Lape, Noreen Groover. "'I would rather be with my people but not to live with them as they do': Cultural Liminality and Double Consciousness in Sarah Winnemucca Hopkins's *Life Among the Piutes: Their Wrongs and Claims*." *American Indian Quarterly* 22, no. 3 (Summer 1998): 261–78.

Lejeune, Philippe. *On Autobiography*. Minneapolis: University of Minnesota Press, 1989.

Lepore, Jill. *The Name of War: King Philip's War and the Origins of American Identity*. New York: Knopf, 1998.

Littlefield, Daniel F., and James Parins. *A Biobibliography of Native American Writers 1772–1924*. Metuchen, N.J.: Scarecrow Press, 1981.

Lott, Eric. *Love and Theft: Blackface Minstrelsy and the American Working Class*. New York: Oxford University Press, 1993.

Lukens, Margo. "Her 'Wrongs and Claims': Sarah Winnemucca's Strategic Narratives of Abuse." *Wicazo Sa Review* 13, no. 1 (Spring 1998): 93–104.

Lutz, Tom. *American Nervousness, 1903: An Anecdotal History*. Ithaca, N.Y.: Cornell University Press, 1991.

Lynch, Deirdre, and William B. Warner, eds. *Cultural Institutions of the Novel*. Durham, N.C.: Duke University Press, 1996.

Mankiller, Wilma P. *Mankiller: A Chief and Her People*. New York: St. Martin's, 1993.

Manypenny, George. *Our Indian Wards*. New York: Da Capo, 1880.

Mardock, Robert Winston. *The Reformers and the American Indian*. Columbia: University of Missouri Press, 1971.

Mark, Joan. *A Stranger in Her Native Land: Alice Cunningham Fletcher and the American Indians*. Lincoln: University of Nebraska Press, 1988.

Martin, Jay. *Harvests of Change: American Literature 1865–1914*. Englewood Cliffs, N.J.: Prentice-Hall, 1967.

Mathes, Valerie Sherer. *Helen Hunt Jackson and Her Indian Reform Legacy*. Austin: University of Texas Press, 1990.

———, ed. *The Indian Reform Letters of Helen Hunt Jackson 1879–1885*. Norman: University of Oklahoma Press, 1998.

May, Antoinette. *The Annotated Ramona*. San Carlos, Calif.: Worldwide/ Tetra, 1989.

McNickle, D'Arcy. *Native American Tribalism*. New York: Oxford University Press, 1973.

———. *The Surrounded*. 1936. Reprint, Albuquerque: University of New Mexico Press, 1978.

McWilliams, Carey. "Southern California: Ersatz Mythology." In *Minorities in California History*, edited by George Frakes and Curtis Solberg, 57–62. New York: Random House, 1971.

Meacham, A. B. *Wi-ne-ma (The Woman Chief) and Her People*. Hartford, Conn.: American, 1876.

Meeker, Josephine. *The Ute Massacre*. New York: Garland, 1879.

Michaels, Walter Benn. *Our America: Nativism, Modernism, Pluralism*. Durham, N.C.: Duke University Press, 1995.

Miller, Nancy K. "Emphasis Added: Plots and Plausibilities in Women's Fiction." *PMLA* 6, no. 1 (January 1981): 36–47.

Mirande, Alfredo, and Evangelina Enriquez. *La Chicana: The Mexican-American Woman*. Chicago: Chicago University Press, 1979.

Moylan, Michele. "Reading the Indians: The Ramona Myth in American Culture." *Prospects* 18 (1993): 153–86.

Munnick, Harriet Duncan, and Stephen Dow Beckham, eds. *Catholic Church Records of the Pacific Northwest: Grand Ronde Register I (1860–1885) and Grand Ronde Register II (1886–1898)*. (St. Michael the Archangel Parish, Grand Ronde Reservation, Grand Ronde, Oregon; St. Patrick's Parish, Muddy Valley, Oregon.) Portland: Brinford & Mort, 1987.

Murdock, George Peter, and Timothy O'Leary. *Ethnographic Bibliography of North America*. New Haven, Conn.: Human Area Relations Files, 1975.

Murray, David. *Forked Tongues: Speech, Writing and Representation in North American Indian Texts*. Bloomington: Indiana University Press, 1991.

Nevins, Allan. "Helen Hunt Jackson: Sentimentalist v. Realist." *American Scholar* 10 (Summer 1941): 269–85.

Nudelman, Franny. "Harriet Jacobs and the Sentimental Politics of Female Suffering." *English Literary History* 59 (1992): 939–64.

O'Brien, Sharon. *American Indian Tribal Governments*. Norman: University of Oklahoma Press, 1989.

Odell, Ruth. *Helen Hunt Jackson ("H.H.")*. New York: D. Appleton-Century Co., 1939.

Oh, Seeiwong. "Cross-Cultural Reading versus Textual Accessibility in Multicultural Literature." *Multiethnic Literatures of the United States* (Summer 1993): 3–16.

Otis, D. S. *The Dawes Act and the Allotment of Indian Lands*. 1934. Reprint, edited and with an introduction by Francis Paul Prucha. Norman: University of Oklahoma Press, 1973.

Parker, Robert Dale. "Text, Lines, and Audiotape: The Ideology of Genre and the Transcription of Traditional Native American Oral Narrative as Poetry." *Arizona Quarterly* 53, no. 3 (Fall 1997): 141.

Pascoe, Peggy. *Relations of Rescue: The Search for Female Moral Authority in the American West, 1874–1939*. New York: Oxford University Press, 1990.

Pearce, Roy Harvey. *Savagism and Civilization: A Study of the Indian and the American Mind*. 1953. Reprint, Berkeley and Los Angeles: University of California Press, 1988.

Peyer, Bernd C., ed. *The Singing Spirit: Early Short Stories by North American Indians*. Tucson: University of Arizona Press, 1989.

Phillips, Catherine Hale. "Helen (Hunt) Jackson and Her Literary Career." Ph.D. diss., Harvard University, 1997.

Pratt, Mary Louise. *Imperial Eyes: Travel Writing and Transculturation*. London: Routledge, 1992.

Priest, Loring Benson. *Uncle Sam's Stepchildren: The Reformation of United States Indian Policy, 1865–1887*. New Brunswick, N.J.: Rutgers University Press, 1942.

Prucha, Francis Paul, ed. *Americanizing the American Indians: Writings by the "Friends of the Indian" 1880–1900*. Cambridge: Harvard University Press, 1973.

Ramsey, Jarold. "Generic and Racial Appropriation in Victoria Howard's 'The Honorable Milt.'" *Oral Tradition* 10, no. 2 (October 1995): 263–82.

———. *Reading the Fire: Essays in the Traditional Literatures of the Far West*. Lincoln: University of Nebraska Press, 1983.

———. "The Wife Who Goes Out Like a Man, Comes Back as a Hero: The Art of Two Oregon Indian Narratives." *PMLA* 92, no. 1 (January 1977): 9–17.

Ramsey, Jarold, ed. *Coyote Was Going There: Indian Literature of the Oregon Country*. Seattle: University of Washington Press, 1977.

Razack, Sherene H. *Looking White People in the Eye: Gender, Race, and Culture in Courtrooms and Classrooms*. Toronto: University of Toronto Press, 1998.

Richey, Elinor. "Sagebrush Princess with a Cause: Sarah Winnemucca." *American West* 12 (November 1975): 30–33, 57–63.

Robinson, Harry. *Write It on Your Heart: The Epic World of an Okanagan Storyteller*. Vancouver, British Columbia: Talonbooks, 1989.

Rolle, Andrew F. Introduction to *A Century of Dishonor*, vii–xxii. New York: Harper Torchbooks, 1965.

Ronda, Bruce A. *Elizabeth Palmer Peabody: A Reformer on Her Own Terms*. Cambridge, Mass.: Harvard University Press, 1999.

———, ed. *Letters of Elizabeth Palmer Peabody: American Renaissance Woman*. Middletown, Conn.: Wesleyan University Press, 1984.

Roosevelt, Theodore. *The Winning of the West, Part I*. New York: Charles Scribner's Sons, 1926.

Ruby, Robert H., and John A. Brown. *The Chinook Indians: Traders of the Lower Columbia River*. Norman: University of Oklahoma Press, 1976.

Ruoff, LaVonne Brown. Introduction to *Wynema: A Child of the Forest*. 1891. Reprint, Lincoln: University of Nebraska Press, 1998.

————. "Three Nineteenth-Century American Indian Autobiographers." In *Redefining American Literary History*, edited by Lavonne Brown Ruoff and Jerry Ward. New York: Modern Language Association, 1990.

Ruppert, James. *Mediation in Contemporary Native American Fiction*. Norman: University of Oklahoma Press, 1995.

Rydell, Robert. *All the World's a Fair: Visions of Empire at American International Expositions 1876–1916*. Chicago: University of Chicago Press, 1984.

Sale, Maggie Montesinos. "Reconceptualizing America." *Legacy: A Journal of Women Writers* 15, no. 1 (1998): 29–34.

Sands, Kathleen Mullen. "Indian Women's Personal Narrative: Voices Past and Present." In *American Women's Autobiography: Fea(s)ts of Memory*, edited by Margo Culley, 269–94. Madison: University of Wisconsin Press, 1992.

Sapir, Edward. *Wishram Texts*. Publications of the American Ethnological Society. Leyden: Late E. J. Brill, 1909.

Sarris, Greg. *Keeping Slug Woman Alive: A Holistic Approach to Native American Texts*. Berkeley and Los Angelès: University of California Press, 1993.

Scharbach, Alexander. "Aspects of Existentialism in Clackamas Chinook Myths." *Journal of American Folklore*, 75 (1962): 15–22.

Scheick, William J. *The Half-Blood: A Cultural Symbol in Nineteenth-Century American Fiction*. Lexington: University Press of Kentucky, 1979.

Scherer, Joanna Cohan. "The Public Faces of Sarah Winnemucca." *Cultural Anthropology* 3 (May 1988): 178–204.

Scott, Lalla. *Karnee: A Paiute Narrative*. Reno: University of Nevada Press, 1966.

Scott, Leslie. "Indian Women as Food Providers and Tribal Counselors." *Oregon Historical Quarterly* 42, no. 2 (June 1941): 208–19.

Seaburg, William. "Collecting Culture: The Practice and Ideology of Salvage Anthropology in Western Oregon." Ph.D. diss., University of Washington, 1994.

Seltzer, Mark. *Bodies and Machines*. New York: Routledge, 1992.

Senier, Siobhan. "American Indian Intellectuals in the Era of Assimilation: Victoria Howard's Oral Stories." *Northwest Review* (September 1997): 46–56.

————."The Politics and Perils of Representing Tribal Discourse: S. Alice Callahan's *Wynema*." Forthcoming. *American Indian Quarterly*.

————. "Victoria Howard." *Legacy: A Journal of Women Writers* 14 (Spring 1997): 51–58.

Sewall, Richard B. *The Life of Emily Dickinson*. New York: Farrar, Straus, & Giroux, 1980.

Shipek, Florence C. "History of Southern California Mission Indians." In *California*, edited by Robert Heizer, 610–18. Vol. 8 of *Handbook of North American Indians*, edited by William C. Sturtevant. Washington, D.C.: Smithsonian, 1978.

Silko, Leslie Marmon. "An Old-Time Indian Attack Conducted in Two Parts." In *The Remembered Earth: An Anthology of Contemporary Native American Literature*, edited by Geary Hobson, 211–15. Albuquerque: University of New Mexico Press, 1981.

Silverstein, Michael. "Chinookans of the Lower Columbia." In *Northwest Coast*, edited by Wayne Suttles, 533–46. Vol. 7 of *Handbook of North American Indians*, edited by William C. Sturtevant. Washington, D.C.: Smithsonian, 1978.

Slotkin, Richard. *Regeneration through Violence: The Mythology of the American Frontier*. Middletown, Conn.: Wesleyan University Press, 1973.

Sollors, Werner. *Beyond Ethnicity*. New York: Oxford University Press, 1986.

Spivak, Gayatri Chakravorty. "Can the Subaltern Speak?" In *Marxism and the Interpretation of Culture*, edited by Cary Nelson and Lawrence Grossberg, 271–316. Urbana: University of Illinois Press, 1988.

Starr, Kevin. *Inventing the Dream: California through the Progressive Era*. New York: Oxford University Press, 1985.

Stewart, Patricia. "Sarah Winnemucca." *Nevada Historical Quarterly* (Winter 1971): 23–38.

Swann, Brian, ed. *Coming to Light: Contemporary Translations of the Native Literatures of North America*. New York: Random House, 1996.

———, ed. *Recovering the Word: Essays on Native American Literature*. Berkeley and Los Angeles: University of California Press, 1987.

Swann, Brian, and Arnold Krupat, eds. *I Tell You Now: Autobiographical Essays by Native American Writers*. Lincoln: University of Nebraska Press, 1987.

Szasz, Margaret Connell, ed. *Between Indian and White Worlds: The Cultural Broker*. Norman: University of Oklahoma Press, 1994.

Takaki, Ronald T. *Iron Cages: Race and Culture in Nineteenth-Century America*. New York: Alfred A. Knopf, 1979.

Tedlock, Dennis. *The Spoken Word and the Work of Interpretation*. Philadelphia: University of Pennsylvania Press, 1983.

Tharp, Louise Hall. *The Peabody Sisters of Salem*. Boston: Little Brown, 1950.

Thompson, Craig. "Gender Representation in Two Clackamas Myths." *Studies in American Indian Literatures* 3, no. 1 (Spring 1991): 19–39.

Thompson, Laurence. "Melville Jacobs." *American Anthropologist* 80 (1978): 640–49.

Thompson, Stith. *Motif-Index of Folk Literature*. 6 vols. Bloomington: Indiana University Press, 1955.

Tibbles, Thomas. *The Ponca Chiefs: An Account of the Trial of Standing Bear*. 1880. Reprint, Lincoln: University of Nebraska Press, 1972.

Tompkins, Jane P. *Sensational Designs: The Cultural Work of American Fiction 1790–1860*. New York: Oxford University Press, 1985.

Tourgée, Albion. "Study in Civilization." *North American Review* 143 (August 1886): 246–61.

Trachtenberg, Alan. *The Incorporation of America: Culture and Society in the Gilded Age*. New York: Hill and Wang, 1982.

Valaskakis, Gail Guthrie. "The Chippewa and the Other: Living the Heritage of Lac du Flambeau." *Cultural Studies* 2, no. 3 (October 1988): 267–93.

———. "'Dance Me Inside': Pow Wow and Being 'Indian.'" *Fuse* 15, no. 5/6 (Summer 1993): 40.

Van Kirk, Sylvia. *Many Tender Ties: Women in Fur-Trade Society in Western Canada, 1670–1870*. Winnipeg, Manitoba: Watson and Dwyer, 1980.

Venuti, Lawrence. *The Translator's Invisibility: A History of Translation*. New York: Routledge, 1995.

Wald, Priscilla. *Constituting Americans: Cultural Anxiety and Narrative Form*. Durham, N.C.: Duke University Press, 1995.

Walker, Cheryl. *Indian Nation: Native American Literature and Nineteenth-Century Nationalisms*. Durham, N.C.: Duke University Press, 1997.

Warrior, Robert Allen. *Tribal Secrets: Recovering American Indian Intellectual Traditions*. Minneapolis: University of Minnesota Press, 1995.

Washburn, Wilcomb E. *The Assault on Indian Tribalism: The General Allotment Law (Dawes Act) of 1887*. Philadelphia: J. B. Lippincott, 1975.

Watson, Margaret G. *Silver Theatre: Amusements of the Mining Frontier in Early Nevada 1850–1864*. Glendale, Calif.: Arthur H. Clark, 1964.

Weaver, Jace. *That the People Might Live: Native American Literatures and Native American Community*. New York: Oxford University Press, 1997.

West, Patsy. "I.laponki.: The Florida Seminoles in the 1930s." *Native Peoples* 9, no. 3 (Spring 1996): 26–32.

Winnemucca (Hopkins), Sarah. *Life Among the Piutes: Their Wrongs and Claims*. 1883. Reprint, Reno: University of Nevada Press, 1993.

————. "The Pah-Utes." *The Californian* (1882). Reprinted in Bernd Peyer, ed., *The Elders Wrote: An Anthology of Early Prose by North American Indians, 1768–1931* (Berlin: Riemer, 1982).

Womack, Craig. *Red on Red: Native American Literary Separatism.* Minneapolis: University of Minnesota Press, 1999.

Youst, Lionel. *She's Tricky Like Coyote: Annie Miner Peterson, an Oregon Coast Indian Woman.* Norman: University of Oklahoma Press, 1997.

Zenk, Henry. "Chinook Jargon and Native Cultural Persistence in the Grand Ronde Indian Community, 1856–1907: A Special Case of Creolization." Ph.D. diss., University of Oregon, 1984.

Zitkala-Sa. "Why I Am a Pagan." *Atlantic* 90 (December 2, 1901): 801–3.

Zucker, Jeff. *Oregon Indians: Culture, History, and Current Affairs.* Oregon Historical Society: Western Imprints, 1983.

INTERNET RESOURCE

Confederated Tribes of Grand Ronde. "CTGR," Web site of the Confederated Tribes of the Grand Ronde Community of Oregon. Online. Available: www.grandronde.org.

INDEX

Abbott, Lyman, 42
Adams, Henry, 218n.33
"Adventures at Zuni." *See* Cushing, Frank, and "Adventures at Zuni"
African-Americans as compared to American Indians, 9–10, 25, 92, 94, 96, 118
Akwesasne Notes, 206n.11
Alcott, Louisa May, 53
Aldrich, Thomas Bailey, 208n.2
Alexie, Sherman, 194
Allen, Paula Gunn, 218n.34
Allotment, 10, 41–49, 135, 195; Dawes Act, 5–7, 35, 36, 40, 42–43, 44, 45–46, 50, 56, 59, 62, 63–64, 80; and Fletcher, 45–46, 62, 63–64; and Indian citizenship, 5–6, 43–44; and possessive individualism, 5, 59; and Ramona, 35, 36–41, 44, 45, 50, 56, 59, 66, 67–68; and *Wynema*, 196–99. *See also* Assimilation; Communal lands; Resistance to Assimilation/allotment
American Indians: as compared to African-Americans, 9–10, 25, 92, 94, 96, 118; attitudes of whites toward, 3, 4–9, 16, 19, 26, 34, 39, 40–41, 42–43, 54, 59–61, 72, 74–75, 79, 84–88, 90–91, 92, 102–103, 108, 128, 131–32, 197, 205n.6, 206n.12, 212n.50; autobiography among, 88–89, 94–95, 134, 138–39, 151–52, 177–78, 183–84, 195, 218n.33; Christianity among, 5, 9, 60–61, 135, 225n.38; citizenship of, 5–6, 9, 43–45, 59, 97, 108, 197–98, 204n.3; community among, 4, 5, 7–8, 13–14, 15–17, 19, 43, 49, 52, 75, 83–84, 97, 101, 109, 112, 115, 211n.27, 220n.50; cosmology among, 13–14; cultural identity among, 9, 12, 18,
19, 20, 113–14, 127, 134–38, 181, 182, 221n.69, 225n.39; education of, 5, 48, 108; literary forms among, 21–22; newspapers of, 196; private property among, 5, 7, 9, 38, 41, 44, 46–47, 49, 200, 220n.50; relations with United States, 4, 5–8, 32–33, 44–45, 48, 67, 72, 74, 91–92, 135, 196–99, 204n.3, 205n.11, 216n.2, 218n.31; relations with white women reformers, 59–64, 79, 87–88, 92, 109, 131; sovereignty among, 6, 7–8, 21, 43–44, 46, 64, 72, 73–75, 83, 101–102, 110, 114–15, 118, 120, 197–98; status of women among, 109, 130–34, 141, 142, 143, 152–54, 156, 163, 179, 182–83, 218n.34. *See also* Allotment; Assimilation; Concealment; Ethnography; Resistance to assimilation/allotment; Tribes
Ammons, Elizabeth, 22
Anderson, Benedict, 56, 58
Anderson, Eric Gary, 81
Anthropology, 6–7, 8, 22, 62, 132, 139, 146; Bureau of American Ethnology (BAE), 6, 23, 127–28, 146. *See also* Ethnography
Assimilation, 4–9, 27, 135; American Indian writers during Era of, 9–15, 19; and education, 5; Fletcher's attitudes toward, 45–46, 62, 63–64; Howard's attitudes toward, 136–38, 157–59, 161, 180–83, 188–92; Jackson's attitudes toward, 36, 45–50, 70–72, 80; and literacy, 22; vs. mediation, 82–83; pace of, 42; vs. sovereignty, 21; Winnemucca's attitudes toward, 74–75, 80, 82–83, 91, 97, 101–102, 114–15, 116–18, 120, 222n.73. *See also* Allotment; Resistance